FIRST
BAPTIST
CHURCH

First Baptist Church

First Baptist Church

GREENWOOD, SOUTH CAROLINA
1870–1999

Ann Herd Bowen

Foreword by J. William Harris, Th.D.

PROVIDENCE HOUSE PUBLISHERS
Franklin, Tennessee

Printed in the United States of America

03 02 01 00 99 1 2 3 4 5

Library of Congress Catalog Card Number: 99-66972

ISBN: 1-57736-165-2

Cover design by Gary Bozeman

PROVIDENCE HOUSE PUBLISHERS
238 Seaboard Lane • Franklin, Tennessee 37067
800-321-5692
www.providencehouse.com

"For all the saints,
who from their labors rest . . ."

CONTENTS

Artist's conception of the first church building on Church (now East Cambridge) Street erected in 1873. Ernest Norwood provided details—window placement, roof line, belfry, etc.—based on his recollection of descriptions by his mother, Leo Golding Norwood, and his Aunt Bessie Waldrop. (Pencil drawing by Betty Coursey Warner)

FOREWORD

History in itself is not the most popular of subjects. High school and college students chafe at having to learn "names and dates" from the past. However, when history relates to personal experience, almost everyone finds it interesting and appealing. Children want to know how things were when their parents were young. Seniors like to share stories from the "good old days." A personal connection with the past makes history a heritage. And heritage is not simply facts, places, and dates. Heritage indicates in part who we are.

A good church history tells a story and conveys a heritage. It originates with accounts of persons and events, but it becomes a portrayal of the essential spirit of a people brought together by God to be a community of faith.

Ann Bowen has told our story in a warm and insightful way. The personality of the church comes through in her treatment. Of only slightly less importance is the readability of her account. I have read many church histories. Some of them are written in such pious fashion that you would wonder whether the church existed in the real world. Some histories deal only with cold facts; they could describe any church. Some are simply dull. Our church history is factual and readable. Even inspiring!

When I completed the manuscript, I felt several emotions. I reflected on a profound sense of gratitude for this church family. It is a congregation of faith and integrity. For nearly 130 years it has proclaimed the gospel of Christ, served this community, and engaged in missions and evangelism in a very distinctive manner. From its inception, First Baptist Church has been *Baptist* in the highest sense of the word. I am grateful for a story that reminds me of such a heritage. Also, I felt the encouragement of a "priesthood of believers" that spans the years. We really are one with those who have gone before and those who will come after us. To recount what God can and will do through a church is reassuring. Finally, I was aware of a feeling of renewal. How can one review so wonderful a story and heritage and not want to be rededicated himself to the body of the church and head of the body who is Christ?

Many thanks to Ann for the diligent work and the gracious use of her talent for storytelling. Thanks to those who have preserved the details of our history by putting aside photos, articles, writings, and memories that now find substance and order in this book. Thanks to all who have lived the story and developed the heritage of First Baptist Church. And thanks to the God who is "our help in ages past, our hope for years to come."

J. William Harris
June 1999

PREFACE

There seems to be no better way to put it than the way it actually was—the history of Greenwood's First Baptist Church needed to be written, and I needed a project. Boykin Curry knew about both needs. End of story. Or, perhaps, just the beginning. . . .

In truth, the challenge to take on the job was quite irresistible once I got used to the idea, particularly since my initial foray into local history had culminated in an actual book, *Greenwood County: A History,* published in 1992. The prospect of producing a companion volume was rather pleasant to contemplate. Besides, as a lifelong Baptist and native South Carolinian, I saw the project as an opportunity to learn more about my denomination as it took hold in the so-called "New World," first along the coast when my state was still a colony, and then moving inland all the way to the backcountry along with the earliest settlers before, during, and after the Revolutionary War.

The church records were lush as well—primary sources all and from the very beginning. Older than the county, the church had wisely preserved the record of its existence, at first in handwritten minute books, and later, as it grew and evolved, in mimeographed newsletters, and finally in the sleek computer-generated, desktop published weekly bulletins of today. In addition, photographs of every one of the fourteen pastors who had filled the pulpit since 1872—more potential material—beckoned from the walls of the main corridor every time I entered the building. I already knew that many members of the congregation were also members of some of Greenwood's earliest families, which meant even more chances to add to my knowledge of the area and its inhabitants. The pastor, too, offered his full cooperation, as did other members of the staff. Had anyone, I asked myself, ever been quite so lucky? And so we began, First Baptist Church and I, a joint venture to discover what we could about each other and to share those discoveries with whoever might be interested.

The biggest problem I faced from the beginning was how to separate my conception of a *church* from the larger and more treacherous realm of *religion*. Years ago someone had defined the latter term in a way that appealed to me strongly: One's religion, he said, is the relationship of that person's individual soul to its creator. If one accepts that definition, then one's church is surely something quite different.

Let us be clear that the "church" in this history does not fit the first definition of the word in my dictionary, which reads: "The company of all Christians regarded as a mystic spiritual body." Someone might write that book, but it will not be I. The second definition is not much better; once again, this is *not* the history of a "building for public, esp. Christian, worship." At least three buildings figured in the case at hand, one of which could be defined as a whole complex of buildings. Things begin to look a little brighter with the third definition, which is "a congregation." Actually, I prefer yet another definition of the word *church* (from another dictionary) as "a body or organization of religious believers." There. Finally. I can live with the idea that what I have tried to write is the story of a particular body of believers, as parts of that story have been understood and preserved in both written and oral form.

In order to do what I thought was necessary, I have physically examined literally thousands of pages of material. Anyone could do the same thing, of course, and come away with the history of First Baptist Church from the horse's mouth, so to speak. But the fact is that we don't as a practical matter get our histories that way. We allow a certain leeway in matters of emphasis and interpretation in exchange for someone's willingness to put in the hours (and sometimes the weeks and months and years) required to research, write, check, and edit a manuscript that finally becomes an actual book one can place on a shelf and browse at leisure.

I could think of no way to accomplish what I set out to do except follow the chronological record and try to provide, for the sake of coherence and flow, some sort of linking mechanism to move the reader from significant event A to significant event B, and so on. In some cases my interest was simply in pinpointing the first time something or other was done; in others, I wanted to insert in the narrative some mention of what was happening politically, or culturally, or socially in the wider world—both to provide context and to remind us of the interconnectedness of things. At times I simply wanted to celebrate an individual who had impressed me in one way or another, whether in appreciation of her uniqueness or recognition of his faithfulness. Of course I wanted most of all to stir memories—of earlier times, of special people, of weddings, funerals, dedications, recognitions, commemorations, memorials, and other moments of great significance in the lives of the First Baptist Church family.

Anyone who works with the records of a Baptist church cannot escape a close look at the single unifying theme of the denomination—the absence of any sort of interchurch form and structure. Each congregation is its own governing body, and each derives its authority by democratic means. Baptists vote all the time and on all sorts of issues. Possibly the most revealing aspect of any Baptist church is how the congregation is prepared for a particular vote. The pastor's hand must be particularly delicate in this area. He must lead without appearing to push; he must educate, but not indoctrinate; he must gather and interpret data, answer questions, offer guidance, and inform himself so that he can inform others. I saw this dynamic in operation again and again as I studied the record.

This is not all, of course, a Baptist minister is expected to do. He must also be able to speak and write clearly; he must visit the sick, bury the dead, dedicate the infants, teach the children, perform the marriages, mediate the quarrels, settle the disputes, maintain the quality, sample everyone's cooking, and sometimes unlock the church. In addition, he is expected to raise money, increase membership, accept responsibility for all auxiliary organizations, attend any number of social functions, join the right clubs, dress well, and above all, never, never embarrass the congregation in any way. Fortunately, the last two senior ministers of First Baptist Church—Jim Bowers and Bill Harris—have made all this look easy. My hat is off to both these remarkable men.

My take on this particular church's history can be discerned from the titles of the various chapters. Far too many authors of church histories have succumbed to the temptation of using the words *in the beginning;* I regret (but only a little) that I am no exception. Who am I to argue with the writers of the Book of Genesis and the Gospel of John? It is surely not my fault that their words just seem to fall at the top of the first page when one sets out to chronicle the history of a church. The title of chapter 2, "A Church Is Born," is not only self-explanatory but also allows the opportunity for assessing the trappings surrounding the birth, and there were many in the case of First Baptist, including other Baptist churches, a couple of terrific preacher-educators, and some early schools, including the seminary at Furman.

Chapter 3, "Years of Growth and Service," is also pretty much what the name implies; it covers the tenures of the first eight pastors, as well as elements of the story of Connie Maxwell, another Baptist phenomenon, and the era of the Giles sisters' educational experiment, Greenwood Female College. Jim Bowers came to town near the end of chapter 4, "The Middle Years," and established himself ever more firmly in chapter 5, "Maturity." This chapter also describes the great building program and the influence of a Philadelphia architect, as well as the turbulent 1960s, a decade that brought far-reaching changes in the church program. Finally, the chapter treats the traumatic events of 1970 that brought to an end the one-hundred-year affiliation of the church with the Abbeville Association.

Chapter 6, "New Directions," ends when Bill Harris assumed the pulpit, and chapter 7, "Milestones of the Second Century," deals with his leadership and the church's emphases after its building needs had been met. The chapter also covers the stresses and strains of intradenominational warfare within the Baptist conventions. Finally, it documents a veritable explosion of missions activity directed outward toward real needs of real people in a real town.

Many people helped with this project. Boykin Curry has been steadfast in his support; Greenwood and First Baptist Church have no greater friend than this gentleman, for without Curry's persistence there might have been no book. Bill Harris has kept me on track in a dozen ways. It is no secret that I consider him the very model of a teacher-minister for thinking Christians; I am honored that he agreed to write a foreword for this volume. I am grateful to Beeka Coleman and Ruth Martin who, serving as the "picture committee," chose the illustrations. Buddy and Liza Jay, Mary McCord, Russie Young, and Ray Young worked with me on the material about their families that appears in the appendix. Dr. Eddie Lieberman shared his memories of Greenwood and First Baptist in a series of letters from his home in Greenville. Janelle Anderson, Carole Mauldin, Joyce Nickles, Jack Parham, Gertrude Sanders, and Joyce Williams helped me out more than once when I had a question about something or other. I had the chance early on to sit in on a staff meeting at the church, and the office personnel got used to my comings and goings with armfuls of old records. Everyone was unfailingly amiable and helpful, and I came away with renewed appreciation for the amount of work that goes into the program of a sizable modern church.

A word or two about perspective is always a good idea in a work of this nature. Unfortunately, it is inevitable that some people will find my treatment of the material in the church records all wrong. Many will be disappointed, perhaps even indignant, that I have included what they consider unimportant details or omitted events of great importance to them or their families. And everyone who feels that way will be exactly right—from his or her particular viewpoint. While I understand this phenomenon very well indeed, I am helpless to correct the problems it creates. I can only say that as far as I know, no hidden agenda has guided me as I worked on this book, and no one attempted the slightest form of censorship as the work progressed.

My membership at First Baptist dates from January 1986. Before that time I had heard a number of good-natured references (at least I think they were good-natured) to the Holy Roman Baptist Church on Grace Street or (in Jim Bowers's time) to St. James' by the Cemetery, and I have always understood how far removed this church is from, say, Bold Spring in Callison where I grew up. It is not quite true that a Baptist is a Baptist is a Baptist. By the time I joined the First Baptist Church in Greenwood I too had moved on; good music and good sermons had become necessary to me as an adult. Oddly enough, another important consideration after a few years was finding a place I actually wanted to be buried—something I had steadfastly refused to consider when I was younger. The prospect of being laid to rest in Edgewood Cemetery, as near as possible to Grace Street where I have lived more or less happily for more than thirty years, was immensely appealing. Thus it must be understood that any claim of total objectivity toward this church is in my case not totally pure; on the other hand, I freely accept responsibility for factual errors and other shortcomings of this work.

First
Baptist
Church

CHAPTER ONE

In the Beginning

The first Baptist church to be established in the town of Greenwood was founded on the twenty-fifth day of September in the year 1870, a brief thirteen years after the town's own incorporation and nearly thirty years before Greenwood County was formed. That historic act, undertaken by only twenty-three citizens at a time of political turmoil and uncertainty that characterized the entire South, would be quite enough to deserve our gratitude and respect; but the truth is that the impulse upon which the act was based is of much earlier origin and has its own bearing on our standing in these, the last days of the twentieth century.

No one knows exactly when the first Baptists came to South Carolina. The Church of England was established in 1706 as the official faith of the young colony that had seen its own beginnings a little more than thirty years earlier. But other religious groups had been welcome from the first to worship in their own way, unmolested. The words of Dr. Joe M. King, in *A History of South Carolina Baptists,* express it well:

> . . . so they came—the Scotch-Irish to Williamsburgh and the back country, the Welsh to the valley of the Great Peedee, the Germans, German-Swiss, and French-Swiss to Orangeburg, Purrysburgh, and the land of the Congaree. These and others, many of whom were

Baptists, were to find a haven indeed in the land from Oconee to Horry, from Catawba to Yemassee.

At some early point in any work of this nature one feels the need to define one's terms, but in this case something as basic as a clear and simple definition of the seven-letter word *baptist* is not easy to come by. The lowercase noun appears to refer only to one who baptizes, while a capital "B" *Baptist* is defined as a member of an evangelical Protestant denomination marked by congregational polity and baptism by immersion of believers only. At least three separate and distinct concepts present themselves immediately—concepts represented by the terms *evangelical, congregational polity,* and *immersion of believers only.* Evangelism, a common theme among Christian denominations, refers primarily to Christian belief and teaching as presented in the four gospels of Matthew, Mark, Luke, and John in the New Testament; "immersion" means a specific form of baptism; and polity defines the denominational form of political organization as the congregational unit. Each of these concepts arises again and again in attempting to trace the movement of the brotherhood of Baptist believers.

The belief system that eventually came to define the Baptist denomination reaches back to the time of the Protestant Reformation at the beginning of the sixteenth century. The name *Protestants* was applied to the Lutheran signers of the official protest presented at the West German city of Speyer in 1529. While the protesters considered themselves fully Christian in the historic sense, they had certain objections to the majority decision among their ranks to rescind an earlier agreement allowing states to enter upon a Lutheran policy of reform in their religious practice. The term *protestantism* in time came to be used without specific reference to the incident at Speyer and was applied to all types of western opponents of the papacy. Most non-Catholic Christians have been able to accept the term in regard to themselves, though some Anglicans who minimize the debt of their church to the Reformation have rejected the word. Similarly, interchurch organizations seem to steer clear of the term even to the present day, no doubt considering its somewhat negative connotations a possible deterrent to their larger objectives.

Because the reformers emphasized so strongly the authority of the Bible and the personal nature of salvation while at the same time repudiating any hint of the medieval system of authority, it is not surprising that the early Protestant movement paid far less attention to overall discipline and order than to multiple and separate forms of organization, each responsible only to itself. The political and social strife of the times often led to disharmony and schism in the religious life and practice of the citizens of western Europe. New and vigorous independent groups might spring up almost spontaneously in the interest of some fresh religious advance. Some, it is true, would expand widely and eventually develop into stable denominations that would cherish their separate traditions and consider themselves firmly rooted in the social fabric of their communities. There seems to be something deeply American in this idea; indeed, an upgrowth of separate sects stressing peculiar tenets and forms of worship, the more eccentric of which bear little resemblance to traditional protestantism, can be traced from the Old to the New World.

The name *Anabaptist* has been given to those persons who broke away from the dominant types of Protestantism in favor of a voluntary religious association coupled with vigorous attention to New Testament ordinances. Since the word was also used pejoratively to define all religious radicals of the sixteenth and seventeenth centuries, it was doubtless applied to at least some of the earliest of the South Carolina settlers from certain regions of Europe. There also arose a distinct Anabaptist movement, one that freely accepted the name, in Zürich, Switzerland, in 1525. Their practices and beliefs were carefully apostolic and gained much ground among the common people in the German-speaking lands of western Europe. Four distinct wings of the movement developed: the Swiss Brethren, the South German Brethren, the Hutterites, and the Dutch Mennonites. American Mennonites claim descent from the Swiss and Dutch branches of the movement; colonies of Hutterites settled in the western regions of the United States and Canada as well as in South America. These groups still preserve the ancient Christian communism based on the practices of the Church at Jerusalem as described in the Book of Acts.

The Anabaptists are generally considered a fringe sect in no sense related to the genteel denominations of modern times;

indeed, they were identified with more than one insurgency movement in sixteenth-century Europe, a link that caused Anabaptists to become known as the "anarchists of the Reformation." This opprobrium has proven somewhat unfair, however, since it is known that the leaders and chief groups of Anabaptists always repudiated violence. Further, contemporary sermons and confessions of faith exhumed from early archives indicate that their chief quarrel with other Reformers was over the union of church and state. Another very significant aspect of Anabaptist belief was that all baptism *not intelligently sought by its subject* was to be rejected, specifically including infant baptism which had been retained by all standard Reformation churches. This stance actually provided the sect's name; both Roman and Reform churches contemptuously labeled these radical individualists "rebaptizers" or "Anabaptists" from the Greek word for "back" or "again."

Using the early church as their model, the Anabaptists taught that a "fall" of the Church occurred under the Emperor Constantine and preached a doctrine of restitution of primitive church life. This view might be considered a foreshadowing of sectarian Protestantism in general and can surely be honored as an early championing of religious liberty.

With a respectful nod, then, to the controversial history of one of the great dissident sects to arise on the European continent during the Protestant Reformation, and in spite of the tantalizing similarity of the names, we must nevertheless hasten to point out that there is no organic connection between Anabaptist groups and the Baptist denomination in America, or elsewhere, today. Recognition of this disconnection or, more accurately, unconnectedness, is quite necessary and might even be considered a defining moment in any attempt to trace any Baptist church as part of some "movement" or other. Baptists will identify easily with the notion that they recognize no need for formal succession or even the concept of continuity. The *United States Census, Religious Bodies* (1936) puts it succinctly: "[I]t is a distinct principle with Baptists that they acknowledge no human founder, recognize no human authority, and subscribe to no human creed. For all these things Baptists of every name and order go back to the New Testament."

Modern Baptists do appear willing to trace their rise in the first half of the seventeenth century in both England and America. They were always considered radical since they held fast to the same movement for independency that produced the Congregational churches. The Baptists stood their ground through various stages and much persecution in England and finally came to an agreement with the ruling orders that allowed full expression of their principles. The development of the Baptist movement in America followed a similar pattern, and the name of an honored early leader finally emerges at this point. Roger Williams came to Massachusetts from England in 1632 but soon found himself in conflict with colonial church authorities over his insistence on personal experience and his opposition to infant baptism. He was actually expelled in 1636, not a surprising move for a colony that a few years later would feel no compunction against burning witches. Williams, along with other persecuted and pioneering souls, made his way to a place he named Providence Plantations and there established what is generally recognized as the first Baptist church in America in 1639.

Another Englishman, Dr. John Clarke, was working simultaneously with the so-called Newport group of Baptists, and a second church was formed around 1641 or 1642. From these beginnings in what is now Rhode Island the American Baptist movement began its slow progression in the face of difficulties and persecutions that persisted until the time of the American Revolution. That struggle, from its philosophical underpinnings all the way to its warring armies, energized the Baptists and received virtually their unanimous support and enthusiasm. The ideals of the new republic were theirs as well, and Baptists were among the leading and militant protagonists of that separation of church and state that was destined to become one of the fundamental principles in the new Bill of Rights of the Constitution of the United States.

The success of the American Revolution was the spur to rapid growth of the movement, so much so that by 1900 Baptists were the most numerous evangelical group in America, though organized quite loosely, if at all, in several separately functioning "conventions." By the late 1950s nearly nineteen million Baptists in the United States could be broken down into four major and twenty-two minor divisions. Worldwide, Baptists constitute the leading free church body in Christendom, or that portion of the world in which Christianity prevails. The one overriding characteristic uniting Baptists is that of the autonomy and final authority of the local church. Even so, Baptists have developed numerous cooperative agencies through which individual churches unite for counsel, missions, and other forms of work and expression. It is clear to all participants, however, that none of these agencies may exert the slightest authority over a local church. Neither do Baptists formulate creeds; even confessions of faith must be voluntary and may take various forms. There is no one organized "Baptist Church" in the United States or elsewhere. There are, however, worldwide groups who are Baptist in name only. The first such group, the Baptist World Congress, convened in London in 1905, and the Baptist World Alliance, an outgrowth of that meeting, was created as an instrument for Baptist ecumenical fellowship. The Alliance is used to voice common ideals and principles of the Baptist denomination, but it exercises no administrative control or function.

A History of South Carolina Baptists refers to the Baptist culture in the New World as "indigenous," by which author Joe King surely means that it arrived with the very earliest settlers from Europe and not that it arose naturally on the North American continent or had anything to do with the Native American population.[1] King also points out that the culture centered around Rhode Island in New England and Philadelphia in the middle colonies, while Baptists in the South appear to have been so scattered among the general population that identifiable enclaves are difficult to place. There exists only a "traditional date" for the beginnings of Baptist work in South Carolina—a date not long after the 1670 landing of the good ship *Carolina* at Charles Town after a month or so at Port Royal. That date is 1683, the year that one William Screven (or Scriven or Scrivine) reportedly migrated from Maine to a place he named Somerton about forty miles above Charleston.

With impeccable Baptist scholarship, an early Furman professor named H. T. Cook, whom Joe King credits with a work dealing with Baptist education in South Carolina, cites Screven as a Baptist pioneer in South Carolina but calls him "one of the three men whose long hands reached down the generations to shape and mold the Baptist denomination." The earliest of these, according to Cook, was a Mr. Blake, identified only as a "respectable dissenter, from England." The Baptists this gentleman brought to the colony were a like-minded group who, "being influenced by his example followed him into exile" in the New World in 1683. Another early Baptist leader was a Scotsman named Lord Cordross who is supposed to have led another band to Port Royal in 1685, "the Baptist part of which removed to the Edisto the next year." If Cook is correct, Screven's group was the third and the most lasting of these very early Baptist settlers.[2]

Screven, no stranger to nonconformity in religious matters by the time he arrived in South Carolina, had emigrated to Massachusetts from England in about 1668 and soon became a merchant of some prominence. He, his wife, and a family friend (who later married a sister-in-law) were baptized at Boston in July 1681, though they actually lived in Maine where Screven had purchased property. Several other citizens followed suit, and by the end of the year the little band had decided to establish itself as a church with its own pastor. Screven was thereupon sent to Boston with a request that the Baptist church in that place license him as minister. This was done in January 1682, so that Screven was a fully licensed Baptist minister by the time he first appeared in South Carolina. Possibly he had no intention originally of leaving New England, but the old persecutions arose again after his licensure, and Screven was eventually fined and jailed for what was termed "offensive speeches tending to blasphemy." It was Screven who offered to move away but not before seeing to it that a Baptist church was established in his adopted hometown of Kittery, Maine.

The records of Screven's movements are quite sketchy and in some cases seemingly contradictory; sightings in both Maine and South Carolina occurred in the late 1600s. Actually, there may have been two William Screvens—father and son; no one is exactly sure. It is known, however, that Screven did establish himself in South Carolina and that he was indeed a Baptist who sought to propagate his faith in a new and more congenial colony than the one he had found farther north. In spite of the lack of conclusive evidence, the Charleston church has traditionally maintained 1683 as the date of its founding and credited William Screven as its founder. As the years passed, names of other Baptists were identified in official records such as land deeds, letters, reports of Protestant missionaries, and so on. The Charleston church has also maintained records that reach as far back as 1699. It is interesting to note that a few of the names of members of that early congregation in another place evoke those of old Greenwood families—there were Elliotts, Bakers, Blakes, Butlers, and Childses among the membership. A meetinghouse had been erected by January 1701, and the church was able to boast a total of ninety members only seven years later. William Screven died in 1713; his burial place is Georgetown where a marker has been erected to his memory. A man of courage, ardor, and energy, one who survived intolerance and persecution in both the Old World and the New, Screven holds the distinction of establishing on a firm foundation the first Baptist church in the South.

A greatly oversimplified fact, but a fact nevertheless, is that the great Protestant Reformation might reasonably be said to have evolved into two camps: those favoring the conclusions reached by Martin Luther and those supporting instead the interpretations of John Calvin. Both men were zealous and brilliant and, it must be admitted, each was completely intolerant of any scriptural interpretation not his own. Neither objected to extreme punishment for what he considered heresy, and both spelled out minutely examined theological premises that might easily be compared in stringency to the excesses of the Roman Catholic Church, which they both deplored. Even so, there was no stopping the reformers' zeal that swept across Europe in the sixteenth century and expanded to the New World as the seventeenth century advanced. The whole question of political and religious liberty on which the United States based its founding documents might have had its roots in the soul-searching of Martin Luther and John Calvin, though neither is remembered as a champion of political liberty. The Catholic Church has itself been forced to deal openly with the monumental effects of the Reformation. Some historians, even Catholic historians, have come to look upon it with more sympathetic appreciation of its spiritual and moral place in human history. Joseph Lorz, for example, puts it well in the closing line of his book *The Reformation in Germany* (1941):

> In the Reformation which transformed the faith, the thought, and the life of a large part of mankind and has had an enormous influence on the living conditions of all the Christian peoples, Catholics included, in the Reformation which brought in the Christian world a contrasting variety of faiths and of prayers, and which for millions of believers changed altogether the path leading to salvation, we see in the background the mystery of the living God in history.

Thanks to William Screven and other zealots of the late seventeenth century, Baptist work found a firm foothold in the coastal regions of South Carolina. Its slow journey to the backcountry followed much the same path as the settlers who came from several directions, all looking for land and a means of subsistence. King points out that in-migration after 1750 was quite steady, partly by inland movement from the coast and partly by overland journeys from Pennsylvania, Virginia, and North Carolina. The new settlers were of western European extraction along with significant numbers of dissenting English people, and it was with these groups that new religious sects, including Baptists, were introduced.

There has always been a strong division—some might call it a mutual aversion—between lowcountry and upcountry South Carolina. For that matter, the whole state has often been depicted in rather extreme terms. Too much about South Carolina has been drawn either in the saccharine fiction of overly romantic books of the "cavalier" variety or, at the other extreme, in a "realistic" turning to themes of bigotry and backwardness in a genre described by Louis Wright as reflecting "a vast Tobacco Road" mentality. Both of these extremes have had their moment in writings about South Carolina, and both are, in and of themselves, utterly erroneous. It is true, however, that the state cannot be understood without recognizing that it is neither Charleston nor the upcountry alone. Some sort of synthesis—unsteady though it may be—must be attained before anything approaching a satisfactory view of the state's history and culture can be achieved.

In view of the unresolved dichotomy between the coastal region and the "frontier," or backcountry, of South Carolina, it is not surprising that Lieutenant Governor William Bull wrote in 1770, exactly one hundred years before the First Baptist Church of Greenwood was formed, that the frontier had become home to any number of new departures in religion, a situation not without certain distasteful overtones to the "orthodox" churchmen of Charleston and its environs. "Our toleration," he wrote, "comprehends every denomination of Christians but the Roman Catholic, and these are subdivided ad infinitum in the back parts, as illiterate enthusiasm or wild imagination can misinterpret the Scriptures."

Among the settlers whose religious persuasion might be termed Baptist were German and English Seventh-Day Baptists, who agreed on little except naming the seventh day of the week as the Lord's Day; German Brethren, who were called Dunkers, Tunkers, or Tumblers in reference to body placement during the rite of baptism; and the so-called Separate Baptists, who had originated in New England and who made up by far the dominant group of Baptists in the upcountry. Originally a result of Congregational churches splitting between the so-called Old Light and New Light groups (based on the idea that Old Lights had lost the "light of scriptural inspiration"), the New Light movement made significant inroads in South Carolina. Because they had withdrawn themselves, the New Lights came to be known as Separates and found solid footing among the sternly self-reliant and independent souls of the Carolina backcountry. The sect was quite rigid, and its practices, all of which members claimed to find in the New Testament, included numerous named rites such as baptism, the Lord's Supper, love feasts, laying on of hands, washing feet, anointing the sick, right hand of fellowship, kiss of charity, and so on. In a rather amazing departure for strict Baptists, however, both ruling elders and deaconesses were allowed. Foreshadowing the revival style of the early nineteenth century, Separate Baptist preachers made use of "powerful exhorting tones and gestures," and many converts cried out or fell to the ground during services. Naturally, the zeal of the Separates caused them to be regarded with much suspicion by Baptists who viewed themselves and their church services as more orderly and decorous. One minister of an early lowcountry church flatly refused to ordain a particularly fiery would-be minister on the grounds that he would hold no fellowship with a group he considered to be a disorderly set who actually allowed women to pray in public, not to mention permitted "every ignorant man to preach that chose" and encouraged noise and confusion in their meetings.

Eventually, at least in the lowcountry, Separate churches allowed themselves to be held to Regular Baptist standards but not so the budding church movement of the upcountry where the "fiery evangelists of Separatism" reigned supreme. One of the most influential ministers of this early period was Philip Mulkey, whose influence can be traced in the history of many early Baptist churches. Mulkey, in fact, established a church on Broad River that later moved to Fairforest on a tract between the creek of that name and Tyger River near Spartanburg. This church is of particular interest as the oldest in the upcountry; in addition, Fairforest served as a sort of link between the Particular and Separate Baptist movements of pre-Revolutionary South Carolina. The combined influence of Mulkey and Fairforest ranged far and wide, and the church branched off into a number of satellite churches which themselves spawned others reaching down to the present day. As a matter of fact, Fairforest, along with the High Hills and Congaree Churches, all of which are detailed in King's book, stand as mother churches of the denomination in South Carolina. While no simple and direct link between Greenwood's First Baptist Church and one of these pioneers has been definitely established, it seems clear that ample precedent exists to support the view that the First Baptist Church of Greenwood was founded in the natural course of events in Baptist history.

It is important to point out that by 1870 the state had endured two devastating wars and the aftermath of each, not to mention the far-reaching implications of the organizational efforts of all the Protestant denominations. One movement, in fact, was sufficiently comprehensive that it revolutionized the whole body of Baptists existing at the time. One particular meeting held in May 1845 in Augusta, Georgia—a meeting that resulted in the formation of the Southern Baptist Convention—has been called "a monumental achievement" and "a benchmark" in the life of Southern Baptists. The division effected at that meeting might just as reasonably be viewed as an inevitable result of the sectionalism that pervaded the entire country and divided its economic, political, and social life during the period just before the Civil War. Indeed, it would have been strange if people's religious life had managed to escape the effects of a movement so fundamental and far-reaching. Though by no means the only issue involved, slavery was undoubtedly among the most critical of those in conflict. Some analysts contend, in fact, that even had other factors not existed, the slavery question alone would have been enough to split northern and southern Baptist brethren. Tensions had been rising for many years and arguments forming and re-forming as a result. Even prominent Baptists such as Richard Furman and Basil Manly Sr. are on record as denouncing slavery as "undoubtedly an evil" as early as the first decades of the nineteenth century. Manly's arguments are particularly cogent. As a young student at South Carolina College, Manly wrote in 1821 that emancipation should occur for the twin reasons of self-preservation for whites and simple justice for blacks. But, as too often happens, such arguments were no match for cultural pressures and economic expediency, and most pulpits and churches at the time raised virtually no moral questions concerning slavery. It is interesting to note that neither Furman nor Manly was able to sustain the conclusion each had reached in the early 1800s. Furman died a slave owner in 1825, and it was Manly who gave the invocation at the inauguration of Jefferson Davis as president of the Confederate States of America in 1861.

CHAPTER TWO

A Church Is Born

(1870–1873)

There are references to thirty-six churches in H. L. Watson's long-running local history series, "Our Old Roads"—a more or less regular column published in the *Index-Journal* beginning in August 1940. For the most part Watson's interest lay in spotlighting a particular family or a site of historical interest, but as his daughter Margaret points out in *Greenwood County Sketches,* he often made use of early church records. Fortunately for historians, minutes of several of these churches are available for research into the attitudes and practices prevalent in an earlier time. Both Watsons seem to stress in their writings the physical manifestations of starting a church—the gathering of a few like-minded people followed by such mundane matters as clearing land, providing accessibility in the form of some sort of road, and, finally, erecting a house of worship. But surely it is important that other matters be considered also, among them the political, economic, and social conditions prevailing in the wider community at a time when forming a new church might be contemplated.

The Baptist denomination was something of a latecomer to Greenwood. Margaret Watson records the existence of at least three pre-Revolutionary churches in the area, all Presbyterian. There is nothing surprising about the preponderance of Presbyterians in the beginning, since most of the early settlers are known to have been "second generation Scotch-Irish Presbyterians." But as settlement quickened over the next few years, log meetinghouses of Lutherans, Associate Reformed Presbyterians, Baptists, and Methodists also began appearing with some regularity, providing not only places to worship but also the first real opportunities for educating settlers' children, since many of the early churches also sponsored schools where their ministers performed double duty as teachers. Two Presbyterian missionaries are known to have visited the upper and middle part of what is now Greenwood County in 1771, ordaining elders, baptizing children, and administering the Lord's Supper for the first time in the settlements. This information provides a date for the beginning of organized church activity in the area. It is clear that Greenville Presbyterian Church on Highway 178 near Donalds and Rock Presbyterian Church just off the Laurens highway must share honors as the first Presbyterian presence in the county. Available evidence gives a slight edge to Rock in the matter of age, but Greenville holds the record for sustained activity, according to Margaret Watson. The third pre-Revolutionary Presbyterian church was at Ninety Six and dates from 1775, perhaps even earlier.

It is quite possible that the Germans who settled in the area around Hard Labor and Cuffeytown creeks established a Lutheran church before the Revolution as well. This supposition is based on a couple of tantalizing references in a 1788 petition to the General Assembly seeking incorporation of "several German-Protestant Congregations in the Back Country. . . ." The petition indicated the location of several churches, and artifacts such as burial stones later found at those sites lend support to the assumption that churches might once have stood there. Watson points out that a lapse of several years between a church's organization and its application for a charter was not unusual at that time.

Evidently neither a Baptist nor a Methodist church was established in what is now Greenwood County until after the Revolutionary War. There is a smattering of evidence that a Methodist Society was formed around 1780 in the Tabernacle community a few miles from Greenwood, but Don Herd's detective work refutes that claim and establishes 1788 as the earliest date such a society could have been formed.[1] This date becomes even more reasonable when one considers that organized Methodism first came to South Carolina with Bishop Francis Asbury in 1785.

Turkey Creek Baptist Church, located just across the line in Abbeville County between Shoals Junction and Ware Shoals, was formed in the same year (1785). Though technically not in Greenwood County, this church's membership was, and is, made up largely of Greenwood County residents. Fifteen charter members were listed, among them a family named Ware, presumably the one for whom Ware Shoals was named. The first pastor, Joseph Redding, moved on after only four years to answer a call to Kentucky. It seems that several Turkey Creek families pulled up stakes and went with him; church records indicate that five households moved west with the Reverend Mr. Redding. As interesting as it is to speculate on exactly why families would decide in what seems such a casual fashion to follow a minister to a new location, the reasons are probably perfectly ordinary and straightforward, having to do with the availability of new land, better opportunities, and the frontier spirit that swept the new republic after the Revolution transformed colonists into full-fledged citizens to whom anything seemed possible.

It is important to note that early frontier churches had a place in the community well beyond that of meeting their members' spiritual needs. The South Carolina backcountry was a virtual wilderness in the late eighteenth century; law enforcement was a catch-as-catch-can affair, and courthouses were few and far between. The church often became an arbiter of economic questions of the day such as the pricing of farm products, as well as societal concerns involving relationships between neighbors and personal standards of behavior. Church records for 1786 report unanimous adoption of a resolution setting selling prices for corn and wheat: a bushel of corn was to be sold for no more than two shillings; wheat could be priced at three. Charges of drunkenness and swearing were heard in church "trials," and reports of dancing brought official reprimands. Slaves were church members from the early 1800s and were fully subject to church discipline. Margaret Watson writes that churches such as Greenville Presbyterian and Turkey Creek Baptist were quite atypical of rural churches of the period. Both reflected a certain continuity and strength that set them apart from others founded with as many, or even more, members and equal fervor. Their history also serves to demonstrate the relative stability—settlement- and population-wise—of the section that would eventually become Greenwood County.

Joe King devotes more than three pages to Turkey Creek Baptist Church. Based on the covenant its constituents signed in 1785, the church was clearly Regular Baptist from the beginning. "Separatist" tendencies still remained in some areas of the backcountry, but regularization became the norm as South Carolina struggled to right itself after the "sad havoc" wrought by the war for independence. Religion sprang into new life after 1790, and Baptist groups grew in number as well as organizational strength. One denominational periodical[2] reported sixty-seven churches—with ninety-one ministers, ordained preachers, and itinerants—serving nearly four thousand communicants in 1790. Ten years later church membership had increased by more than 40 percent, easily outpacing population growth during the same period. In addition, the shift of Baptist strength to the backcountry had become pronounced by 1790. And, though Baptists had gained a reputation as "the most zealous" of all the sects, they seemed to engage in remarkably little political activity in the earliest days, less than their numbers would seem to warrant. This fact could be explained by the difficulty of travel and communication during that period as well as the lack of organization and the basic independent nature of the denomination itself. Still, there are records of a few forays by Baptists into political affairs, including one in 1768 that involved the Regulators (a backcountry group which attempted, not very successfully as it turned out, to provide a semblance of order before law enforcement through a court system reached the hinterlands). After the Revolution, however, names of known Baptists began to appear with increasing frequency among members of the General Assembly as well as delegates to national conventions. There is evidence, according to King, that prominent South Carolina Baptists demonstrated a leaning toward the Federalist Party during the early days of independence.

King's research also revealed that South Carolina Baptists were, in general, men of limited means—few large land grants are recorded for known Baptists, and those few went to prominent

Charlestonians. Also, nearly two-thirds of church members, nearly all backcountry men, owned no slaves at all. Oddly enough, however, 40 percent of Baptist preachers in 1790 owned slaves, a fact that places this group among the more prosperous citizens at that period (unfortunately, slave ownership must be considered as evidence of wealth).

Though reports of the attitudes of early South Carolina Baptists toward education are sometimes contradictory, it appears that a certain orthodoxy of faith and a blameless life were valued more highly than an educated ministry or congregation. Still, there are a great many documented instances of genuine scholarship among early ministers, and a number of South Carolina Baptists contributed to an institution established in New Jersey "for the promotion of learning amongst us" as early as 1756. The school was Hopewell Academy; King writes that it provided the germ of an idea that eventually led to the founding of Rhode Island College in 1764, an institution that evolved into the present-day Brown University in Providence. James P. Boyce insisted that South Carolina narrowly missed being chosen as the home of this Baptist school.[3] Also, the voluminous mass of extant articles, confessions, covenants, and rules of decorum drawn up by Baptists for guidance of themselves and others in both faith and practice represent what King calls "the upper level of training and ability" to be found in early Baptist churches. Excerpts from a number of these documents demonstrate a remarkably uniform style and grammatical construction. King concluded that the writers were more sincere and zealous in their faith and exhortation than in the reasoned and scholarly presentation of their ideas. They may have been forceful writers, he noted, but they were nevertheless obviously men of limited education.

There is no point in exploring the question of education for women in early Baptist history. No one will be surprised to learn that though women frequently made up two-thirds of a given church's membership, females generally took no part in church business. While questions involving "female discipline" (whatever that was) were sometimes delegated to women of the church, for the most part their share in church life was passive and their influence indirect. With a few exceptions, Baptist interest and activity in education for both males and females would be a phenomenon of the future.

As for their theology, early South Carolina Baptists, while largely Calvinistic, managed to simplify and modify the system in order to appeal to the "active but untrained" minds of the population.There were few symbols and forms to deal with; baptism was the most vivid in that it represented starkly the death of the "old Adam" followed by renewal and regeneration of the subject into conscious membership in the body of Christ. King writes that an early Baptist church was an excellent spiritual home to those who felt comfortable in an atmosphere of simple but rigid theological requirements. This rigorous morality and doctrinal simplicity found its strongest appeal in the newly settled backcountry and provided a firm foundation, while standards in other areas tended to shift as civilization progressed. Joe King's simple prose describes the straightforward appeal of early Baptist discipline:

> The dramatic act of immersion publicly proclaimed one's intention to walk with the elect; the tonic sting of discipline held waverers in the right way; closed communion emphasized separateness from the world and membership in the family of heaven. The power of public prayer and exhortation might descend upon any man, however untrained, and only his own weakness could prevent its being exercised. . . . Church organization being congregational, the business meetings furnished an outlet for further activity and trained the members in the practice of direct democracy. Other groups made a strong appeal, but Baptists presented a peculiarly attractive combination of rigid theology and democratic activity.[4]

While methods of handling church business might differ from church to church, one main feature virtually defined continuity among nineteenth century Baptists: a group of baptized believers constituted the church, and the minister and two deacons normally carried out decisions reached at full-congregation business meetings where a clerk recorded minutes.

As time passed churches began to see certain advantages of cooperation with other Baptist churches, and local differences gradually gave way to associations, an idea that gained more and more currency as time went on; the terms *Separate* and *Regular* also gradually disappeared. Some later critics charged that the associations of this period went beyond their supposed functions of advice and deliberation, and individual churches were often too tame in their submission. King indicates that the churches repeatedly assured themselves of their complete independence even as they became ever more standardized through association.

Spiritual depressions and revivals appear throughout church histories in cycles not unlike other areas of human activity; indeed, it would be odd if such were not the case. Some fluctuations can be linked to other events such as wars, economic conditions, or natural disasters, but writers seem loath to connect the so-called Great Awakening with any specific cause. Perhaps such movements defy explanation in any case, but this surge of interest in spiritual matters appeared first in New England as revolutionary fervor took hold in the political realm and reached its apex in the Southeast with the "Great Revival" of 1800. Both religious fervor and congregations grew until they could no longer be contained by church buildings, and tent or camp meetings came into vogue. Greenwood County, in fact, retains a vestige of this phenomenon in its Epworth Camp Grounds just off Highway 178 a few miles below Greenwood where a revival is still held every July.

While Baptists participated in these revivals, their involvement was somewhat more tentative than that of other Protestant denominations since they held firmly to the practice of closed communion. In at least one instance recorded by King, a Methodist minister named James Jenkins complained in 1802 that "the Baptists reaped the fruit of our labors" due to the lack of "some one to nurse our converts." Among the more startling features of the great revival in the South was the general prevalence of what King terms "bodily exercises." Converts often underwent rather extreme physical manifestations of their religious fervor, from "mild swoons" to "convulsive spasms." For the most part, Baptists tended to disavow these extremes and instead concentrate their revival efforts within their own congregations, presumably to avoid the growing extremism of the so-called "general meetings" which some critics had begun to regard as devices of the devil. While Baptists embraced the notion of revival, most wished their own services to proceed "in an orderly and truly spiritual manner" at all times.

The effects of the great revival were felt both in increased membership of existing churches and the founding of any number of new churches. Thirty-five new churches and branches sprang up in the period 1802–1804, with a marked concentration in the larger towns of the upcountry. The number and makeup of associations increased accordingly. Church membership during this period grew by 80 percent; most of this growth would prove to be permanent.

While Mount Moriah is credited as the immediate forebear of Greenwood's First Baptist Church, a couple of other local Baptist churches are older. Margaret Watson names Mountain Creek, founded in 1798, as the earliest in the county. Siloam, which followed a year later, is also noteworthy in that its founder was the Reverend John Waller, a rather famous Baptist preacher from Virginia who moved to the area with a sizable contingent of settlers in the year 1793. Waller is also notable as an ancestor of the county's first senator, Captain C. A. C. Waller, among many other Greenwoodians.

If Watson is correct, Mount Moriah was the third Baptist church established in what is now Greenwood County, having been organized about 1810 on one of the area's very earliest thoroughfares, Barksdale Ferry Road. This road derives its importance not only from its official authorization date of 1784 but also because it was built to serve as a link between two valuable resources, the Savannah and the Saluda Rivers. Remnants of the road still essentially define the eastern and southern edges of the town of Greenwood, including Kirksey Drive, New Market and Creswell Streets on one fork and from Scotch Cross to old Cambridge (Ninety Six) along another. Mount Moriah appears on the Mills' Atlas as "Mt. Maria M.H." (Meeting House). Mills also named other meetinghouses nearby, including Sylome (Siloam), Smyrna, Cedar Spring, and St. Patrick's. Smyrna and St. Patrick's are now extinct, according to Watson, but Cedar Spring and Siloam can still be seen, albeit not in their original form.

One of the early pastors at Mount Moriah was the Reverend Nicholas Ware Hodges (1797–1841), a member of one of Greenwood's very earliest families and a name associated with both Baptist pulpits and Baptist education. As a young man Hodges read law with a cousin in Edgefield. He took over the cousin's practice when the latter moved on to Augusta and a political career in Georgia.

According to a family story recorded in *Greenwood County Sketches*, the cousin abandoned his protégé, declaring he would have nothing more to do with the young man when he decided to become a preacher. Hodges was past thirty when he was ordained, yet the record shows that he organized several Baptist churches in the upstate as well as played a prominent role in early Baptist education. As an educator he was among those leaders who advocated manual labor as part of the curriculum. Operating under the conviction that such labor met the twin requirements of economy of operation and the health and good order of students, proponents of the provision stood their ground even as the fad rapidly came and went at the institutions that implemented it.

The same experiment was tried for about nine years at nearby Cokesbury, where even the name of the school was changed at one point to include the words *Manual Labor*. Don Herd believed the idea was always more popular with clerics than with the young scholars and their families. Parents who might have been expected to embrace the notion often felt themselves cheated; one of the reasons they sent their sons to school was to help them become "gentlemen," and the role of "field hand" did not set well. The manual labor phenomenon in denominational schools lasted, all told, about ten years; it seemed to run its course at most institutions, including Furman Academy, in three or four. One Methodist minister, writing in 1898 about the manual labor experiment at Cokesbury, called it "the delusion of our fathers." There is no evidence that the Reverend Hodges ever considered himself delusional in this regard, though he did differ with a colleague, the Reverend Dr. William B. Johnson, who was strongly opposed to the idea of a laboring student body and who argued against it with the classic line: "Ardor, sir, not perseverance, is our southern characteristic." Hodges actually headed the fledgling Furman Institute for a year or so before he moved to Greenwood where he spent the last years of his life. An early school for boys in Greenwood was named in his honor. He is buried in the Mount Moriah Church cemetery.

Margaret Watson points out that Mount Moriah had replaced its original log building with a brick structure by 1834. She also writes that the congregation was both large and wealthy before the Civil

War; nearly half of its membership of 241 in 1854 were slaves. Clearly, this apparent bond between slaves and their owners was not able to withstand the much stronger tides of dissension that came with sectionalism, secession, and war. A "Ladies Soldiers Aid Society," believed to be the first such group in the Confederacy, was organized at Mount Moriah in 1861. Whether or not this group had any black participants (it is extremely doubtful that it did), its formation does tend to indicate a level of activity that was probably typical of the stronger churches of the period. As a matter of fact, the church at Mount Moriah was considered adequate to meet the spiritual and worship needs of a number of Baptists who had settled in and around the village of Greenwood from its earliest days. It is interesting to note that two Baptist schools were established in the village well before a church appeared. Hodges Institute for boys and Fuller Institute for girls opened in January 1847. As noted earlier, the preacher for whom the boys' school was named was a native of the area. Fuller's namesake, on the other hand, was the Reverend Richard Fuller (1804–1876), a native of Beaufort and a leading figure in South Carolina Baptist history who never, so far as is known, so much as visited Greenwood.

Fuller was born into the slaveholding aristocracy. His early education was broad and thorough, and he was admitted to Harvard at the age of sixteen. A superior record allowed him to graduate with his law class in 1824 even though a consumptive illness had laid him low for many months. Following his mother's example, Fuller joined the Episcopal Church soon after his return to Beaufort where he planned to practice law. Although his first baptism was by immersion at his request, Fuller counted his actual conversion as a later occurrence. That event came in 1832 as he knelt in group prayer during a revival effort. As a result of that "transforming experience," Fuller joined the Baptist Church, was rebaptized, and for several days remained so transported by joy that he was unable to eat or sleep. Fuller's new convictions, coupled with numerous dissatisfactions with his law career, led him to enter the ministry at the age of twenty-eight. He never looked back. Harvard granted the Doctor of Divinity degree to Fuller in 1853, some years after Greenwood Baptists named a school in his honor.

Richard Fuller's career was rich and full even though his health was never robust. About the time Greenwood Baptists gave the new girls' school his name, he was leaving the large and prosperous church at Beaufort to serve a small and struggling congregation in Baltimore. Evidently he possessed a magic touch; that church grew to a membership of twelve hundred in a few years, and Fuller left it to organize the Eutaw Place Church in his native state which he served for the last five years of his life.

Fuller was both an active and effective minister; King lists him among the ablest preacher-debaters in the South and a leader in the organization of the Southern Baptist Convention in 1845. No doubt it was his prominence in this activity that recommended him so strongly to local Baptists, since there is no record that he spent time in the upcountry. From 1846 when he preached the sermon celebrating the convention's first anniversary, it was understood that a Fuller sermon would be part of the annual proceedings, a record that lasted for thirty years. He served a term as president of the convention, as a member of both the foreign and home mission boards, and as a trustee of Furman University. He also supported ardently the new Southern Baptist Theological Seminary whose first president, James Petigru Boyce of Charleston, was a convert of his ministry.

Fuller was also a compelling writer, particularly on the burning questions of the day such as the philosophical underpinnings of the slavery issue. In one heated polemic with President Francis Wayland of Brown University, Fuller took the simple position that since the Scriptures sanctioned slavery, modern Christians were forced to the conclusion that the institution "was not always and in every case a sin." Wayland's view was much more abstract and did not lend itself to conclusive positions, with the result that Fuller was credited with "best verbalizing the dominant opinions in the South on slavery." While countless other ministers took up his position over the course of the long debate, it must be added that Fuller's personal leanings were toward peaceful abolition. After the war he urged his fellow Baptists to take the gospel to the freedmen as "equal citizens of the American Republic." Fuller spoke from his own experience. Even before he left Beaufort in the 1840s, either he or an assistant regularly preached every Sunday to a black Baptist membership of two thousand. Historian D. D. Wallace credits this brilliant Baptist minister with the success of the denomination among the black population of the state and calls this work an example of "common Christian brotherhood." Clearly, Baptists chose well when they determined to affix the name of Dr. Richard Fuller to their new school in Greenwood.

The Fuller Institute building burned in 1849 but was rebuilt on the same site—the present 400 block of East Cambridge Avenue immediately adjacent to Greenwood Health Care Center. It is not clear how long the school lasted, but its second building became the home of the first Methodist church in the village when its organizers "bought a brick building which had been the Baptist girls' school." The old cemetery that can still be seen at the site was the graveyard established at the rear of the Methodist church during the 1850s.

The appearance of schools and churches, as well as a few mercantile establishments and other businesses that began to cluster themselves along the east side of the first railroad tracks to traverse the town, meant that Greenwood was on the move even before the Civil War. The Greenville and Columbia line, which arrived in 1852, served not only to link the village with two much larger and more commercial (almost) cities, but its depot also became a sort of natural town center and a symbol of what must have seemed a bright future to the leading men of the little town. The Greenville and Columbia line survived the excesses of the war itself until hostilities were almost over. On their last foray through the upcountry from Columbia, Sherman's troops destroyed the railroad between the capital city and Alston, presumably by their trademark method of heating the tracks until they were pliable and bending them around tree trunks. Historian D. D. Wallace is unsparing of the infamous general and his attitude toward the state. He quotes part of a letter from Sherman to General H. W. Halleck: "The . . . whole army is burning with an insatiable desire to wreak vengeance upon South Carolina. I almost tremble at her fate, but feel that she deserves all that is in store for her." Modern historians have tended to exonerate Sherman in the matter of Columbia's burning, but Wallace clearly does not share their view. He also names Greenwood's first railroad as the prize in a spectacular piece of corruption in the early 1870s when nine public officials, through a combination of bribery and manipulation of public policy, sold shares in the railroad that had originally cost the state $20.00 to themselves and their associates for $2.75. The road failed to prosper and was bought under foreclosure in 1872 by the South Carolina Railroad. Jimmy Wade summarizes the final days of Greenwood's "First Line" thusly:

> On April 15, 1880, the bankrupt company was sold at auction and reorganized as the Columbia & Greenville Railroad. Eventually the new corporation became a division of the Richmond & Danville Railroad System, a party to the formation of the Southern Railway Company in 1894.[5]

The little village of Greenwood was not a particularly prepossessing place in the year 1870. Actually, the entire state—indeed, the whole of the South—was not a pretty sight in the immediate aftermath of the Civil War. Greenwood's own Louis Booker Wright demonstrated his skill as a phrasemaker when he entitled a chapter in his South Carolina bicentennial history book "Triumph of Extremism and Devastation of War." This seven-word description speaks volumes about both the rhetoric employed by certain politicians and the cost involved in playing out that rhetoric on the battlefield. In retrospect it is clear that the most glaring shortcoming of too many of the state's leading men was their willingness, even eagerness, to secede and go it alone. This defiant attitude was the direct legacy of John C. Calhoun, a towering figure in sheer reasoning power but one whose prescriptions (and whose successor in the U.S. Senate, Robert Barnwell Rhett) brought not only his native state but an entire region to utter ruin.

Calhoun's argument—that the Constitution had established merely a confederation of sovereign states and not an indivisible nation—made such sense to South Carolinians that many participants did not believe their actions in signing the Ordinance of Secession would precipitate war. That belief is the basis of an insistence, even to the present day, on calling the conflict the "War Between the States" rather than the "Civil War," a term that carries the idea of a revolt against a unified nation. In short, everything in the South, even the religious life of its people, appeared to take second place to the blazing issue of states' rights from about 1850, the year of Calhoun's death, until the ignominious end of a hideously destructive war. A single example can illustrate this point. In the aftermath of the infamous Brooks-Sumner Affair of 1856 in which Congressman Preston S. Brooks, representing Edgefield (now Greenwood) County, administered a sound caning to Senator Charles Sumner of Massachusetts on the floor of the U.S. Senate, public opinion in South Carolina was so blindly pro-Brooks that a Baptist minister in Orangeburg was forced to resign his position and leave the state because he criticized Brooks's action and "expressed opposition to Southern institutions," presumably slavery.

But well before this galvanizing public attack that focused the eyes of both the nation and the world on South Carolina, sectional differences had already begun pulling apart the loose fabric of American society. Opposing politicians seized on issues such as the tariff and the question of extending slavery into new territories in the West, not to mention John C. Calhoun's extremist "nullification" rhetoric, to fan the flames of sectionalism. The upcountry of South Carolina was also facing agricultural problems because profits from its one-crop cotton economy were declining due to diminishing fertility of its fields. New and fresher lands in the rapidly developing Southwest were threatening an uncomfortable competition with fields worn out from overplanting a single crop. And always there was the overriding question of slavery. Wright points out that only those owning the largest number of slaves were eager for an immediate break with the Union. Plantation owners, primarily from the lowcountry, were not above using scare tactics to convince small farmers in the upcountry that they too had a stake in maintaining the system even though they might own no slaves themselves. Abolition would "Africanize" the whole state, they cried, and quite possibly unleash another Haiti-style uprising of ex-slaves against the white population. Perhaps the bitter seeds of racial prejudice were sown in just this way.

Whether or not one agrees with Louis Wright that it was "an unnecessary war," the devastation and death were there for all to see when the Civil War came to its bitter end in 1865. If South Carolina carried a special burden of guilt for its part in precipitating hostilities, it paid many times over in the loss of its men and wealth, the sacrifices and contributions of its heroic women, and the privations suffered by all its citizens during four years of conflict. South Carolina sent about 44,000 fighting men to the front; its casualties numbered more than 10,000, or about 23 percent. The result of such loss was comparable to England's when a generation of its best blood fell in World War I—men whose leadership potential would be sorely missed during the years following the conflict. Louis Wright's final paragraph in his chapter on extremism and devastation is a gem; it paints a realistic picture of the South Carolina upcountry about the time the idea for a new Baptist church in the village of Greenwood was beginning to take shape:

> The small farmers of the Up Country fared a little better than the planters in the tidewater region. Few had ever owned slaves, and they were accustomed to heavy labor. But former slaveowners who themselves had never worked in the fields found it necessary to pick up a hoe, or, if lucky enough to find one, to follow a plow. One dignified ex-Confederate soldier who lived near Greenwood was often seen plowing—but not without his small black string tie. Even some professional men, lawyers and bankers, . . . had to turn to farming because they had no income from the former occupations. No one despised any honest labor that would keep body and soul together. In some fashion, people raised subsistence crops of corn, wheat, sorghum, and vegetables, as they scratched out a living from the soil in the first year or two after Appomattox. The war was over; life had to go on. South Carolina's men and women followed Lee's injunction. They resumed their occupations or adopted new ones and prepared to rebuild a civilization that in time would be vastly different from the one they had defended.[6]

The little village of Greenwood was virtually defined in its earliest days by the growth and development of the railroad industry. A true pioneer in the field, South Carolina was the site of the second American railroad when the Charleston and Hamburg line was completed in 1833 as the first in the country expressly designed for steam locomotion. Its primary purpose was to facilitate trade between the lowcountry port and the cotton belt of central Georgia, but it also set in motion the idea that small towns everywhere were only a railroad line away from the progress represented by the new innovation. Certainly Greenwood was no exception, and its first railroad followed the Charleston and Hamburg by less than twenty years. It is interesting to note that the time span between Greenwood's first and second railroad lines was thirty years; no doubt decades of sectional politics, war, and reconstruction are sufficient to explain the gap. Perhaps it is also significant that the Greenwood Baptist Church was formed during the period between the arrival of the first railroad line in 1852 and the second in 1882.

This thirty-year span also covered the entire Civil War and the period of intense political upheaval called Reconstruction. When the smoke cleared after the war, the state found itself not only exhausted and impoverished but also under the heel of a state government made up of carpetbaggers (northerners who came south after the war for political or financial advantage) and scalawags (defined as southern white men who joined the Republicans) and a central government bent on a method of reconstruction never anticipated by the framers of the Constitution. D. D. Wallace calls Radical Reconstruction the "outstanding failure of American statesmanship," citing its glaring inconsistencies and blatant laceration of the public welfare. According to Wallace, the state at the end of the war was generally reconciled to the notion of reunion with the North, even though extremes of opinion certainly existed then, just as they do now. "South Carolina had lost her appeal to the court of her own choosing," he wrote, "and was ready loyally to abide by the issue." But the state would have much to endure before that reunion became a reality.

Among the less baleful results of Radical Reconstruction was a new state constitution, one that greatly advanced the concept of democracy and, among other significant changes, established the public school system that still exists. While echoing the U.S. Constitution in affirming religious liberty, the document also gave married women, for the first time, full control over their own property. Moves to wrest political control of the state from the Radical Republicans began about 1870 and continued unabated until the election of 1876 installed former Confederate General Wade Hampton as governor. Wallace does not bother to conceal his scorn for the criminals, opportunists, and similar types who made up the political class during the nine years or so of Radical Reconstruction; his word for them is "corruptionists." He excoriates Governor Robert K. Scott, whom he characterizes dismissively as a "carpetbagger from Ohio," as weak but not malicious, a man whose "feeble instincts of decency" tended to dissolve in the face of the "circumambient corruption" that was the order of the day. It was during this period of profound public unrest and private despair that Greenwood area Baptists finally mobilized themselves to form a new church in their little town.

The village could trace its own beginnings to the name given by Charlotte Dozier McGehee to the summer home her husband built about 1823 on a six-hundred-acre plantation between Cambridge (Ninety Six) and Abbeville. She called her new home, located on what is now lower East Cambridge Avenue between Elm Court and Brewer School, Green Wood. Even though a small settlement had grown up around the first house within a few years, the first post office established in 1837 was called Woodville for some unknown reason for the first thirteen years of its existence. By 1850 post office and village bore the same name—Greenwood—but the town center was soon to shift from the "old chapel" of the Presbyterian school, the heart of the original village, to a new and bustling area around the railroad tracks.

When twenty-three people, most of them members of Mount Moriah, presented themselves at Waller Hall for the purpose of organizing a Baptist church, most probably understood that the groundwork for this venture had been carefully laid by a few prominent men. The Reverends N. W. Hodges and Richard Fuller have already been mentioned, but two other local Baptist preachers, James M. Chiles and W. B. Jones, also deserve credit as leaders in the movement. Margaret Watson traced the Chiles family to a Revolutionary soldier named William who purchased land along Hard Labor Creek near Bradley in 1791. A grandson of the first settler, James Chiles (1809–1862), led a very active ministry. Not only a prime mover in founding two county churches—Damascus and Horeb—he also worked tirelessly on behalf of both Hodges and Fuller Institutes in nearby Greenwood. Though Chiles moved to Georgia a few years before his

The Reverend W. B. Jones, the "very active, energetic, and progressive man" who organized the church and founded the Abbeville Association in 1870.

death, Greenwood's first Baptist church surely owes something to his pioneering spirit and belief in Baptist institutions.

Another leader, W. B. Jones, was a more direct participant. He is called, in fact, the actual founder of the church in a long article in the *Index-Journal* of January 22, 1933. The reporter describes Jones as a "very active, energetic, and progressive man" who had also founded the Abbeville Association of Baptist Churches the same year. According to the historical table in King's history, Greenwood's church was a charter member of the new association, along with Beulah, Buffalo, Damascus, Fellowship, Friendship, Horeb, Mount Moriah, Pine Pleasant, Providence, Olive Branch, Siloam, and Sister Springs Churches. The other churches had previously belonged to the much older Edgefield Association which dates from 1807.

Jones performed another public service when he led the movement to mark the gravesite of the Reverend John Waller a few miles below Greenwood and near the settlement at Phoenix where Jones made his home for a time. W. B. Jones began his drive to form a new church during the winter of 1869–70 with a series of lectures on the life and ministry of Jesus and the missionary work of Saint Paul. While no record remains as to the actual size of his audiences, the lectures must have been well attended; the local Methodist church offered its facilities, and the meetings continued through the summer of 1870 when Jones concluded the time was right for setting his organizational plans in motion. The church's own records emphasize the single-minded dedication of the Reverend Jones to the task at hand:

> At considerable expense, no little labor, and almost alone, Bro. Jones secured & fitted up what is known as the Waller Hall for the use of the Church. This Hall is the property of Sister J. E. Waller,[7] who generously offered it free of rent—thus indirectly contributing, at least, $100 per annum to the Church.

With the foundation laid and prior notice given, a meeting was held on September 25, 1870, for the purpose of organizing a church in the regular manner. Jones and Professor C. H. Toy (from the seminary) conducted the meeting with Toy acting as moderator and W. P. McKellar as clerk. The names of the very first members can be found on page 1 of the church's original record book; surely they should also be included here. Founding members included eighteen Mount Moriah members and five from Bethany. They were F. G. Parks, M. E. Parks, S. H. Parks, G. C. Parks, F. A. Parks, W. P. McKellar, A. L. McKellar, G. M. Harrison, M. A. Harrison, Amelia Crews, Eliza Crews, Bettie Crews, Sudie Crews, Mary F. Isaacs, Mary Norrel, Emily Silks, Lizzie Arnold, W. T. Farrow, C. Richter, S. Richter, Lou Richter, Kate Richter, and C. E. Patton. Oddly enough, W. B. Jones is not listed as a member.[8]

After enrolling themselves as charter members, the little group adopted its first covenant and articles of faith, with resolutions, at the same meeting:

COVENANT

> Having been, as we trust, brought by divine grace to embrace the Lord Jesus Christ, & to give ourselves wholly to Him, we do now solemnly & joyfully covenant with each other, to walk together in Him, with brotherly love, to His glory, as our common Lord. We do, therefore, in His strength engage—
>
> That, we will exercise a Christian care & watchfulness over each other, & faithfully warn, exhort, and admonish each other, as occasion may require;
>
> That, we will not forsake the assembling of ourselves together, but will uphold the public worship of God, and the Ordinances of His House;

That, we will not omit closet & family religion at home, nor neglect the great duty of religiously training our children, & those under our care, for the service of Christ, & the enjoyment of heaven;

That, as we are the light of the world & the Salt of the earth, we will seek divine aid, to enable us to deny ungodliness, & every worldly lust, & to walk circumspectly in the world, that we may win the souls of men;

That, we will cheerfully contribute of our property, according as God has prospered us, for the maintenance of a faithful and evangelical ministry among us, for the support of the poor, & the spread of the Gospel over the earth;

That, we will, in all conditions, even till death, strive to live to the glory of Him, who hath called us out of darkness into His marvelous light.

ARTICLES OF FAITH

We believe the Holy Bible has God for its author, salvation for its object, & truth without any mixture of error for its matter; that this salvation is secured through Faith, Repentance, & Baptism; that Faith is implicit confidence in the teachings of the Bible; that Repentance is real sorrow for past sins because displeasing to God, & a determination to sin no more; that Baptism is the immersion of a believing penitent in water into the name of the Father, the Son, & the Holy Spirit; that all who honestly & conscientiously exercise this Faith, feel this Repentance, & submit to this Baptism, thereby become Deciples [*sic*] of the Lord Jesus, the Christ; that a Church is a congregation of such Deciples [*sic*], worshiping statedly in one place; that the Officers of a Church are an Elder or Bishop, & Deacons; that the first day of the week is the Lord's Day, & should be devoted to public worship and private devotion.

RESOLUTIONS

1. This Church shall be called the Greenwood Baptist Church.
2. In an Election for officers, all the members shall have the right to vote.

3. All business meetings of the Church shall be conducted according to parliamentary usage.
4. To keep full & fair records of the proceedings of the Church, a Clerk shall be annually elected from the members.

The first deacons elected by the new church were F. G. Parks and G. M. Harrison; the latter was ordained on the spot, but Parks's prior ordination at Mount Moriah was recognized. Farrow, Harrison, and McKellar accepted appointment as delegates to the Abbeville Association. Since no regular pastor was available at the time, the church arranged for students and faculty members of the seminary at Greenville to supply preachers until such time as it could fill its pulpit. This arrangement lasted about eighteen months, according to church records; Gerald Smart makes it only fifteen. Smart's little history also indicates that, at first, preaching services were held only once a month.

Thanks to the detailed newspaper story we can place most of the original church members firmly within the context of early Greenwood history. Five were direct descendants of John Waller: Amelia Crews was a granddaughter and M. A. Harrison a great-granddaughter, as were her sisters Eliza, Bettie, and Sudie Crews. The Parks family was another sizable group consisting of Dr. and Mrs. Felix G. and their three daughters. Originally from Edgefield, Dr. Parks moved to Greenwood in 1851 where he attained the unique distinction of serving as postmaster for three separate terms. Deacon Harrison moved to Alabama only two years after the church was formed.

Mary Norrel, Emily Silks, and Lizzie Arnold were longtime residents of the area, while the Reverend Mr. W. T. Farrow would shortly move on to Newberry to hold a pastorate in that town for some years. (Is it fair to speculate why the church did not see fit to use one of its charter members in the pulpit? In the light of its actions in later years, this omission just might be significant.) Farrow's son married one of the Parks daughters; we do not know whether they continued to live in Greenwood. Mrs. Isaacs's husband worked for the railroad. The five people who brought letters from Bethany Church were all members of the Christopher Richter family. Richter had emigrated to America from Germany in 1841, settling first in Hamburg. The family affiliated with Bethany in 1857 and had been living in Greenwood for several years when the new church was formed.

At the time the article was written, more than sixty years after the church was founded, only two of its charter members were still alive, and only one, Lou Richter Waldrop, lived in Greenwood. Her sister, Kate Richter Anderson, was a resident of Williamston. The article also notes that S. H. Benjamin was received as a transfer member from Siloam Church at the October conference less than a month after the official founding date of the church. It seems clear that Benjamin's name should be included as a charter member. Still another article from a much later source, an item signed by the pastor in the newsletter of September 19, 1995, puts the whole question of charter membership into the proper perspective. Dr. Harris wrote:

> When I heard the story of Mr. Benjamin and thought about what membership really means, it occurred to me that every one of us is a charter member of this church. We are deeply indebted to the past. As we celebrate 125 years of proclamation and service through this congregation, we are aware of the blessings we have received from those who have gone before us. But today we are the church. First Baptist Church will have life today and a life in the future only as we receive and share the love of Jesus Christ. In a sense we are all beginning anew in each service and in each attempt to minister. We and the original twenty-three are all one.

But that view was part of the distant and unknown future when the fledgling church held its founding meetings in 1870.

As the new church sat in conference after services on December 4, Deacon Harrison evidently felt it necessary to clarify Resolution No. 2 which had been adopted at the founding meeting; accordingly, his motion that "the Female members of the Church" be granted the privilege of "voting upon all questions" was passed. The deacon seems to have been uncharacteristically sensitive to the importance of women's contributions to the new enterprise, or possibly his wife had prodded him on the issue before they left home that morning. Either way, the action was portentous. Greenwood's First Baptist Church can point to an outstanding record in regard to the full participation of women in church business; women members of today need to know they were valued from the very first. It was also felt necessary to set forth a few clear terms of stewardship at the same conference. Members adopted the following preamble and resolution:

> Whereas our Association has urged upon the Churches the adoption of the plan of Systematic Benevolence, & we are convinced that it is good policy, to say nothing of duty in the matter. Therefore be it Resolved:
>
> 1st That each & every member of this Church shall feel bound to contribute something to the Treasury of the Lord every Lord's Day.
>
> 2nd That it shall be the duty of the Junior Deacon to pass through the audience, during the singing of the 2nd hymn, & give everybody an opportunity to contribute.
>
> 3rd That these contributions shall be appropriated as follows: three fourths (3/4) for the use of the Church, & the balance equally divided between the Abbeville Association & the indigent young men at the Seminary.
>
> 4th That the amt. recd. each day shall be reported to the Clerk to be duly recorded.

The clerk's entries for the first three quarters of the year 1871 are laconic, even somewhat lackluster. A committee was named in January to approach Mrs. Waller for permission to use the hall for another year. This seemingly simple and straightforward piece of business had not been accomplished by conference time in February; as a matter of fact, no further mention of using Waller Hall appears in the record that year.

The little group seems to have limped along, holding sporadic services and picking up a member or two here and there until January 1872 when the first pastor was officially called. He was the Reverend Thomas Herbert Pope, a thirty-three-year-old Newberry native and Confederate veteran who had been ordained as a minister only nine years before. Pope, whose father was a well-known member of the Newberry Bar, was a graduate of Furman University. He began his seminary training at Princeton, New Jersey, and later finished the course at Greenville. Clearly, Pope was a denominational stalwart;

the record shows service as state missions secretary, general agent of the Executive Board of the State Baptist Convention, and moderator of the Abbeville Association. He also was instrumental in forming new churches at both Ninety Six and Hodges. Evidently Pope was much loved by the Greenwood congregation; when his health began to fail in the third year of his pastorate he was given sick leave in the hope he would recover. The church called Dr. J. A. Broadus as supply pastor during Pope's last illness.

It is surely worthwhile to pause for a bit to consider the quality of the man who filled the pulpit at the Greenwood church during a crucial period. John Albert Broadus was born in 1827 to a refined and literate family in Culpeper County, Virginia. His father served in the usual capacities of a country squire—he farmed, taught school, and sat in the legislature—but he was also a devoted parent and an active Baptist layman. He was known as a "Christian politician and a firm advocate of missions, temperance, and ministerial education." Broadus's mother, while less church-minded than her husband, saw to it that her family was exposed to the finer things of life, such as music, books, and flowers.

The Reverend Thomas H. Pope (1839–1875), first pastor 1872–1875.

Young Broadus was a child of his era; he grew up in the accepted system of an agricultural economy based on slave labor. Schooling was a haphazard affair, and he studied either in small field schools with itinerant teachers or at home with his parents. The family farm and home constituted his world. An exceptionally bright young man, Broadus longed for a college education and a career. He had embraced Christianity at the age of sixteen at a revival meeting but explored several other options before deciding on a career in the ministry. Once decided, however, he lost no time in throwing himself wholeheartedly into the work. He enrolled in the University of Virginia, one of the best schools in the country, where he made good use of the elective system then in effect and established himself as the best debater in the Jefferson Society. The skill with words Broadus developed in college would serve him well throughout his life. A sermon on the work of the minister was the determining factor in his choice of a profession, and his own contribution to the art of preaching was the historic volume, *On the Preparation and Delivery of Sermons* (1870), a treatise that has been in continuous use for more than a century.

Broadus was a man of broad scholarship and deep understanding of humankind, and he operated with the urbanity typical of a cultured Virginia gentleman of the period. He was continually exasperated with the careless treatment of the Scriptures by students whose familiarity with their meaning he considered superficial. "The main difficulty with students of the Bible," he wrote in a *Seminary Magazine* article, "is they think they know more than they do and want to know more than they can. . . ."

Well-known also as the biographer of James Petigru Boyce, a friend as well as an academic colleague, Broadus was one of the first four men named to the faculty of the new Greenville seminary which was preparing to open in 1858. Perhaps convinced that the proposed opening date was a bit premature, Broadus and another nominee declined the honor after weeks of anxious consideration, an action that delayed the opening of the school for another year. By 1859 he and the others were ready to accept. King called the four-man group of Boyce, Broadus, Basil Manly Jr., and William Williams "an excellent faculty, comparing favorably with any in the nation at that time."

When the Civil War forced the seminary to close, Broadus occupied his time with writing and preaching. As evidence of his commitment to faith and works, he and the other faculty members met in the summer of 1865 to consider the fledgling seminary's prospects for the future after the war which had left the whole state as if "swept by a cyclone." The question was clear: should the four men press on in the face of worthless seminary subscriptions and dim hopes? They had prayed over the question again and again; finally, someone in the room said: "Suppose we quietly agree that the seminary may die, but we'll die first." All heads were bowed once again and so the matter was decided. The seminary remained at Greenville until 1877 when it was moved to Louisville, Kentucky. As one of the guiding spirits behind the Southern Baptist Theological Seminary, Broadus became its second president, serving from 1889 until his death in 1895. He always believed in institutions for the good they could do in the everyday world and placed particular faith in the seminary he had helped shape from its earliest days. So strong was his belief in its potential that he turned down offers of more prestigious posts—at the University of Chicago, Brown University, Vassar College, and many others—in favor of furthering the work at Louisville. He also served a term as president of the South Carolina Baptist Convention.

John Broadus developed cordial relations with a wide range of notables through travel and correspondence and spoke frequently from pulpits in the North and Midwest. He was neither a narrow sectarian nor a provincial southerner. His scholarship was more universal in scope, and he dealt little with the social and political issues of his day, preferring to concentrate on the ages-old questions of biblical scholarship and interpretation. He supported a liberal arts education for preachers and considered no branch of knowledge useless. He believed it was particularly important for ministers to read the "best books in every subject" and be familiar with not only the great authors but also the natural world and human nature. His viewpoint was large and his whole nature sympathetic. He once remarked, in fact: "If I were asked what is the first thing in effective preaching, I should say sympathy; and what is the second thing, I should say sympathy; and what is the third thing, I should say sympathy." The Greenwood church was indeed fortunate to obtain the services of the eminent John A. Broadus at a critical moment in its early history.

As for the church's first official pastor, Thomas Pope undertook his charge at the beginning of 1872 with a group that had baptized presumably its first new convert, W. H. Patton, the previous August. The congregation had also gone on record the next month with the first move to erect a house of worship and to seek aid from the

Abbeville Association and the American Baptist Missionary Society to that end. The first pastor was offered an annual salary of four hundred dollars to preach twice a month, morning and night. Siloam Church called Pope at the same time to fill its pulpit on alternate Sundays, but this arrangement caused a problem that was not resolved for several months. Evidently Siloam wanted the same Sundays for their services as Greenwood had arranged with the Reverend Mr. Pope. A discussion with two visiting brethren from the older church at a conference in December appeared to resolve the question in Siloam's favor when a motion to change to the second and fourth Sundays instead of the prevailing first and third was adopted. But a short entry in the record a few months later reads: "Febr., March, & April, no business transacted except to change the meeting days back to the 1st and 3rd Lord's Days."

Another important move came at the beginning of the year 1872 when a "neat organ worth $150" was purchased for the sum of $85. A penciled note in a different hand was added to the record at some point, presumably by a subsequent clerk or perhaps pastor. This note indicates that the organ came from the firm of H. Waters of New York which had in effect made its own donation to the church by reducing the price by $65. The local financing came from "friends of the church" who agreed to pay half the cost. C. A. C. Waller paid the balance. A brief note in the same hand appended to the minutes of the December 17 conference named Miss B. Crews as church organist. The church's long tradition of receiving significant gifts from its members had begun; so, incidentally, had its emphasis on the musical component of its worship services.

To no one's surprise, probably then or now, a building committee was named at conference on Pope's first Sunday in the pulpit. Five prominent Greenwood men were named as members: W. P. McKellar, G. M. Harrison, C. A. C. Waller, Dr. J. C. Maxwell, and Thomas F. Riley. The last two named were not at the time members of the church, though Maxwell would subsequently join. Evidently it was not uncommon to have one or more "outsiders" named to such committees. Perhaps it was felt that the project could thus be viewed as something of a civic enterprise; besides, there was an implied compliment in naming men not formally connected by ties of membership, and there was always the possibility of attracting subscriptions from still other outsiders. At conference on May 5, 1872, the "balance of the Male members" of the church were added to the building committee by resolution and consent, and by June the committee was able to report a total of nine hundred dollars raised toward the estimated fifteen hundred dollars required to purchase a suitable lot. The committee was instructed to continue its work, to accept either cash or notes as pledges, and, finally, to mortgage the property for any balance that might be needed. It was also charged with selecting a lot at the proper time. The program of building—in all its ramifications—that would characterize the church for many years was on its way.

Though the new church was careful to put "first things first," so to speak, by securing a pastor and appointing the all-important building committee, one recorder obviously thought it necessary to add notes here and there in the first minute book so that the contributions of auxiliary church groups would not be lost forever. Thus we learn from a notation on page 13 that an average of about forty scholars took part in the "Lord's Day School" under the guidance of Dr. W. A. Williams as superintendent.[9] Another note on the same page credits the pastor with organizing a Ladies Aid Society to meet weekly and make weekly contributions. That group managed to raise more than two hundred dollars in its first year, an amount it "invested in a communion sett, chandelier, carpeting, sofa, chairs & the bal[ance] applied to painting." Doubtless this type of contribution from its women was common to most early churches.

CHAPTER THREE

Years of Growth and Service

(1873–1911)

Though the twenty-two months from February 1872, when a building was first mentioned, to December 1873, when the new church home was formally dedicated, must have been a veritable beehive of activity, the official minutes are strangely silent on the matter. Possibly some sort of auxiliary records were kept by the building committee and were subsequently lost. No one can really be sure. Officially, we know only that the structure was the second church building within the town limits (the Methodist church was the first). It was situated, appropriately enough, on what was then named Church Street, and its dedication on "the 3rd Lord's Day in Dec. 1873" was considered a great day in the life of the church. The minutes indicate that no less than seven ministers participated in some way in the program. Dr. John Broadus's sermon with a text taken from John's Gospel must have been inspired; the minutes call it one "long to be remembered, for it melted many to tears, and made many hearts throb with thanks. . . ."

The location of the church was squarely between that part of town known as "old Greenwood" and the newer business section that had grown up beside the railroad tracks (only the east side of the present-day square existed at that time). A contemporary newspaper article describes the structure only as a frame building and places it about sixty feet back from the street, at some point in the third block of the present-day East Cambridge Avenue. Thanks to the detective work of John Blythe, formerly historic preservation officer of the Upper Savannah Council of Governments, the location of the first church building can be determined by means of identifying the families who subsequently built houses on three lots that were once church property. The street numbers in the old records (and still on the houses themselves) are in the 200s, which would normally indicate the second block, but it must be remembered that Jennings Avenue did not exist in the 1870s (nor, for that matter, for another sixty years). The second block of East Cambridge became the third when Jennings was opened sometime between 1930 and 1936. Blythe's discoveries from early newspapers and interviews clear up a few mysteries:

> 215 East Cambridge Avenue—lot #1 of Baptist Church property. Sold to Mrs. Ella Turner (Mrs. John Durst) Seago 3/27/1899. House constructed 1900. (on site of church)
>
> 223 East Cambridge Avenue—W. V. Blyth, contractor. Lot #2 of Baptist Church property. Sold to J. G. Mattison 3/27/1899. House constructed 1899.
>
> 229 East Cambridge Avenue—lot #3 of Baptist Church property. Sold to Janie A. (Mrs. A. J.) Sproles 3/27/1899. House constructed 1899. Some of the lumber was reused from the old Greenwood Baptist Church.

The notation that some of the timbers from the first church building found their way into the A. J. Sproles house is particularly interesting. This sort of thing happened quite a lot in the early days; there is something oddly satisfying in these accounts of recycling building materials. As evidence of the physical impact of the new church building, the minutes record naming a committee to employ a sexton about seven months after it was dedicated. His name, unfortunately, is not recorded.

An interesting controversy arose in 1874 when a former member was denied "letters of dismission" needed to join another Baptist church on account of "his silence in reference to his subscription to

First Baptist Church members and children, Greenwood, S.C., about 1905, at the church location, North Main and Bailey Circle. First row left to right: Mrs. Joel Burnett, Mary Sue Sproles, Genevieve Singleton, Mrs. DeShaze, Mrs. Napier, Mrs. Mary Beaudrot, Mrs. Wideman, Mrs. Susan Hill, Mr. J. R. Leavell, Mr. Cowan (pastor), Elizabeth Cowan, and Theodosia Sproles. Second row left to right: Gerald Smart, D. M. Nixon, Mr. DeShaze, N. B. Norris, J. C. Burns Sr., Mrs. Duckett, Mrs. A. F. Hagan, Mrs. Bessie Andrews, Mrs. Lizzie Harrison, Mrs. J. W. Sproles, Joe Beaudrot, L. C. Craig, J. W. Sproles, and Press Devore. Third row left to right: Mr. Watts, Mrs. A. T. Jamison, Mrs. J. G. Mattison, Mr. A. F. Hagan, Mr. Youngblood, and Mr. Graham.

the pastor's salary for the year 1872." This intriguing motion, however, also included the proviso that letters would be granted provided he gave a "satisfactory answer" to the subscription question. Fortunately, the satisfactory answer was forthcoming, and the former member was provided the letters he needed to associate himself with another congregation.

Although the little church and its first pastor seem to have suited each other's needs admirably, their association was destined to be short-lived. The Reverend Mr. Pope died on July 8, 1875, only four days after his thirty-sixth birthday. The minute book contains a three-and-one-half-page "Tribute of Respect" signed by a committee of three prominent church members: Dr. J. C. Maxwell, Thomas Duckett, and C. A. C. Waller. An example of the flowery prose typical of the period, the tribute offers remarkably little in the way of hard fact. We do not learn, for example, what killed Pope at such an early age, only that he died "after a lingering illness of seventeen days." Neither do we discover any objective measures of the strength of the church at the end of its first pastor's tenure; the tribute goes no further than crediting Pope with turning "a very small membership . . . into one of the most self-sustaining churches of the Association and a beautiful church building . . . , a lasting monument to his indefatigable industry, energy, and zeal." And, lest anyone fault the tribute for erring on the side of too much praise, the committee permitted itself the luxury of extremely mild criticism, allowing that as a preacher Pope "was not a finished pulpit orator"; rather, the writers believed that his "earnest conversational style" both won the attention of his audience and carried a deep conviction of its own. The tribute to Pope ends with a preamble and resolution:

> Whereas it has pleased God, the Sovereign Dispenser of all events, to send the swift-winged messenger of death to garner in our beloved pastor, Thomas H. Pope,
>
> Resolved, 1st, That we bow in humiliation and prayerful resignation before this mysterious dispensation of his providence.
>
> Resolved 2nd, That forasmuch as the deceased had so endeared himself to us by his "winning gentleness and loving patience" and Christian example, we will ever mourn his irreparable loss, strive for the impress of his high intellectual and moral character, and emulate his example and pray for his virtues.
>
> Resolved 3rd, That we erect in our church building a tablet to his memory.
>
> Resolved 4th, That we extend to his bereaved family our deepest sympathy in their severe affliction and rejoice with them in the

glorious hope that their loss will be an immortal gain to our departed brother and pastor.

Resolved 5th, That a copy of the above preamble and resolutions be furnished to his family, and also to the *Working Christian*[1] for publication.

Three pastors having declined to accept the pulpit of the Greenwood church from November 1875 to January 1876, the relief of the pulpit committee is almost palpable in the clerk's note entered on page 41 after Elder J. S. Jordan answered the church's call. "May he be imbued with wisdom from on high," he wrote, "and the humble instrument in God's hands of leading the people to do their whole duty and build up the waste places both near and far and to God be all the honor and glory." The new pastor's salary would be eight hundred dollars per year for three morning and two night services per month. It is surely not insignificant to note that the salary of the second pastor was exactly double that of the first.

The records of this period also indicate a small but significant step toward developing a music program. In April 1876 C. A. C. Waller made a motion during conference that "three seats near the organ be reserved for the singers of the congregation." In another concession to the importance of music, the minutes of the conference session of May 14 report that Mr. Anderson's singing class would be allowed the use of the church. It is quite clear as well that the church was diligent in its duty to the Abbeville Association from the beginning. Even before the building was finished the church had extended an invitation to the association to hold its next meeting in Greenwood.

Dr. John Maxwell, lately a member of the building committee, had followed that important service with joining the church as a full-fledged member in late September 1874. He was one of fifteen new members who responded to calls issued during a "meeting of days" which followed an "agreeable and harmonious" meeting of the Abbeville Association held on the fourth Sunday. (Note: At this point the minutes begin using a simple "Sunday" designation rather than the more cumbersome "Lord's Day.") Maxwell's decision to join was a genuine coup for the church. Not only was he a prominent and highly respected physician, a Confederate veteran who had made a reputation as a regimental surgeon, and a civic leader whose presence was felt in virtually all of the town's most progressive ventures, his is also the name most strongly associated with a Greenwood institution whose purpose and influence loom large in the history of the Baptist denomination in a ministry then known as "orphanage work." Maxwell had been a member of the Greenwood church nearly twenty years when his most notable act of philanthropy occurred, one that would bring the spotlight of Baptist attention statewide to the little town of Greenwood. Connie Maxwell Children's Home would be the long-range result of that attention, one that still stands on its original site on the western boundary of the city of Greenwood.

South Carolina Baptists had not embraced this particular ministry with the enthusiasm of other Protestant denominations, notably the Episcopalians and Presbyterians, both of whom had founded orphanages in the upcountry. Actually, it was the president of Thornwell Orphanage in Clinton, Dr. W. P. Jacobs, who brought the problem of children's needs to the attention of an editor of the *Baptist Courier* in 1888. An editorial in the magazine met with immediate response; only two weeks after it appeared the state convention voted to consider the advisability of establishing an orphanage under the auspices of the Baptist Convention. Public sentiment, while overwhelmingly in favor of the idea, nevertheless seemed to support the notion of providing care restricted to "orphan children of Baptist parentage." Perhaps this approach, which seems rather narrow-minded more than a hundred years later, made sense in an earlier time, particularly when one remembers that the canvass was conducted among Baptists who might understandably respond in purely denominational terms. Fortunately, church leaders were able to avoid this pitfall and concentrate on the issue of providing a basic and much needed service as their primary goal. Somehow they managed to confine their intraconvention bickerings to less potentially explosive issues than the church preference of potential clients.

Offers of free sites for the proposed facility were made even in the first year of exploring the feasibility of the idea itself, but the original committee did not allow itself to expand its charge to anything as specific as site deliberation, nor did it consider obligating the state convention in any manner. In fact, after a year the study committee limited itself to reporting a favorable response to its most basic inquiries and recommending an entirely new committee to explore possible sites and receive any gifts or bequests that might be made.

The Reverend J. L. Vass of Darlington, who would be named the first superintendent, not only chaired the second committee but also recommended a single site, Limestone Springs, to the 1890 convention where he immediately ran into opposition from members who felt the search had been entirely too limited in scope. Accordingly, yet another committee was named to work with Vass's group. The membership of the joint committee, totaling twenty-two persons, was charged with a list of duties, including final choice of a location, a draft of proposed management policy, and gathering "as many facts as possible touching upon the establishment, management, and support of some of the orphanages now in successful operation." As evidence of the convention's firm intention to proceed, a resolution was adopted calling on each pastor in the state to secure a collection "at or near Christmas" for the support of the proposed institution. Dr. Maxwell's detailed and generous offer was made to this expanded committee.

It was well that the Maxwells and the town of Greenwood got together on the offer since theirs was in direct competition with proposals from ten other locations, all the way from Williamston and Greer in the upstate and Lake City, Florence, and a spot called Cat Fish,[2] all located nearer the coast. Perhaps Maxwell's promise of 470 acres of land in one body lying near the town limits to the west, as well as ten acres near the center of town and virtually all the Maxwells' personal property to be conveyed by will, was the clincher. The proposal's two conditions must have seemed simplicity itself to accept: a permanent home for the facility in Greenwood and a name memorializing the last of the Maxwells' four children and the only one to survive infancy. Constance Pope Maxwell had succumbed to scarlet fever at the age of seven in 1883. Compounding the tragedy of Connie's death was the belief that Maxwell himself had brought home the bacteria that would kill his daughter from the bedside of another patient, one whose illness he had not diagnosed correctly. Scarlet fever was among the most virulent killers of children at that time; Alan Keith Lucas points out that a noted English bishop lost every one of his four children to scarlet fever in just one week about the same period.

Convinced that he had found the perfect means of honoring the memory of a beloved child, Maxwell nevertheless felt justified in adding a caveat to his gift. The property would revert to his estate at the first indication that the orphanage was not being maintained properly or that any of the conditions of the conveyance were being violated. Maxwell's crusty nature was further revealed in a warning contained in a letter dated 5 April 1891: "Though if the Baptists do not keep up said orphanage in more businesslike and liberal manner than they sustain their pastors, churches and University the will would probably be revoked." Lucas believed the acute economic depression of 1891 loomed large in the early deliberations.

Doubtless no one was surprised when Dr. J. C. Maxwell was elected president of a thirteen-member board of trustees named by the joint orphanage committee, which also stipulated that a majority of this board would be residents of Greenwood or its environs and would constitute a local board in immediate charge of the institution. This decision turned out to be a mistake in that it pitted Maxwell and two of his handpicked associates, Greenwood businessmen J. K. Durst and J. W. Sproles, against the Reverend Vass, who had somewhat reluctantly agreed to accept the office of superintendent. Details of the internecine conflict of Connie Maxwell's very earliest days are hard to come by but seem to consist of a great many little things that added up to rather unsatisfactory administrative relations. For one thing, Maxwell was not above calling board members to sessions at his home, and it appears the local board may have been a bit too zealous in its oversight. In addition, Vass was a promoter by nature and a good businessman. Love of children was not high on his list of desirable character traits; he was much more likely to come down on the side of economy, discipline, and corporal punishment than that of compassion and empathy with the plight of his charges. Maxwell, on the other hand, was almost solely concerned about the welfare of the children themselves. His views can be summed up in one sentence from his report to the board in 1896. "I would especially suggest," he wrote, "that the high aim of the Orphanage should be not to increase the number of inmates, but to improve the facilities for better education and preparing the children for the definite trades and professions."[3]

The uneasy state of affairs between the board and the superintendent continued to simmer for years, affecting both the Greenwood church and eventually the entire state as it ebbed and flowed. Neither side emerged a clear winner in the struggle, which actually amounted to little more than a philosophical difference of opinion between two strong-minded individuals; only Maxwell's death in 1899 and Vass's resignation the same year brought an end to years of acrimonious bickering. Since modern writers accord both men more or less equal status as Connie Maxwell pioneers and visionaries, it is clear that the skirmishes of its first seven years brought no lasting ill effects to the institution.

One quite serious contretemps in 1897 did, however, cause a troubling rift within the church itself. At least one member, the outspoken A. J. Sproles, brother of prominent Greenwood citizen J. W., saw fit to align himself strongly with the Vass faction and against his own pastor, who at the time was the Reverend E. J. Forrester. So deep was his bitterness, in fact, that he wrote a sort of open letter to Dr. C. C. Brown of Sumter in which he thoroughly castigated Forrester, charging him with an "insatiable desire to rule" and hinting that the pastor had few supporters within the church and would probably soon be moving on. When Brown subsequently shared the letter with other Baptists—Sproles had specifically termed it "not confidential"—the church found itself in a most uncomfortable spotlight statewide. Accordingly, in conference on April 18, a resolution supporting Forrester and condemning Sproles was passed and submitted to the *Baptist Courier* for publication. Obviously stung, Sproles protested and asked for a hearing in a letter handed to a deacon and recorded in the minutes. That hearing came and went on June 6. Sproles was heard, in a "talk of some length," according to the minutes, and was asked some pointed questions "to which he made no satisfactory answer." And there the matter rested until January 1898 when the conference minutes record granting "Letters of Dismission to Bro. & Sister A. J. Sproles."

But final settlement of the great rift would not be so easy. At conference the next month a question was raised over the form of the letter issued by the clerk; a member termed it "irregular and not in accordance with the action of the church" and requested instead a letter stating that Mr. and Mrs. Sproles were "in good and regular standing or fellowship" with the church. An amendment that this instruction would apply only to the letter for Mrs. Sproles was offered, and the amended motion passed. Even at this juncture, the church made an effort to reconcile with Sproles; a committee of five was charged with the task. It is probably safe to assume that this effort at peacemaking never really had a chance. The minutes of March 6 record the sad end of the matter as well as the formal discharge of the reconciliation committee. The letter offered in January was summarily withdrawn and fellowship discontinued upon Sproles's failure to apologize to the church and to the pastor personally for the infamous letter. The church rolls record the action under a column labeled "losses by Exclusion." Mrs. Sproles's letter was allowed to stand as originally granted. This is probably the most extreme episode of growing pains from the orphanage's earliest days.[4]

Despite this embarrassing incident, Connie Maxwell gained an early foothold as one of Greenwood's most cherished institutions, no doubt in part because of the involvement of Maxwell and other prominent citizens but also because of the nature of its mission. There was a time when the phrase *widows and orphans* implied more than federal welfare programs. The orphanage also profited from several sociological theories and practices that were rather advanced for their day. For example, Connie Maxwell was notable for the ideal of making its cottages self-contained units. This concept, which is rather difficult to envision today, meant that each individual cottage had its own vegetable garden, poultry yard, and so on, and even its own source of milk—a cow. Only a lack of certain teaching skills on the part of houseparents, among them the correct method of milking, ended this experiment in individualized provision.

Other innovative fund-raising techniques were used to finance new cottages as the orphan population grew. The second cottage was named Memorial House because its subscriptions were raised largely by means of selling space "in transoms, window panes, and other parts of the building for memorial inscriptions." Still another charming innovation was Children's Cottage, so named for the dual reason that it was designed for very young children and largely financed by small gifts from Sunday schoolers throughout the state.

Thanks to Maxwell's generosity there was ample space to build the campus originally, and one striking characteristic of Connie Maxwell even today is its physical spaciousness. The fact that eight buildings were erected in the first seven years of the home's existence, none within a hundred yards of another, has been cited as a tribute to both Baptist generosity and the industry and promotional skills of its earliest leaders.

The second superintendent, unanimously elected by the State Convention in 1899, was a dark horse, a compromise candidate who belonged to neither faction of the divided convention. Serving that year as assistant secretary, A. T. Jamison was so taken by surprise that he required a full two weeks to make up his mind to accept the appointment. As it turned out, that decision was a master stroke for the institution; Jamison's importance in the history of Connie Maxwell Orphanage is impossible to overstate. His tenure of forty-six years stands as mute testimony that the man and the institution were uniquely well suited to each other. A chapter of his own book lists the qualities he thought a good administrator needed to possess: he should be spiritual, a nonmaterialist, and a gentleman with "fairly good ability" as a public speaker. In addition, he should be studious, progressive, and exhibit common sense. Many people felt that Jamison was simply, albeit inadvertently, describing himself when he wrote those lines. He also left a strong personal legacy when his only daughter, Sarah, married Joel Smith Bailey Jr., a member of perhaps Greenwood's most prominent early family. Their only child, Margaret Wallace Bailey Tinsley, still lives in Greenwood. The record shows that Jamison and his wife joined the Greenwood church by letter from Camden Baptist on June 3, 1900.

The history of Connie Maxwell Children's Home is inextricably linked to the tenure of two of the six superintendents who have served since the institution was founded. Jamison and his successor, Dr. Sam M. Smith, together headed the home a remarkable seventy-six years. There can be no doubt that Connie Maxwell owes a large part of its excellent reputation to the work of these men and the staff they entrusted to carry out their policies. The story of Connie

Maxwell Children's Home is one of ongoing success whose mission continues to unfold. Its early connection to Greenwood's First Baptist Church is one of the most significant in the church's long history of community service.

The Connie Maxwell Children's Home story places us somewhat ahead of ourselves in chronicling the progress of the church itself. Some years before Dr. Maxwell undertook his most notable philanthropy, the church had found itself struggling with potentially serious problems among the membership. In late 1876 a committee was appointed to inform the pastor that it would be "unable to employ as much of his time next year" as it had previously; the Reverend Jordan's preaching was cut to four services per month—two Sundays morning and night—and his salary reduced proportionately. While surely no one would suggest a connection, the minutes for the very next month contain the first reference to inappropriate behavior on the part of certain church members:

> Whereas we are painfully conscious that as a Christian Church we are less influential for good than might and should be, and whereas we recognize in the baneful evil of intemperance one of the causes of our inefficiency, therefore Resolved that in a spirit of affection for our brethren who have fallen into this evil we entreat them to make humble confession of their fault to the brethren, and to turn from it, and that we will pray that the grace of God may lead them to true repentance. Resolved that it is the plain duty and the firm determination of this Church to remove this hindrance to our usefulness by a prompt exercise of corrective Church discipline when admonition and entreaty shall have been tried and failed.

Nor did the matter end with adopting the resolution; the culprit was actually named in the conference minutes and a committee appointed to admonish and "cite him to appear before the Church and answer charges of intemperance and profanity." The case was concluded about a week later when the erring brother appeared and made "satisfactory acknowledgements" of his misdeeds. A resolution to excuse his past offenses and join him in praying for strength "to be led no more into the same error" was adopted. An interesting coda to this sad story appears in the minutes for February 18, 1877. The member who had been singled out for chastisement requested that the record of the case of discipline against him be expunged. Possibly a more detailed accounting of the proceedings against this unfortunate brother once existed and was destroyed; clearly, however, no one felt an obligation to remove the references to the case in the official minutes since they are still there for anyone to see.

The church also paid careful attention during this period to defining the role of its board of deacons. Several sessions of what amounts to instruction, conducted by leaders from both within and without the congregation, were held, sometimes in lieu of preaching services. This close scrutiny resulted in the discontinuance of the finance committee in favor of direct oversight of financial matters by the diaconate as of May 1877.

It seems clear from the record that all was not well between Pastor Jordan and his flock at this period. There is even one strong hint that Dr. Maxwell was fully prepared to give up his church membership; his request for his letter was tabled, presumably to get at the root causes of his discontent.[5] And there was other turmoil as well. Anyone reading the minutes more than 120 years after the fact will come away conscious of a certain tension resulting from changing pastors during this period, though the record is sometimes at pains to conceal it. A Virginia minister by the name of Kemper was offered the position, and plans were laid to confer with two other churches in regard to sharing his time, but Kemper declined the call. Another minister, the Reverend Ebleloft, also declined, but Elder J. K. Fant accepted.

The Reverend J. S. Jordan, pastor 1876–1878.

The Reverend James K. Fant, pastor 1878–1879.

Fant was already serving Beulah Church and simply added the Greenwood church to his charge. He moved his membership to the latter from Belton. Jordan and his family requested and received their "letters of dismission" in December.

In addition to several blank spaces in the minutes of this period, caused by what appear to be applications of ink eradicator, the entry for September 22, 1878, contains a startling sentence: "The Sisters of the Church were relieved from voting on all cases except the election of Pastor." Thus was a tradition dating from the church's founding set aside. It is difficult not to wonder why this action was taken. Possibly cases requiring church chastisement had reached beyond such mundane matters as intemperance and profanity and now threatened feminine sensibilities in ways their husbands, fathers, and sons could not permit. On the other hand, perhaps the church was merely conforming to common practice of the period. Sometimes it is better not to know. Similarly, it is useless to speculate on the reasons for Elder Fant's decision not to accept a call to serve the church for a second year. The minutes of January 12, 1879, record his request for his letter as well as the church's decision to call the Reverend H. C. Smart for two services monthly at a salary of three hundred dollars per year. The Greenwood church would be one in a charge of four to share Smart's services; the others were Ninety Six, Siloam, and Fellowship. Smart's four-member family were received by letter from Beech Branch Baptist Church in the lowcountry. Beech Branch was one of the state's oldest, having been organized in 1759. It was formerly named Coosawhatchie and was originally a member of the Savannah River Association formed in 1802.

Evidently the church still exists; King places it in the Allendale-Hampton Association which was organized in 1958, many years after Smart lived in Greenwood.

Smart's tenure lasted for seven years and seems to have been a period of peace and progress for the little church. Conference minutes record routine transactions routinely; membership growth appears to have been steady but not spectacular; and local church, missions, and association business seems to have proceeded apace. An entry in June 1881 stands out as another landmark in the music ministry when Sister L. Sheppard (presumably Laura, or possibly Lura or Lizzie, all of whose names appear in various listings of membership rolls; Sheppard was not an uncommon name) was appointed church organist (the minutes read "requested to take charge of the Organ") and granted permission to use the old instrument for practice purposes until it was sold. The church seems to have come into possession of a new organ at some point; the minutes do not state how this came about. Another entry nearly a year later documents building a small house to enclose the church well. That work was reported complete two months later at a cost of $30.80. Members were still being canvassed in February 1883 when a balance of $7.25 remained outstanding.

The Reverend H. C. Smart, pastor 1879–1886.

The first mention of a parsonage came in November 1882. By April of the next year plans had progressed to the selection of a site, and work was slated to begin as soon as the amount of eight hundred dollars was in hand. Nor was the church delinquent in organizing new congregations in outlying areas. A group was sent to Bradley in

1883 to meet with delegates from other churches to "consult and advise and organize a Baptist Church there if deemed expedient." A new church was up and running shortly thereafter. Still another, this time in Mt. Carmel, was organized in August 1884.

The parsonage matter blew hot and cold for months. One 1884 entry records the pastor's reluctance to proceed without more wholehearted support from the entire membership; evidently he felt the deacons and committee had moved a trifle too precipitately on so important a matter. A month or two later all seemed ready to go. Captain Waller reported that funds had been secured by mortgage on the lot purchased earlier from a Mr. Hill, and arrangements had been made to build at once. An amusing sidelight to this entry is the fact that at the same meeting the treasurer reported a balance of $19.03 on hand in the church treasury.

The minutes dwell hardly at all on Smart's resignation, apparently due to illness, in the fall of 1885. As a matter of fact, the same entry that records the resignation also notes a call to the Reverend O. M. Miller to the post, a call that was evidently declined. The next pastor mentioned in the minutes, G. H. Carter, agreed to preach every third Sunday for fifteen dollars per month. The minutes of March 21 record issuing letters of transfer to Smart and his family to join Troy Baptist Church. By September the church had agreed to call Carter for one year to preach two Sundays each month for a salary of five hundred dollars per year "without reference to Parsonage." The church had been struggling with the parsonage question for some time. Considering the fact that committees were continually named to raise funds to pay the pastor, it is not surprising that the church seemed reluctant to commit itself to the ongoing expense of a house and lot. The church treasury was usually found to be on the brink of insolvency; even mundane matters such as securing a new stove were referred to ad hoc committees, and one entry records the minister's earnest request to the ladies of the church to consider special offerings "towards adding to the appearance of the interior of Church." Budgeting in the style of today seems to have occurred to no one. On the other hand, there is something quite stirring in the notion of truly directed giving such as the early church employed.

The first mention of using sealed envelopes to collect funds occurs in the minutes for February 9, 1888. Probably because of limited use—the collection envelopes would be solely to receive gifts to missions—the committee empowered to carry out the envelope mandate consisted of five women and only one man; members' tenure would be one year and included monthly reports to the church. Could it be that the sole male committee member would be the one expected to make the report?

The Reverend G. H. Carter, pastor 1887–1891.

A remarkable entry in the fall of 1890—actually, a preamble and set of resolutions—makes clear to anyone the church's view of its duty to itself. The resolution reads:

> Whereas the Greenwood Baptist Church has from the time of its organization, to a large extent, been too lax in its disciplinary methods, for the welfare and spiritual growth of its members, or to restrain them from the violation of the spirit of religion. And whereas, the failure of the church in this particular respect has a tendency to lower the standard of spirituality, and prejudice the outside world against the cause of true righteousness, and paralize [*sic*] the efforts of the church in bringing men to Christ, therefore be it resolved,—
>
> 1st That we, the members of the Greenwood Baptist Church, do hereby pledge ourselves to maintain a more thorough and rigid discipline, for the twofold purpose of advancing the spirituality of those who are seeking to adore Christ & to restrain those who [are] going astray,

> 2nd That such things as intoxication, profanity, fraud and dancing are looked on as being opposed to the spirit of Christ, & that hereafter any member who may be guilty of any of these things, or anything else which the church should decide as wrong, such member shall be held amenable [accountable?] to the church for the same.
>
> 3rd That the deacons of this church are hereby appointed a standing committee, whose business it shall be to look into & bring before the church, such matters for discipline, as in their judgement, they shall deem best.
>
> 4th That a copy of these preambles & resolutions be spread upon the minutes of our church book.

Thus was the church's position in matters as widely disparate as fraud and dancing spelled out, in Spencerian script so elegant that no computer can ever duplicate it, in the early fall of 1890.

Dr. E. J. Forrester (1853–1932), pastor 1891–1902.

Carter's resignation came in January 1891 before the church was ready to accept it, but a committee appointed to ask him to reconsider found the pastor adamant in his refusal. Accordingly, he was granted his letters of dismission, and a committee was appointed to draft the customary resolution of appreciation for his services. The church resigned itself to seeking temporary pastors until such time as a permanent replacement for Carter could be found. That replacement was finally named in July: E. J. Forrester would serve the church for the next eleven years. The minutes recording his election at a salary of one thousand dollars per year also dwell on plans for a new church building. There may be no connection whatever, of course, but it is interesting to note at this point that Greenwood's most prominent builder ever, the notable William V. Blyth, had joined the church only a few months before. Four members of the Vass family were also received from Swift Creek Church in Darlington at this period. The reader will remember that Vass had just accepted the position of first superintendent of Connie Maxwell Orphanage.

A new church membership roll was prepared at this period, and the names of 177 members were entered in the minute book. Among the names with echoes in today's rolls are Abney, Benjamin, Beaudrot, Richter, Snead, and Sproles. The question of building a parsonage was also attacked with renewed vigor. The entire board of deacons plus seven prominent members were named a standing committee to push the project forward.

A new clerk, E. S. F. Giles, replaced C. W. Crews in late 1891. An attorney, Giles had moved to Greenwood in the early 1880s to practice his profession as well as try his hand at editing a newspaper. The first issue of the *Greenwood Light* appeared on August 1, 1885, but the enterprise flared only briefly and disappeared in less than a year. Giles was one of only three attorneys named in an article about Greenwood that appeared in a Charleston newspaper in 1899. While the young man's Greenwood career seems not to have been wildly successful, that of his sisters who followed him to the little town would bear fruit in the field of education and link Greenwood with the lives of five truly remarkable women.

The E. S. F. Giles family of North Carolina was so devoted to the ideal of learning that the widowed matriarch, whose name was Nancy, moved to the village of Trinity in Randolph County in 1874 so that her son, the seventeen-year-old Edward (E. S. F. Jr.), might have the benefit of higher education offered by Trinity College (now known as Duke University). The school dates from 1838; its first charter (1841) was issued in the name of Union Institute. But that name would be changed twice in the next decade, and the school had been known as Trinity College for fifteen years when the Giles family set their collective sights on enrolling there. Edward had no problem since his was the correct gender; however, his three sisters—Theresa, age twenty-eight, Persis, twenty-five, and Mary, twenty-one—knew perfectly well they could be neither formally admitted nor enrolled because the school policy excluded women. Clearly the three sisters did not accept the prevailing notion that education for women was at best unnecessary and, at worst, a positive danger to the fabric of society. They lived at a time when conventional wisdom held that women should receive no more than the barest possible academic instruction, even in the basics of reading and writing. If women learned to write, some people feared they might forge their husbands' signatures (!), and sufficient reading skills meant they would probably neglect their household tasks. Reading just a little—enough presumably to take in those passages of Scripture dealing with their own regulation—was considered the ideal.

The three Giles sisters had been teaching school for some time before they quietly began their own college training. Their salaries were absurdly low; still, they managed to pay their tuition and set aside funds to nurture a private ambition to open a school of their own. At first they read and studied with their young brother, but when it became clear that more instruction was needed they found a Trinity professor, Lemuel Johnson, willing to offer private lessons after his regular work at the college was done. There was never any question that the sisters were serious contenders for college degrees; indeed, they bearded the president early on with the challenge that they expected course work no less stringent than that offered to males and would expect the exact same reward for their industry. To his credit, he agreed, so that Professor Johnson was able to take his students' ambitions seriously and line up other professors who were also willing to instruct the Gileses privately. The records indicate that they attended only one class—metaphysics—with Trinity men, and that in their senior year. All three continued to work to pay their own tuition, at teaching jobs that paid about twenty-five dollars per month for five months' work, a great deal less than men's work in the same field commanded.

There is no evidence that the Giles sisters found their busy lives particularly onerous. When bachelor's degrees were granted to all three in 1878, they calmly set to work to earn the master's in order to enhance their standing as scholars and their shared goal as educators. The dream was to open a school for girls and young women, and the town they chose for this venture turned out to be Greenwood, South Carolina, where their brother had moved to open a law practice after his own education was finished.

The three Trinity-educated Giles sisters, along with their mother and youngest sister Susan, who had graduated from Wesleyan Female Institute in Staunton, Virginia, moved to Greenwood and opened their school, Greenwood Female College, in September 1885. At first they contented themselves with remaining quietly in the background and receiving all inquiries through the good offices of E. S. F. Giles, Esq., even though almost the entire burden of the school was on their shoulders from the start. Their reception in the little town, however, seems to have been entirely positive, and the whole family soon regarded Greenwood as home.

The school itself, unfortunately, lasted only six years. It closed in 1891, the building was sold, and the sisters moved to the mountains of Tennessee for some much needed rest and recuperation. They came back in 1897, built a house on West Cambridge next to the railroad tracks and not far from the Presbyterian church, and opened a school in their home early in 1898 when Greenwood's own boom was at its height. That school lasted until Lander College began its operations in Greenwood just a few blocks away in 1904. Evidently none of the four sisters ever married, and all, along with their mother and brother, are buried in Magnolia Cemetery. Edward turned out to be the only Baptist; the rest of the family were staunch Presbyterians. Everybody lived long enough to see attitudes toward education for women change completely, though several Gileses had died before Trinity College became Duke University in 1924. Duke officially opened its doors to women in December 1896, four years after its move to Durham and eighteen years after three sisters were privately granted bachelor's degrees and went on to influence the lives of a number of Greenwood's young women.[6]

Of course a case could be made that there is no rationale for including the story of the Giles sisters in a history of Greenwood's First Baptist Church, particularly since their denominational allegiance was always Presbyterian. But surely there is room in our narrative to pay tribute to these learned women, three of whom shared a singular honor as the first female graduates of Duke University. And, if a solid connection with the church is required, the record is clear that E. S. F. Giles Jr., joined the church on May 10, 1891, and served as clerk from December of that year until his resignation in October 1896.

Though Forrester's tenure was destined to last nearly twice as long as any of his predecessors, it is not at all clear from the record that his selection was universally sought in the beginning. The minutes show that his name was among the first two submitted, but the Reverend W. T. Hundley also received the call, twice actually, a call he finally declined. C. T. Herndon was offered the position next, but he too was not inclined to accept. Thus Forrester was actually the third choice when he accepted the call in July; the minutes for August record the church's decision to "pay the Freight on Bro. Forester's House Hold Goods." Clerks persisted in spelling the new pastor's name without the double *r* in the middle until he had occupied the pulpit for more than five years.

During the period from Carter's resignation to his successor's appointment the church had offered its support, both financial and otherwise, to a general revival meeting held in Greenwood by an evangelist whose name was Fife. A couple of cryptic references to the "Fife meeting" in the Bailey, Barksdale & Company hall appear in the minutes for February and March 1891. Perhaps an infusion of eleven new members, also reported in March, was directly attributable to this emphasis on what was evidently a nondenominational revival meeting. Such a result, in fact, is not unknown in our own day; Billy Graham's evangelistic crusades always contain a plea to affiliate with local churches. The Reverend Fife's name is by no means a household word in Baptist circles, but his ministry was doubtless one of the remnants of the Great Awakening that swept the South during the nineteenth century.

With its pulpit secure at last, the church was free to return to the burning issue of a building program; dreams, not merely of a parsonage but a whole new church building as well, began to claim the attention of the church's leading men. A standing committee consisting of the deacons plus seven members (J. W. Duckett, C. I. Cummings, J. W. Sproles, J. R. Abney, W. H. Mays, J. C. Hill, and J. H. Milford) was named in April "to devise a plan to build a parsonage, with instructions to continue their efforts till the object was accomplished." Thus was the serious nature of the committee's charge spelled out in no uncertain terms.

In the meantime, however, a committee charged with updating the membership roll for the first time since the church was organized nearly twenty-two years earlier found more problems than it had anticipated when it tackled the task. The committee's report, spelled out in March 1892, outlined those problems and contained three recommendations: present and all subsequent clerks were charged to record with greater accuracy and clearness "all the business proceedings of the church . . . without unnecessary delay"; deacons were admonished to examine the records regularly, revise the membership roll, and report to the church by March 1 each year; and the clerk was charged to make sure every name in the church book carried the date the member was received as well as the manner, along with a marginal note that only names so annotated would constitute the official membership of the church. The same committee was expected to correspond with nonresident members to ascertain their status and location.

As month followed month in the early 1890s all seemed serene, if the official record is any indication. Treasurer's reports were received routinely as information with no mention of what they contained; ad hoc committees came and went, taking care of small tasks such as "repair[ing] the choir box at a cost of not exceeding $10.00"; or "waiting on" a recalcitrant member whose record of attendance was found wanting. A protracted meeting was held in August 1893 at which "Bro. Ramsey of Charleston" assisted. Even though the clerk spelled his name with a final "e" instead of "a," this was surely the noted David M. Ramsay who was to become the ninth president of Greenville Female College in 1911, serving in that capacity until 1930 and becoming, in Joe King's words, "singularly identified" with the school. If the church was fortunate enough to secure Ramsay's services while he was pastor of Citadel Square Baptist Church in Charleston, its efforts paid off handsomely; the minutes record the names of forty new members received over a three-day period, presumably as a result of Ramsay's performance in the pulpit.

Meanwhile, the all-important report of the building committee was postponed for three straight months. Evidently the chairman, W. L. Durst, was making himself scarce for reasons we cannot know. He showed up at the November 3 conference, however, to ask for yet another week's delay. The fact that the church had voted to raise the pastor's salary by two hundred dollars per year only a few months earlier might be an indication that its fiscal health was sound at this period and a whole new beginning symbolized by a new building was just around the corner. The report, when it came at a meeting on December 1, only reinforced that spirit of confidence:

> Your committee appointed to consider the question of church building have made inquiries of a large number of our members and have decided to recommend:
>
> 1st That we are in need of a larger and better church building, and one more conveniently located to a majority of the congregation
>
> 2nd That we are able to build a house at a cost of $10,000 payable in two installments, one half this winter, the balance next
>
> 3rd Dr. Maxwell be requested to act with a committee composed of J. R. Abney, J. K. Durst, F. M. Allen, C. I. Cummings, J. L. Carr, J. L. Vass & W. H. Mays to solicit subscriptions
>
> 4th That should the subscription list show a willingness on our part to honor God, by erecting a fit Temple in which to worship Him, then this Committee be increased to twenty in number and they be instructed to select a suitable lot and recommend to the Church its purchase for carrying forward the work.

Though the committee scrupulously asked for help to take charge of soliciting and receiving members' subscriptions, the financing was actually nearly all in place by early in the new year. As usual in such cases, six members had already pledged more than half the projected cost, and nearly all that figure was in sight from subscriptions solicited earlier. By July the site had been purchased from prominent businessman William H. Bailey for the sum of $1,650. Another site had been offered by the Durst Brothers—part of the "very valuable Bank Hotel Lot . . . at an exceedingly low figure"—but the committee felt that location was not the best choice for the new church. They were surely right. The spot on the east side of the square at the present location of Bank of America and the Grier Building became the very heart of downtown Greenwood shortly thereafter. The site that was chosen served the church's needs for about fifty years, even though it too was quite near the center of town.

And so the walls of a brand new church building, carefully planned to meet the specific needs of a growing congregation for the foreseeable future, rose steadily on their strong foundations. As for the first parsonage, a 1933 newspaper article indicates it was built in 1892 on Magnolia (or Byrd, as it was called for a time) Street and subsequently sold. According to the article the Reverend Smart was the only pastor to live in the parsonage. This brings up a problem with dates: Smart's pastorate ended in 1885, and Forrester was pastor when the parsonage is supposed to have been erected.

Plans for the new church were drawn up by a Columbia architectural firm, Wilson & Edwards, and W. V. Blyth was placed in charge of construction of the new facility, the building of which just happened to coincide with a boom period for the town; Greenwood was also in process of becoming the seat of a brand new county at the time. A third railroad line had just been completed, and the entire business climate of Greenwood was approaching a new high. Its attractions were advertised widely by many admirers, and new citizens seemed constantly to be moving to the area in search of opportunity.

No one will be surprised to learn that the building exceeded its budget by some 40 percent. The important thing was that the new church home fit the congregation like a glove, and the church's own membership proved itself equal to the task of supervising and financing the enterprise. The dedication ceremony on November 7, 1897, along with a sketch of the church's history, was featured prominently in the *Baptist Courier* that week, and the story was front page news in the very first issue of the *Greenwood Index*, a weekly newspaper launched during that eventful year. A drawing featured in the *Courier* story shows a building dominated by a 108-foot tower located between two main entrances, one to the side adjoining a covered carriage way and the other facing the street, each with triple doors and a set of stone steps. This arrangement allowed for a sort of wrap-around vestibule inside, as well as space in the tower section for a parlor on the ground floor and a classroom upstairs. The main auditorium, designed to seat five hundred worshipers, was octagonal with curved inside gables and a handsome central chandelier. The heating system was state of the art, and furnishings were of oak and leather. The coping for the baptistery was of white marble and was raised more than a foot above the pulpit floor. The design featured several gables of various sizes which allowed for a number of memorial windows. The six largest of these were dedicated to former Pastors Pope and Smart, Mrs. W. L. Durst, Supply Pastor Broadus, Albert Waller, and Mr. and Mrs. Enoch Simmons. Five smaller windows honored other Greenwood families and Pastor Forrester. Among these was one dedicated to Mr. and Mrs. Stanley Crews by their children and grandchildren. It was noted that thirty-six members of the Crews family had joined the church at one time or another since its founding. The memorial windows, made of the best "opal glass," were described by the *Courier* as "beautiful and costly."

All three of Greenwood's largest churches—Baptist, Methodist, and Presbyterian—took part in the dedication ceremonies, their massed choirs performing the anthem "Gloria." The dedicatory sermon was preached by Dr. William H. Whitsett, president of the seminary, who was well-known in Greenwood, having preached on occasion at several Baptist churches in the area. The offering that day went to the seminary students' fund and was not applied toward retirement of the building debt as was the custom. It seems that Forrester himself was the instigator of this act of generosity; one hopes he consulted the board of deacons beforehand.

Actually, there were three services on that special day: R. W. Sanders, who had recently completed a term as president of the South Carolina Baptist Convention, spoke to another full house in the afternoon, while Dr. Whitsett returned for the evening service. As his part on the afternoon program, Forrester read a sketch of the Greenwood church which was also reprinted in the *Baptist Courier* of

November 11. The church's history, according to Forrester, could be divided into three distinct periods lasting fifteen months, eighteen years, and eight years respectively. He based this division, naturally enough for a Baptist church, on pastoral service. At first the church had been able to hire only supply pastors, usually seminary students, about once a month. The second period, he said, began with the Reverend Pope and ran through the tenure of the first pastor to accept a call to full-time service, G. H. Carter. Forrester's own pastorate constituted the third segment of church history, one that had culminated in the most visible of the church's many accomplishments—its impressive new building.

Forrester's sketch also included details of other aspects of the church program, such as the Sunday school, which had operated from the first, and weekly prayer services that reached back almost as far. He also saw fit to report that "the ladies were organized for special work" as early as 1873 "and continue to be efficient helpers." Membership numbers were revealing. From the initial complement of 23, the church had grown to 291 members by 1897, double the number recorded in 1890. Financial data were even more impressive: contributions totaling about $15,000 over the first nineteen years had jumped to more than $32,000 for the last eight.

Finally, Forrester read off the names of those individuals who had contributed at least $500 to the building fund, from W. L. Durst who gave $2,100 to F. M. Allen, a subcommittee member whose gift was $600, and concluded with a sort of blanket tribute:

> It is to be doubted whether any church ever had a better building committee, and whether any such enterprise was ever carried through with more beautiful harmony. Here we raise our Ebenezer, and give God all the glory, and ask him to give us grace to consecrate ourselves wholly to him, and humbly to depend upon him in all our work.

Three weeks after Dedication Sunday the church appointed four of its most prominent members to serve on "a special committee to have charge of the house of worship & the grounds." One committeeman announced on the spot that planting trees should be undertaken straightaway and that twenty-five cents would procure a tree, whereupon, according to the minutes, "a large number of trees were taken." Many of those same trees had to be taken down when the county library was built on the site some sixty years later.

The first mention of ushers appears in the minutes of April 9, 1899, when four men were officially named to that office.

With its impressive new edifice as a base, Greenwood's First Baptist Church prepared for the dawn of the twentieth century with great expectations and lofty purpose. Now and then the minutes record reprimands for laxness of one kind or another, most frequently irregular attendance and inattention to financial stewardship. Unpaid insurance and fuel bills had become troubling by early November 1899 and critical a couple of months later, so much so that the church took action in the form of a resolution to ascertain the names of members "who have from year to year failed to contribute to the support of the Gospel," call upon those members, and report to the church the cause of their failure to discharge their financial obligations. A group of ten members was cited in May 1900 for financial delinquency and given six months to make reparations.

When Deacon W. L. Durst reported in October that a debt of $10,300 was due the Bank of Greenwood, everyone seemed at last to sit up and take notice, and several suggestions were offered to meet this serious demand. One, a motion that each member voluntarily double the amount assessed for the pastor's salary and church expenses, was adopted the following week. While there is no information on how much additional money was actually realized from this idea, Durst was able to report soon afterward that funds to pay the debt were coming in steadily. Finally, the pastor was forced, in effect, to hold the congregation hostage until members came up with the money. The minutes of April 28, 1901, read: "Regular business was dispensed with. Bro. Forrester explained that we would proceed to raise an amount sufficient to liquidate church debt. The Brethren responded, amt. of Twenty Six Hundred Dollars was raised, which amt. was sufficient to pay said debt." The question of electric lighting came up in September when deacons were assigned the task of disposing of the chandeliers and putting in electric lights. The pastor was charged with choosing a time for holding a protracted meeting, or revival.

Forrester tendered his resignation in June 1902, to take effect in three months. A pulpit committee of seventeen men appointed on the same day eventually recommended that the church call Dr. H. A. Bagby of Richmond at a salary of fifteen hundred dollars per year and parsonage; Bagby accepted effective November 1, 1902. The minutes for the first years of Dr. Bagby's ministry are remarkably sketchy. The clerk actually recorded at one point that the minutes for ten whole months had been lost, but no harm was done as "there was nothing of importance transacted." No one knows whether this laxity reflected on the clerk or the pastor; it could well be that church business was so well established by this time that matters virtually ran themselves. Such events as were recorded seem to have been routine: accepting new members, issuing letters to those transferring to other congregations, inviting groups of one kind or another to hold annual meetings in Greenwood, etc. Now and then committees would be appointed to check out various parts of the physical plant, such as the heating system, or look into enlarging a classroom in response to a request from a growing Sunday school class, but for the most part the church seemed to hum along like a well-oiled machine.

Dr. H. A. Bagby, pastor 1902–1908.

A special meeting was called for January 14, 1906, to hear reports on various branches of the church's work. One report—that seventy-three new members had joined the church by letter and baptism over the preceding year—seemed entirely positive. On the financial front, the church had spent a little over $2,300 for expenses and benevolence during 1905 while raising another $2,300 for missions, the orphanage, and various other charities through its organized subdivisions—a special missions treasurer, the Women's Missionary Society, the Sunday school, and three youth organizations. At the same meeting the church passed a resolution neither to lend church furniture to anyone nor allow its removal from the church building. If the motion triggered any discussion the minutes do not reveal its thrust. Surely some inconvenient or inappropriate request prompted this action; on the other hand, the church might simply have moved to forestall difficulties its members realized could easily arise in an area so sensitive. Still another general church conference in March concentrated on the report of the committee to revise the church roll. The entire membership at that point numbered 607, of whom 56 lived out of town and were considered inactive. The cadre of active members in 1906 consisted of 551 people, a figure that represented about 7 percent of the estimated population of the town of Greenwood at the time.

Perhaps one way the maturation of a church can be measured is by the number of its members who enter the ministry. The minutes of this period mention two such candidates: M. B. Whittaker, who was wished Godspeed at a church conference in February 1906 and J. H. Washington, who received the church's good wishes in the form of a request to the Columbia church to "call a presbytery to examine" him and if they were satisfied "to proceed to ordain him to the gospel ministry." Joe King provides enlightenment regarding this procedure. Ordination in a Baptist church "consisted in the church's choice of a man to office, and needed not the laying on of hands to make it valid." Still, most denominational leaders leaned toward a bit more investigation of a candidate's strength, and examination by a "presbytery" was the accepted means of judging. The word must not be confused with the Presbyterian denomination, though they obviously spring from the same root. A presbytery is defined as that part of a church reserved for the officiating clergy; an examining presbytery would normally consist of two or more ministers. King points out that early Baptist associations tended to pronounce ordinations illegal if both examination and laying on of hands were omitted. Clearly the church at Greenwood subscribed to proper form.

When the church decided to install carpeting in the spring of 1906, it appointed women to committees charged with determining the needs, selecting the actual carpet, and raising the necessary funds to pay for the project. The estimate of five hundred dollars, installed, turned out to be too modest; the finished job amounted to seven hundred dollars, still a surprisingly small sum by today's standards. The committee obviously set to work with a will and was able to report in July that the carpet had been selected, manufactured, and shipped though it had not yet arrived in Greenwood. The church must have been quite pleased; the same committee was instructed to have the auditorium walls "tinted," presumably to set off the new carpeting, at a cost of about eighty-five dollars if the Baptist Young People's Union (BYPU) would be willing to foot the bill.

The minutes record an odd little controversy during this period that is completely unexplained. A routine resolution to "take a collection one day during each year for support of aged ministers relief" was passed by the church in regular conference on July 4. Three months later a called meeting was held for the purpose of voting on a resolution offered by a prominent member, John R. Leavell. The resolution read:

> Whereas we prize above everything else in church life the unity and harmony of the church, and in the spirit of our master are willing to do anything within our power to secure it; therefore be it resolved
>
> 1st That any and all actions heretofore taken by this church relative to the support of the board for the relief of aged ministers be and hereby is abolished;
>
> 2nd That the clerk of the church is hereby instructed not to record the action of the monthly conference held in July last bearing on this matter.

The resolution passed, but the clerk obviously failed to carry out his instructions. We are left to wonder why the church withdrew its support from the fund to aid aged ministers. Possibly the problem lay with the board that administered the fund.

In other areas, the church was clearly making steady progress. Operating debt was reviewed and measures to pay up passed promptly so that the treasurer could announce six months into the new year a balance of $44.06 after meeting church expenses and retiring nearly $800 in indebtedness from the preceding year. There was progress in other areas as well. First, a "plan of succession" was put in place for the board of deacons whereby staggered terms of office would ensure smooth rotation on and off the board. Also, as evidence of the church's satisfaction with the Reverend Mr. Bagby, the minutes of January 12, 1908, report a salary increase from $1,500 to $1,800. At the same meeting a total membership of 695 was reported, along with collections of $3,403 for regular expenses and more than $2,400 raised and spent by subsidiary groups for their activities.

Bagby, after a six-year tenure, submitted his resignation in a beautifully written letter to the church dated July 26, 1908. He assured the brethren that he had hoped to remain in Greenwood, "but an unexpected call to a congregation of unusual possibilities" had dictated otherwise. A committee of twenty-five members was immediately appointed to search for a successor. As it turned out, the church that offered those "unusual possibilities" was located in Liberty, Missouri, which must have seemed a land of opportunity indeed when compared to little Greenwood. Bagby was praised in the resolution adopted on August 2 as a "true pastor" with "an intelligent conception of the teaching of the word of God" who, among other things, had visited the sick, ministered to the needs of the dying, and comforted and consoled the sorrowing among the congregation. This was obviously no hollow tribute; the church's gratitude for Bagby's services and good wishes for his new work shine through in every line.

While the church wrangled over choosing Bagby's successor, it managed to secure the services of Furman president Edwin McNeill Poteat as supply pastor. A North Carolinian by birth, Poteat had been elected Furman's fourth president and moved to Greenville from a pulpit in Philadelphia. Joe King describes him as a pastor of brilliant personality and successful experience. His service to Furman lasted nearly fifteen years and covered an important period of the school's growth and development. It was during his administration, for example, that the complete separation of Greenville Female College from Furman University was finally effected. Poteat not only brought new energy to the religious life of the institution with a renewed emphasis on the Bible as a source of broad culture and learning, he also advocated a healthy combination of Christian teaching and scientific exploration. The Greenwood church was always quite selective in regard to supply pastors; the choice of E. M. Poteat is simply another case in point.

With no replacement for Bagby in sight but having extended a call to Dr. George N. Cowan of Bristol, Tennessee, the church moved into the year 1909. The financial report for the previous year was combined for convenience to show overall collections and disbursements by category. An impressive total expenditure of $5,037 included operating expenses of $2,644 as well as gifts to missions, the orphanage, the seminary, and miscellaneous agencies in varying smaller amounts.

Dr. Cowan accepted the church's call effective in March 1909. It is not clear whether he was the cause, but a significant development in budgeting occurred in September of that year when the church formally adopted a plan of giving to denominational causes endorsed by the Abbeville Association, of which it was a charter member (actually, the tie was even closer—Greenwood's First Baptist Church and the Abbeville Association were established in the same year). From the record it appears the committee simply subdivided a preset total of twenty-five hundred dollars into the seven categories of Orphanage, Foreign Missions, Home Missions, State Missions, Men's Education at Furman, Other Furman Support, and Seminary Support, arranged in descending order. Later pencil entries expressed the dollar amounts as percentages; these percentages were applied in subsequent budget years. Clearly, the church was moving steadily toward a more businesslike approach to its finances. When the annual report was made on January 9, 1910, the figures seem to have fallen into place rather easily. For example, though there had been a net decrease of two in membership, the church had received sixty new members by letter, baptism, and statement, and the two categories of "death" and "erasure" accounted for 29 percent of the sixty-two-member decrease. The church fell somewhat short of its dollar goal in missions and charitable giving but met the previously set breakdown and even managed two dollars for the Aged Ministers' Fund. Also, the church's regular operating expenses were met handily, with current

The Reverend George N. Cowan, pastor 1909–1914.

funds sufficient to cover the cost of a small lot "with cabin thereon, situated immediately back of the present parsonage lot" purchased nearly a year earlier. The recapitulation showed that slightly more than six thousand dollars passed through the church's coffers in 1909, an increase of 20 percent over the previous year.

As of February 1910, a little over twelve years after the new church building was dedicated, the chairman of the board of deacons reported at a regular conference session that both the congregation and the Sunday school had outgrown the facilities provided for them and that the church's "cause was suffering because of this condition." To underscore the urgency of his report Chairman J. B. Hughey recommended that immediate steps be taken by the church to remedy the situation. Sunday school superintendent J. R. Leavell spoke in support of the deacons' position and pointed out the need also for "better equipment" to aid the Sunday school in its work. Three days later a committee of eight men was appointed to investigate the situation and bring its recommendations before the church.

Another significant event of the spring of 1910 concerned the proposed opening of a street adjacent to the church. The new owners who had bought up the property in the area were prepared to deed thirty-four feet to the city along the proposed street, which would curve from Main Street and continue to Cambridge "between the residences of T. J. Bolton and J. P. Jennings," if the church would deed sixteen feet along the northern boundary of its lot. After a good deal of discussion lasting nearly a month, the final resolution to go along with this plan passed in committee by a vote of twenty-three to eleven. Thus did Bailey Circle, which was soon to become a premier residential street, have its beginnings in a series of negotiations among town, church, and private property owners.

The committee charged with investigating the need for more space got rather more than it bargained for when it recommended on April 10, 1910, that the church build a whole new "modern Sunday School room at a cost of about $5,000." The discussion that followed this motion revealed that a majority of those present actually favored the building of a whole new church building, or, in the words of the minutes, "a second church." The minutes are unclear as to whether this sentiment meant a replacement church building or a sponsored, or "daughter church" with an entirely new congregation. Whichever, the discussion promptly escalated, as did the proposed fund-raising goal, from the initial $5,000 to $12,000 and all the way to $25,000, a figure that appeared to cause consternation as

North Main Street, Greenwood, S.C. early 1900s. First Baptist in the foreground flanked by First Presbyterian.

well as a quick negative vote. But a compromise goal of $20,000 was actually adopted and a committee of fifteen appointed to look into the feasibility of raising such a sum, $5,000 of which would "go to the improvement of the SS room and $15,000 to the building of a new church." The committee was forced to report three months later that its canvass revealed a high improbability of raising more than $12,000 for the church's purposes. The response to this piece of news was dramatic: the church simply passed a motion that the committee continue in operation until the fall and "prosecute further their work until the amount of $20,000 was subscribed." This motion was, however, withdrawn after some remarks by G. W. Gardner and A. T. Jamison, and the church settled on receiving the committee's original report as information and discharging the group.

A rather revealing episode appears in minutes of two consecutive conferences, both of which also dealt with highly significant business

Another view of the 1897 building.

matters. In brief sentences, the first entry noted that a brother had been "correctly charged with immorality" and recommended withdrawal of fellowship. The church complied, evidently without discussion. At conference the next month the same deacon announced that the erring brother "had made a full statement . . . expressing his great regret, and asked for restoration." The church dutifully restored fellowship on the spot. Perhaps second guessing this sort of thing more than eighty years after the fact is a bad idea for many reasons; still, it is impossible not to speculate on what this action must have been like for the participants. Similarly, it is convenient to believe the "immorality" in the case meant some sort of sexual indiscretion when it might just have easily been lying or petty larceny; such is our conditioning in this area.

In addition to this excruciating exercise, the church took care of other business at back-to-back conferences that fall. First came the question of looking into the advisability of organizing a Sunday School Association, a proposal initiated by the Abbeville Association. Since Sunday schools had been part of the Baptist movement from the first, and since a committee on Sunday schools had been established as a standing committee by the South Carolina Baptist Convention in 1894, it is not surprising that the Greenwood church was eager to participate in this new venture and named its delegates on the spot.

But an even more momentous event occurred only a month later, in November 1910 when, sandwiched between withdrawing fellowship from six members "because of their having joined a church of different faith and order" and restoring fellowship to the repentant petitioner described above, the church heard the following resolution:

> We, the undersigned members of the Baptist Church of Greenwood, believing that it is for the best interest of the cause in Greenwood, hereby signify our willingness to become members of another Baptist Church in Greenwood to be known as the 3rd Baptist Church or some other appropriate name, to be selected at some subsequent time by the members of this Third Church. We wish to put ourselves on record as being in the fullest harmony & brotherly feeling towards the entire membership of the Baptist Church of

> Greenwood, to be hereafter designated as the First Baptist Church of Greenwood, and this expression of our feelings as regards another church is actuated by the sincere belief that it is best for the good of the cause in our growing community.

This resolution, with its thirty-two signatures representing seventy-eight members, was received as information and with "hearty approval of this action." The church also pledged to the movement its moral, financial, and fraternal support. Clearly, Greenwood's first Baptist church considered itself fully mature and ready to sponsor a whole new congregation. That group would eventually form the nucleus of South Main Baptist Church, another thriving Greenwood institution, but not for a few more months.

Membership as of January 1, 1911, stood at 805, a net increase of 77 over the previous year's figure. As for the church's finances, the record shows that a sum of just under six thousand dollars was received and disbursed during 1910.

The question of more room and better equipment for the Sunday school was raised yet again at the first conference of the new year when supporters tried to pass a resolution containing an offer of $1,000 from the Baraca Class as an incentive for the church to act in the matter. Before the vote could be called, however, another member reopened the question of "a new church" and proposed a goal of $20,000 for a fund-raising appeal. When the smoke cleared the church found itself naming a building committee of five to look into the church's building needs and devise both a building and a fund-raising plan. The brethren named were J. W. Sproles, W. V. Blyth, H. B. Ellis, W. C. Strawhorn, and H. A. Graham.

Two weeks later the church called a special conference during the midweek prayer service to take the necessary steps to establish a new congregation at another place. Some fifty-two individuals representing twenty-eight households received "letters of dismission" along with recognition of their intention "to constitute a new Baptist Church in Greenwood." The name of the church had been decided by February; minutes for the eighth record requests for letters from eight additional members who wished to unite with "Sou Main St Church." Still another group were released a short time later.

The Sunday school seems to have received a new level of attention about this time, or perhaps merely a new emphasis on its organizational structure. Whatever the reason, the church named eight members (all men except the pianist, Miss Carrie Wideman) as general officers with titles such as Classification Superintendent, Superintendent Absent Pupils, General and Assistant Secretary, and Treasurer. In addition, six superintendents called departmental officers were named to lead departments ranging from "Primary" to "Home," which presumably meant shut-ins who still wished to receive Sunday school instruction. A whole list of teachers, twenty-three women and seven men, were also elected at a conference that appeared to deal solely with instructional matters within the church. The names of two prominent school teachers, Sunbeam Andrews and Maude Pratt, appear on this list; doubtless others were Greenwood teachers as well. As further evidence of this preoccupation with educational matters, it is interesting to note that the church drew up and adopted a full constitution and by-laws for the Sunday school; this all-inclusive document required ten full pages in the minute book when it was entered in November 1911.

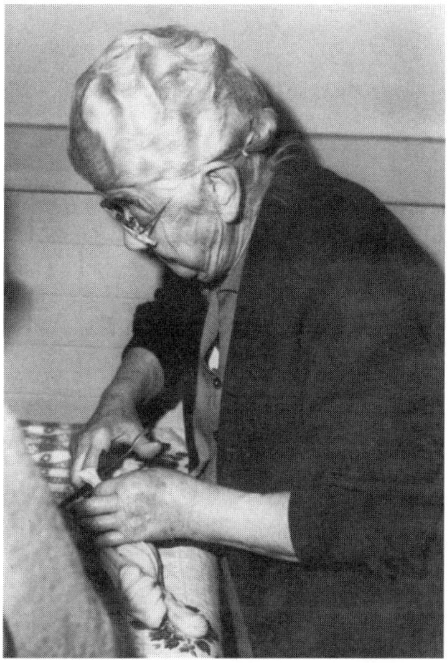

Emma "Sunbeam" Andrews (1887–1972), faithful church worker and everybody's favorite algebra teacher for about forty years.

An entry for May 14, 1911, reads as follows: ". . . the Treasurer was authorized to pay for the Individual Communion Service, which would hereafter be used." While no direct evidence has come to light, the form of communion (i.e., the use of a common cup as opposed to individual glasses) is said to have been one of the reasons for the withdrawal of those members who decided to organize a new church. As the year wore on, other members left the mother church from time to time to join the newly formed congregation. Those who were found to have united with churches "of different faith and order," however, had their names summarily removed from membership rolls.

Though the church demonstrated its stability and maturity again and again during this period, as for example when it confidently borrowed sixty-five hundred dollars for the new Sunday school room as well as "some necessary repairs to the church building" and a new heating plant, the congregation was not above a little petty bickering over hymnbooks! It seems that one faction, led by Dr. Jamison, wanted Baptist hymnals without notes, while another headed by Gerald Smart was equally determined the books should contain musical notation. The matter was tabled, according to the resolution, for a period of thirty days, but (probably to no one's surprise) was back on the floor a mere week later. This time Smart was able to circumvent Jamison's motion again and substitute his own—to appoint a committee of three to study the question and report to the church. When the report was made on November 12, a full two months after the matter was first broached, its recommendation as proposed by Smart was to purchase two hundred "Baptist Hymn & Praise books." Another motion to defer action for three more months greeted this report; the motion carried.

In the meantime the church was making plans to host the South Carolina Baptist Convention at its December 5, 1911, meeting. Three prominent churchmen accepted chairmanship of committees charged with hospitality, transportation, and arrangements at the church. Each was free to appoint the other members of his committee. In what seems an afterthought, the church appointed a committee "of six ladies" to "look after and see that the church and Sunday school building was properly cleaned and otherwise put in shape for the State Convention." One assumes their job, after the work was done, was to report to the male chairman of the arrangements committee.

The new Sunday school room was formally dedicated on December 3 with the assistance of the state Sunday school secretary, who spoke at the Sunday school hour, and Dr. D. M. Ramsay, president of Greenville Female College, who preached the dedicatory sermon. The Sunday school facilities were pronounced the best in the state, "certainly among Baptists."

Smart began the new year with moves to place the church's music program on a more stable footing. He proposed a standing music committee (consisting of "three male members") to be charged with general oversight of the music program of the church, securing singers, and managing the music fund (nonexistent, but to be raised by another committee). The motion passed; accordingly, three men—J. E. Burnside, J. C. Burns, and T. B. Meacham—became the music committee, and six women were given the job of soliciting subscriptions to form a music fund.

Among the church offices at this point was that of trustee, and while the duties incumbent upon this office are nowhere described in detail, the assumption is that trustees were authorized representatives of the church in matters such as signing notes and executing similar transactions relative to the everyday business life of the church. Evidently there were two trustees at the beginning of 1912, but W. C. Strawhorn proposed that the number be increased to three, with a term of office of one year. His motion passed, and businessmen J. K. Durst, Strawhorn himself, and A. F. McKissick became the official board of trustees for that year. The church also discovered after a careful search of the records that its very name, The First Baptist Church, though designated by resolution in 1910, was actually unauthorized, having resulted from common usage alone, and that, unlike the Sunday school, the church had no constitution. A four-part resolution followed, the terms of which were meant to place Greenwood's First Baptist Church on solid legal grounds, with a corporate charter, a constitution and by-laws, and a standing committee charged with electing the various officers of the church. In a sweeping move to bring itself into the mainstream of corporate life, the motion passed, evidently with no discussion.

And so began the year 1912.

CHAPTER FOUR

The Middle Years

(1912–1950)

The decade before World War I was a time of growth and consolidation for the town and county of Greenwood just as it was for the South as a whole. Though the agricultural depression of the 1920s had not yet hit with its full force, such were the ominous portents that the upcountry of South Carolina had already begun its transition away from the family farm to the manufacturing and service industries that still define the region's economic base. The reasons for this transition are quite plain: with the end of the Civil War came the need to rebuild an entire society, not merely an economy and its supporting institutions, but every aspect of southern life on every level. Not only was such rebuilding necessary if the region was to survive, but the task had to be accomplished in a time of changing realities, among them very different attitudes toward government, shifting population groups, women's issues which would eventually lead to universal suffrage, the race question in all its disturbing ramifications, the rise of a new social class of mill workers called "operatives," and financial problems connected with everything from a stable tax base to infrastructure to education and venture capital.

Many writers characterize this period as the end of one era and the beginning of another in the American South, and they describe its effects according to their own biases. Robert West Howard, whose slant can be deduced from the title of his 1985 book, *The Vanishing Land*, sketched it this way in his chapter entitled "Transition":

> Between 1865 and 1915, farm and ranch and plantation were maneuvered toward total dependence on technology and its edict of cash and credit. The self-sufficiency of horse, mule, ox, and donkey power was abandoned for machine power and the expensive by-products of distant oil wells. Farm and ranch prices were fixed by professional gamblers in the cities' grain exchanges and stockyards. Tick fever, the boll weevil, potato bugs, grasshoppers, and other crop ravagers forced the first widespread use of such poisonous insecticides as Paris green. The need for more cash crops necessitated extensive use of chemical fertilizers on overworked soils. The rural preacher gradually lost his leadership to the educational upsurge caused by public schools, public libraries, Chautauquas, land-grant colleges, and easier access to cities. Eagerness for advertising revenue persuaded farm publications and newspapers to promote more mechanization, hence greater dependence on middleman manufacturers. Books, dime novels, and then the movies sang a Lorelei song of rags-to-riches in the cities.

Other writers saw the problem rather differently and cited the changes as positive. They believed an economy supported by wages paid to workers had the potential to extend personal independence to an ever-growing group who might reasonably be expected to attain solid middle-class status as time went by. Considering the era of Radical Reconstruction that had been visited on South Carolina by a Congress bent on vengeance, coupled with the possible political plum of a resulting one-party Republican South made up of newly enfranchised black freedmen, it is not difficult to imagine a worse situation that might just as easily have resulted from the chaos that reigned from about 1868 to 1877. As it turned out, a sane government under former Confederate General Wade Hampton, whom Louis Wright described as "a political realist, as well as a man of great humanity," and a governor who "pursued a policy of justice and fair play toward all classes, black and white," slowly turned the tide back to the tough task of rebuilding a state forever changed by war and its aftermath.

The little town of Greenwood at this time found itself busily consolidating the hard-won gains of the period Louise Watson called its "great upsurge" as the nineteenth century ended and the twentieth got under way. County status had been achieved in 1897, bringing with it a whole new set of priorities to occupy the attention of its so-called "leading men." The county seat could not afford to rest on its laurels and set out to prove its mettle in a number of different areas. In fact, it might be said that the town was preparing to play its part in a new drama that, clearly in hindsight, was being enacted throughout the region. The South was beginning the process of, for want of a better term, its return to Americanization, or a rejoining the union on terms much more of its own choosing than the previous decades had allowed. The election of Woodrow Wilson in 1912 marked the reappearance of southern political influence on the national scene, and memories of the Lost Cause and Reconstruction were sufficiently diminished to allow southerners to share in the national enthusiasm for wars. Both the Spanish-American War, which gave Greenwood's Oregon Hotel its name, and World War I provided national rather than merely regional heroes to a population that had always cherished its men-at-arms. In addition, while World War I brought a level of economic advancement in production, employment, cash income, and population mobility, its end heralded a decline in the southern economy with the abrupt drop in the price of cotton, the onset of the boll weevil scourge, and the realization that too much emphasis on cotton production had effectively destroyed much of the farmland of the region. So serious was the situation, in fact, that the South was defined as the nation's number one economic problem during President Franklin D. Roosevelt's first term.

As debate over state and national issues swirled about the heads of Greenwood's body politic, the town's now officially named First Baptist Church plunged full tilt into activities designed to achieve its apparent goal as the town's largest; the minutes record the addition of 152 new members as the result of a revival meeting in May 1912. There was a great deal of activity on the membership front throughout the year; many conferences seemed to deal solely with receiving or dismissing whole lists of candidates for either fellowship or disassociation. But as the year drew to a close the question of music again came to the forefront. After routine votes almost month by month to table the

One of Gerald Smart's little "surprises"—Daffodil Day when the chancel area of the church on North Main held "a crowd, a host, of golden daffodils." Not all Smart's ideas were as successful.

hymnbook motion that had so occupied the congregation the previous year, followed by a final motion to extend the table vote indefinitely, those members most passionate about the church's music ministry, led by the ubiquitous Gerald H. Smart, opened a campaign to purchase a new pipe organ. Following what the minutes describe as "considerable discussion . . . as to the need of an organ in keeping with the church, new SS room, Choir, and the times," the members present voted to canvass the entire membership and secure subscriptions to an organ fund.

The annual report for 1912 which was, in the quaint terminology of the times, "spread upon the minutes" of January 13, 1913, revealed membership of 638 (a net loss of 76 from the previous year and reflecting "erasures" of 45 people), a deficit of more than $300 in operating expenses, and an outstanding banknote of $6,862. There had been a good deal of parsonage activity in 1912, and the report on that matter was a bit rosier. The sale of the old building had brought in a little more than $6,500 with which the church was able to purchase a lot and build and equip a brand new parsonage with nearly $50 left over.

The long-awaited report from the organ committee came in September 1913 when Smart brought the information that nearly $3,700 was in sight. Part of that figure, the amount of $1,250, was listed as "Carnegie Donation" with no further explanation. Obviously, none was needed. This reference testifies to the generosity of philanthropist Andrew Carnegie (1835–1919), the Scottish-born steel magnate who devoted the last twenty years of his life to giving away a large part of a fortune amassed from involvement in American industry, primarily its iron and steel works. Carnegie's gifts to libraries and educational institutions are legendary; numerous institutions, foundations, and trusts, both in this country and abroad, still honor his name. If Greenwood's First Baptist Church did secure a Carnegie grant toward the cost of a new organ, it was in good company indeed; better still, the gift was received during the lifetime of a truly remarkable man, one who gave away an estimated $300 million.

Smart's report was received with a motion to place the organ question in the hands of the music committee with power to act and with the understanding that the cost of a new organ would be held to whatever amount could be raised through subscription. The church met in special conference about a month later to formalize its commitment. It authorized the committee to "contract for the extension of the church building for the purpose of installing the new organ, this work to be done under the supervision and with the approval of the trustees." The trustees were also empowered to handle the actual purchase of the instrument, including arranging for deferred payment. The music committee was twice reminded of its responsibility to raise the money for the whole project. Even the hymnbook question seems to have been laid to rest at last. An entry for January 11, 1914, notes authorization for the music committee to purchase such number of Baptist hymnbooks as in its judgment were needed.

Membership had declined to 620 as of January 1, 1914, but the church showed no sign of cutting back either its program or its financial obligations. Quite the contrary, in fact; a motion was made to revisit those members who had already paid their pledges if the deacons were unable to collect enough to liquidate the deficit in current expenses.

George N. Cowan tendered his resignation as of May 1. The minutes give no clue to the reason but pass along the full text of Cowan's letter to the chairman of the board of deacons in which he assures everyone connected with the church of his love and affection. The resignation was accepted and a pulpit committee of fifteen authorized on the spot.[1] The church also acted early that year to release forty-two members for the purpose of organizing a church in the Greenwood mill village. This was the beginning of West Side Baptist Church, which dates its organization as March 1, 1914. Several other members left the congregation to join West Side as the year wore on.

The church found itself without a pastor when Cowan left, and Gerald Smart resigned his posts as both organist and Sunday school superintendent in September. Smart was moving away, but before leaving he tried to make sure the church would work with an organization called the County Interdenominational Sunday School Movement. Ever the ecumenist, Smart obviously wished to remind the church of its duty to like-minded groups in the community. The response to his motion was lukewarm: a motion of sympathy with the organization's work and a desire to "co-operate with others in the movement so far as we could" was passed.

Guest pastors such as a Reverend Nelson from the Rock Hill church and Dr. Howard Lee Jones, president of Coker College, filled the pulpit that fall. The minutes, in fact, indicate no particular urgency in securing a pastor. Perhaps the quality of the lay leadership at this period explains the delay. Members of the same group seemed to succeed themselves as deacons, attend associational meetings, and handle church business routinely; men named Snead, Sproles, Durst, McKissick, Turner, Strawhorn, Beaudrot, Giles, Graham, Singleton, and Leavell appear on nearly every page of the minutes. No doubt in recognition of this fact, and perhaps giving vent to certain ambitions and frustrations of his own, Gerald Smart had offered a resolution a few months before he left that no deacon could succeed himself immediately but could be named in a subsequent election. The resolution passed but was rescinded about a year later.

Dr. Byron H. DeMent, pastor 1914–1917.

Ready with its recommendation by November, the pulpit committee put forward the name of Byron H. DeMent, at that time professor of Sunday School Pedagogy at the seminary in Louisville. The committee must have been impressed with this gentleman; their salary recommendation was twenty-five hundred dollars "and home," and they also advocated paying his moving expenses. DeMent's salary would be seven hundred dollars more than Cowan's, an increase of 39 percent in one fell swoop. The record shows that the Cowans subsequently departed for North Carolina, taking their letter to the Baptist church in the little town of Apex, near Raleigh.

DeMent was accorded rather extravagant expressions of welcome to his new charge, not only in church on a December Sunday morning but also at a "formal welcome service" held that evening in which other churches joined. Welcome addresses were delivered by the editor of the *Baptist Courier* and the president of the state Baptist convention, who spoke on behalf of the entire membership. In addition, the Reverend Louis J. Bristow, pastor of Abbeville's first church, brought greetings from the Abbeville Association of which he was moderator. City Baptists were represented by the South Main pastor, Reverend J. B. Green. No wonder DeMent responded to this enthusiastic welcome "in a very happy way."

The first conference in the year 1915 marked a significant moment in the life of the church, one that could be regarded as a clear sign that it was becoming a force in the life of Greenwood. Upon recommendation of the board of deacons, the church voted unanimously to take a special collection "for the relief of the suffering in our community." No details of the discussion made the minutes, and this historic move into local missions work was matter-of-factly recorded in only eight lines of handwritten text. Church membership at that conference was reported at 552.

The first description of an ordination service appears in the minutes for Friday evening, June 18, 1915, when John A. Langley, presumably a church member, was publicly examined and ordained by a presbytery consisting of five pastors including DeMent, who served as chief examiner. The minutes describe the ceremony as "unusually impressive" and note that the candidate "stood a creditable examination." It might be interesting to compare ordination examinations of that period with those of today.

Another momentous change occurred in 1916 when typewritten minutes began to appear pasted in the minute book. In several cases corrections were made within the text, and it is not unusual to find recommendations and resolutions added by hand, no doubt in an effort to reflect exact wording. The researcher who finds rather tedious the task of deciphering eighty-year-old penmanship that might change every few pages is pleased to note this move toward state-of-the-art methods of recording business matters.

It must have struck the church like a thunderbolt when DeMent, whose acceptance of the pulpit had been the occasion of so much rejoicing, tendered his resignation in the fall of 1917, not quite three years after his arrival. The offer he had been unable to refuse had come from New Orleans where he was invited to create a new position as president of the Baptist Bible Institute established by the home mission and Sunday school boards of the Southern Baptist Convention. This institution, which eventually became the New Orleans Baptist Theological Seminary, was brand new and was intended to provide, in DeMent's words, "the very best possible advantages to pastors, evangelists, missionaries, laymen and women in order to equip them for the most efficient work in the various spheres of Christian service at home and abroad." As a former seminary professor, DeMent must have been delighted at the opportunity to return to an academic environment, even though it meant leaving "noble people . . . whose tender love, thoughtful consideration and wholehearted cooperation" had made his sojourn in Greenwood so pleasant. He gave the church thirty days' notice.

Dr. John R. Jester, pastor 1918–1922.

The month of September 1917 was not enough for the church to find a suitable replacement for DeMent, but matters had moved along sufficiently by the middle of December. Clerk J. E. Burnside made a firm offer to Dr. J. R. Jester who was serving at that time as one of three field secretaries on "The Million Dollar Campaign" in an attempt to provide new buildings, a scholarship program, and an endowment for Richmond and Westhampton Colleges, identified as "co-ordinate colleges" on the letterhead and presumably both located in Richmond, Virginia. Because both Burnside's typed offer and Jester's handwritten reply have been preserved in the minute book, the temptation to quote them verbatim in these pages has been too strong to resist. One is a matter-of-fact offer couched in cool business terminology, and the other is a somewhat convoluted discourse typical of churchmen of an earlier period, in the middle of which an acceptance of that offer can be discerned. Both the salutation, "Brother," and the complimentary close, "fraternally," echo the accepted code of address among Southern Baptists of the period:

> Dear Brother:
>
> At a special conference of the First Baptist Church on Sunday morning, Dec. 16th, a call was unanimously extended you by the Church to become our Pastor, at a salary of $3,000 per annum, and the use of the parsonage free of rent to you.
>
> The Church also agrees to pay the necessary expenses incurred in your moving to Greenwood, should you accept our call.
>
> I was authorized by the Church, as Clerk, to convey to you the above facts officially.
>
> Yours fraternally,

Dear Brother:

Your official communication notifying me of the call to become pastor of the First Baptist Church, of Greenwood, S. C., has been received. The spirit of unanimity on the part of the church in extending the call, has deeply impressed me with the hope that your action in the matter has been of the Lord's leading, and has greatly aided me in ascertaining what seems to be my course of duty.

As you urge that I give my reply as early as I can "consistently do so," and also a letter from the Chairman of the Pulpit Committee brings the same request, I have endeavored to reach a decision as quickly as possible. Therefore after earnest prayer for guidance from Him who makes no mistakes, and following what seems to be His will, I hereby convey through you to the church my acceptance of the call.

May I request that the church join with me in earnest prayer that this union may be one of mutual helpfulness, as we seek to advance the Master's Kingdom.

My relation to the Million Dollar Campaign for Richmond College is of such a nature that it will require a short time to finish up some work, for which engagements have already been made; but I shall begin my pastorate in Greenwood as early as my present relations will permit, which will not be later than the first Sunday in February. If I find that I can terminate my present work earlier, I will do so.

Please convey to the church the foregoing communication.

Fraternally yours,

Jester was not able to wind up his affairs in Richmond earlier than February 1918. Until he came on board the church made use primarily of the services of South Main's pastor Dr. E. J. Smith. In its resolution acknowledging his help the church commended Smith for "visiting the sick, comforting the distressed and burying the dead of this church and congregation" during the "four or five months" between regular pastors. One hopes Dr. Smith also received a tangible token of appreciation for his services.

Gerald Smart reappears about this time. The record shows that he was elected statistical secretary on February 6, and his part-time salary of thirty-five dollars per month was entered in the conference record a month later. He wasted no time in his zeal to improve efficiency; the minutes for May 8 include a resolution that printed "report cards" be provided to the various church organizations by means of which they could keep Secretary Smart fully informed of their activities.

At this point the church records come to an abrupt halt. The minute books for the period from May 1918 to September 1937 are missing. A number of people have no trouble envisioning these books carefully stored in somebody's attic, but no one seems to know whose. Unfortunately, this means that the official record covering a period of eighteen years and four months is unavailable for research. When one considers that this period covers almost the entire time between two great world wars, the Roaring Twenties, the Great Depression, and the administrations of seven governors and five presidents, the true impact of this loss becomes apparent. Even so, not every church can point to anywhere near the rich legacy of primary material still available for study that remains to the First Baptist Church of Greenwood, even though that trove is incomplete.[2]

Because of the missing official records, a small cache of church bulletins (called *calendars*, probably because of the listing of activities we call *opportunities* today), mostly from the 1920s, takes on special significance. The earliest of these is dated November 11, 1917, when the church was between pastors. Supply ministers filled the pulpit at this point; the speaker that day is identified only as "Lieut. Butler." Deacon J. R. Leavell put together the bulletin for this particular Sunday; some of the items he contributed read very well more than eighty years later:

> The congregation greatly enjoyed the sermon of Prof. Lawton[3] Sunday morning. He was at his best. He certainly preaches good Baptist doctrine. That only goes to show that we are not so far apart after all. . . .
>
> Attention, good ladies! Do you think the parsonage needs painting before the new preacher moves in?

> Bro. A. J. Sproles has been appointed a committee of one on ways and means. Ways to keep us cool in the summer and means to keep us warm in winter. We are very sure that he is the right man in the right place.

Another calendar, this one dated October 30, 1921, contains a paragraph that manages to combine two very different themes:

> The Greatest Question before the world to-day is shall we have disarmament, or continue in the old way of building up armaments, and thus laying the foundation for a future war of unparalleled proportions? It is a matter of such paramount importance that we have yielded to the request made to the pastors of America to speak upon this subject. To-night the theme will be "War or Civilization,—Which?" Surely no matter of public concern is more important just now. Next Sunday night we shall resume the series on "Bible Types of Womanhood of Yesterday and Today."

The most complete group of bulletins (calendars) is for the year 1923. Nearly every issue from June to the end of October was included in someone's box of memorabilia. Dr. Vines was in the pulpit during the period and Baptists were involved in the great $75 Million Campaign of the Southern Baptist Convention. A reminder of this appeal appears in nearly every issue:

> Every member of the church should make a pledge to the current expenses of the church and to the 75,000,000 Campaign. . . . This is a duty and a Privilege. To fail to do this is disloyalty to your church and to Christ. How can you afford to fail to comply with the plain command of the New Testament and the appeal of your church and of your denomination?"

An issue in July announced a series of four Sunday evening sermons entitled "Themes from the Poets," a wonderful notion that allowed a nod to writers as diverse as Robert Browning, John Greenleaf Whittier, and Joyce Kilmer. In addition, W. L. Feaster,

Dr. William N. Vines, pastor 1923–1927.

who must have been choir director, though he is not so listed, was to "lead the congregational singing and render a solo each evening appropriate to the subjects of these sermons." The title of the first sermon was from Whitman: "I Love Flowers and Children and God." The program of evening worship during this period was billed as "People's Popular Services" beginning at 8:30 P.M.

At the request of the pastor, A. J. Sproles took over the church calendar while Vines was on vacation (the "vacation" included supply visits to the first churches in Richmond and Bristol, Virginia, as well as a revival in Taylors, South Carolina). Sproles took his responsibilities seriously and provided a most entertaining column week after week. A few excerpts follow:

> [August 5] In keeping with my promise to undertake whatever our Pastor requested I will occupy the Bulletins Sanctum for the next few weeks and ask your assistance, your sympathy and your prayers, that my observation may not be too secular.
>
> Despite the excessive heat a great congregation heard Dr. Vines Sunday evening, among whom was the student body of the Lander Opportunity School[4] which was an inspiration to us all. . . .
>
> It devolves on the officers and leading lay members to keep our Sunday School and Mid-Week Service up to standard during our pastor's absence. Therefore let them be up and doing. The ability

of our pulpit supplies as announced is sufficient guarantee that the preaching services will be all that could be desired.

This congregation is unanimous in granting its pastor a five weeks leave for recreation and such rest as comes to a preacher from preaching old sermons to new people.

[August 12] This congregation extends Maj. J. Rion McKissick most cordial greetings this morning, almost as one of our own; certainly he is no stranger to us. We have known him as an able editor whose terse writings on current topics are quoted extensively in the leading magazines and periodicals throughout the nation; we have known him as a fluent speaker and fine orator very much in demand on memorial, patriotic and other extra occasions; we have known him as the younger brother of a former member and ranking officer of this church, Mr. A. F. McKissick; we have known him as the baby boy of a Christian mother, Mrs. Sarah F. McKissick once an honored and active member of this church, now a Saint in glory, but the memory of her sweet life and acts of Christian benevolence live on in all our hearts and the activities of the church—mother McKissick as we were delighted to call her. . . . we bid him thrice welcome believing that the message he brings to us this morning in his own courageous, forceful and inimitable style will encourage, stimulate and inspire us all to a higher and better life.

[August 26] Good morning, Brother Rhett.[5] We are delighted to have you with us this morning; so rejoiced in fact that the poorest sermon you ever preached—if there ever was such a one—would sound mighty good to us because we love you for your genial and fraternal nature as well as your ability; we love you for the cause you espoused early in life and the great denomination you represent; we love you for its companion cause in which you are now engaged as President of our greatest Educational Institution . . . ; and we love you because you are now as never before identified with the highest and best interests of Greenwood and we trust that you may go in and out among her people, doing good for many many years yet to come.

> An example worthy of emulation by all of us is that of three young ladies who are sisters, all members of this church and married; who with their husbands rarely, if ever miss a church or Sunday school service, yet they do not believe that religion ever was designed to make our pleasures less; consequently they attend picture shows and other places of innocent amusement, when they like, which is eminently proper for young people to do.

> [September 2] We have with us this morning another noted educator, Dr. D. M. Ramsay, president of one of our own leading educational institutions. Dr. Ramsay is too well known to this congregation to need an introduction.[6]

The calendar for September 9 describes a program called "Welcome Service to the Pastor" with R. B. Curry presiding. This sounds very formal, but actually the church was simply welcoming Dr. and Mrs. Vines home again after an absence of a few weeks. Sproles put it this way: "We are delighted to have Dr. and Mrs. Vines back home again. We have missed them, indeed, but we are catholic enough to be glad they have had these few weeks of recreation and relaxation. Now we welcome them back with open hearts." Another item in the same issue concerns the great earthquake in Japan that devastated Tokyo and Yokohama with severe fire damage and loss of life. Nearly half the population of the two cities lost their homes, and more than 100,000 people died. Vines preached that Sunday on "The Religious Significance of the Great Earthquake," and Sproles inserted a plea for contributions to aid in the worldwide call for assistance that was sure to come through the churches. The amount of $165.33 had been subscribed by the following week.

The issue of September 9 also contained Sproles's swan song: "In this issue my valedictory should appear, but I can't write one, however, I want to thank you all for your patience and kind words which have materially aided me in the discharge of a very pleasant task these five or six weeks, and simply bid you an affectionate FAREWELL."

An unexpected piece of information appears in the calendar of September 23, one that begs to be recorded here. Probably in recognition of the opening of school, the church extended a special invitation to the teachers of the city schools to be welcomed from the pulpit at the Sunday evening service. The pastor would set the tone with a sermon entitled "The Fundamental in Education." A listing of Greenwood's schools and the teachers in each followed:

> Magnolia Street School:—Miss Josephine Kerr, Miss Dorothy Hart, Miss Loree Smith, Mrs. B. S. Boyd, Miss Mary Leslie, Miss Nannie Major, Miss Maude Pratt, Miss Rebecca Sligh.
>
> High School:—Miss Annie Jones, Miss Eva Williams, Miss Cora Neil Arnold, Miss Sunbeam Andrews, Miss Lois Steele, Miss Georgia Wardlaw, Miss Edna Harvey, Mrs. George Dickson, Mrs. John Lyon, C. L. Hood, H. B. Mulkey, D. L. Harper, J. C. Martin, Principal.
>
> Blake School:—Mrs. Gussie C. Crum, Miss Rebecca Wideman, Miss Thelma Bailey, Mrs. B. F. Olive, Miss Marie Still, Miss Alice Wilson, Mrs. P. W. Jayroe, Mrs. W. L. Daniel, Miss Claudia Townes, Mrs. W. F. Huiet Jr., P. W. Jayroe, Principal.
>
> Leslie School:—Miss Mary Calhoun, Miss Marie Martin, Miss Margaret Calhoun, Miss Camille Jennings, Mrs. A. D. Calhoun, Miss Lucille Harvey, Miss Hortense Padgett, Miss Louise Burnett, Miss Louise Kern, J. R. Hooten, Principal.
>
> Durst School:—Mrs. W. H. Page, Miss May Bell Cooner, Miss Ruth Cain, Miss Ella Mays, Principal.
>
> Jordan School:—Miss Lucy Agnew, Principal, Mrs. J. E. Bolton.
>
> Grenola School:—Miss Dorothy Lumley, Miss Evelyn Dallas, Mrs. W. G. Gambrell, Principal.

As of October 1923 the church claimed 1,030 members. That was the good news; the bad news was that a third of that number had contributed nothing at all to current expenses. Even worse (or not, depending upon one's point of view), the calendar reported that a full 48 percent of the membership had taken no part in the $75 Million Campaign.

The calendar of January 18, 1925, contains the announcement that an address by Greenwood attorney Douglas Featherstone would be part of a service honoring the memory of Confederate General Robert E. Lee to be held the next morning at 11 A.M. The fact that Lee was born on January 19 explains the date of the service; the surprise is the realization that such tributes were still being held, probably throughout the South, a full fifty-five years after the general's death.

The minute book placed in service in 1937 contains on its first page a most convenient listing of pastors with their dates of service, a listing that might well be regarded as one of the missing links caused by the missing minute books. While their records cannot be detailed from firsthand sources, the pastorates of J. R. Jester (1918–1922), William M. Vines (1923–1927), and Charles F. Sims (1928–1943) can at least be acknowledged. And the final entry, James A. Bowers (Sept. 1, 1943–), carries a significance of its own, for it was Bowers who would lead the church through perhaps the most turbulent period of its existence and into what might reasonably be viewed as its postmodern era.

Dr. Charles F. Sims, pastor 1928–1943.

More than half of the minute book for 1937–1941 is devoted to a conscientious effort to record the church's membership in chronological and alphabetical order, with the date and method of entry, awarding and receiving of letters, gains and losses broken down by category, and even an extensive double-entry system noting name changes when young female members married. Though this exercise was doomed to failure in the long run, the meticulous listing did allow for some of the most elegant Spencerian script imaginable (as well as some virtually illegible entries added in other, less refined hands). Indeed, one wishes the scribe had seen fit to identify himself so that he could receive a well-deserved "Bravo" in these pages for the beauty of his penmanship.

By 1937 the church had settled into a practice of pasting typed, albeit very badly typed, conference minutes and bulletins in the official record. Many well-remembered names, such as Seymour, Beaudrot, Leavell, and Sproles, continue to appear in listings of deacons, but new ones are clearly moving into prominence as well. Among the names familiar to much of today's membership are Benson, Jay, Penn, Curry, Bradford, and Sanders. Gerald H. Smart is listed as organist and choir director; the Sunday school general officers are male (except for the music director) while the workers are overwhelmingly female; women's work and the BTU departments are firmly in the hands of women except for L. H. Rowell and Bryan Dorn who serve as secretaries for the Training Union; women chair two of the nine listed committees and represent about one-third of the total membership of that group.

The church had also taken the giant step of formal budgeting at some time between 1918 and 1937. The budget adopted for 1938 anticipated $7,300 for "local work" and a similar amount to meet all obligations to the cooperative program, including missions and all benevolent gifts. It is always interesting to compare institutional costs and priorities from one generation to the next. In 1938 the music department of the church was projected to cost $700, supply ministers only $100 (to cover the pastor's month of vacation), and the church secretary's stipend was budgeted at $120. While the pastor's salary accounted for nearly half the budget, the second costliest item was debt liquidation, which the church pegged at $1,300. Fuel, water, and lights in those days were expected to cost $350 for the year. A treasurer's report for January shows expenditures running a little over $600 for the month; the budget appears to have been quite realistic.

The church entered, one hopes enthusiastically, upon a new venture sponsored by the general board of the state convention—

the first minister's retirement plan—in the summer of 1938. No doubt an emphasis on old age and survivors' insurance, which was the original name of the New Deal program now known simply as Social Security, was at least part of the reason for the denomination's actions during this period. A form letter from the general secretary-treasurer of the convention makes clear that the program is meant to provide retirement income for Baptist ministers in the state; ministers had been among those groups allowed to opt out of the federal social security program. In its simplest terms the program provided for contributions from the employing church, the pastor, and eventually the convention, to provide a retirement income of up to 50 percent of the pastor's active salary. Full retirement pay depended upon attaining age sixty-five and a minimum of twenty-five years of service. First steps are always important, and this one was particularly significant. Joe King records that the first ministerial relief organization in the South had been established in South Carolina in 1813. A better means of providing for retired pastors came 125 years later. The treasurer's report persisted in calling the $7.50 monthly contribution "Ministers Relief," a term that was quite incorrect but that probably reflected the general understanding of the program at the time. The word "annuity" was finally adopted to describe the contribution in March 1940.

The church budget continued to hover around $14,000 to $15,000 in 1939, 1940, and 1941, and conferences appear to have covered only routine matters of election to various church offices, processing new members, and issuing letters to those who wished to transfer their memberships to other Baptist churches.

An interesting situation presented itself in early 1941 concerning a member, Edward Lieberman, who is listed in the alphabetical register with the notation "Jew" in parentheses beside his name and in another place as having been received upon profession of faith in 1932. Oddly enough, Lieberman's surname is also written as "Lee" in the chronological register,[7] where he is again identified as "Jew" and a New York City address is inexplicably recorded. Lieberman wrote to the pastor (Dr. Charles Sims), explaining that he had received a call to the ministry and wished to be examined and ordained by his own church before accepting the call. Gerald Smart offered a resolution to the effect that the church thought it best for him to continue his preparation work; in other words, if Smart had his way the church *would not* offer the ordination ritual.

Smart's resolution, fortunately, did not prevail. Only a week later Sims chaired a conference that began with a report from a five-member presbytery which had examined Lieberman in the interim. Sims reported that the presbytery had found him fully eligible for ordination, and the conference ended with an ordination sermon, prayer, and laying on of hands by the ministers of the presbytery. The minutes conclude, one senses rather defiantly, with the line, "Benediction pronounced by Rev. Eddie Lieberman." The gentleman's name is spelled with an "ie" in some places and an "ei" in others, but regardless of the spelling it is impossible to escape the feeling that his request for ordination to the Baptist ministry, as well as the conditions of his original membership, might have stirred some ancient religious passions. Even so, the church comes off reasonably well in handling the matter. Lieberman moved to his first pastorate in Hugheytown, Alabama; his letter from the Greenwood church was granted soon afterward.

Actually, there is more to the Eddie Lieberman story than is revealed in the church's minute book. Both the current pastor, Dr. William Harris, and Boykin Curry had something to add. Harris recalled that Lieberman went on after his ordination to a full-fledged career as an evangelist, one who used as the centerpiece of his pulpit repertoire his compelling personal story—a Jew who consciously experienced conversion to Christianity as a young man. Curry's recollection was a little more personalized since his father had played a significant role in Lieberman's link with Greenwood in the 1930s. It seems the young man had fled New York in a stolen car and got as far as Greenwood before being apprehended by the long arm of the law. Lodged in the old city jail on Edgefield Street, he must have been ideally situated for the missionary zeal of Mrs. A. F. Hagan, the mother of Miss Carrie Hagan and a longtime member of the church, and Mrs. E. F. (Lucile Parks) Jay. An extraordinary Sunday school teacher who went so far as to call her students on

Miss Carrie Hagan who, along with her mother and Lucile Jay, ministered to Eddie Lieberman in jail.

Saturday nights to remind them to be in church the next day, Hagan also possessed a strong missionary instinct and was particularly active in personal witnessing and work in the local jail. So thorough was the influence of the two women on the young man from New York that he was actually released from jail in Hagan's custody. Part of that custody meant that Lieberman was sure to be found in church at every possible opportunity, and it seems that conversion, ordination, and a life dedicated to spreading the gospel followed as the night the day.[8]

Dr. Eddie Lieberman lives today in retirement in Greenville. He added a few compelling details of the courtroom segment of his personal drama in a letter to the author dated February 27, 1999:

> My trial in Federal court, under federal Judge Watkins of Anderson, made headlines on the front page of the *Greenwood Index.* The headline read, "Judge says Red Letter Day in Greenwood." What that was all about concerned the trial. I had been jailed six times in four different States, winding up as a Federal prisoner. I pled "guilty" and asked for the mercy of the court. The judge peered at me and said, "With your record I am not inclined to grant you any mercy." Then he did an amazing thing. He said, "Before I pronounce sentence is there anyone in the courtroom who has anything to say on behalf of this prisoner?"
>
> Mrs. Hagan stood up in the crowded courtroom and told him how she had witnessed to me and I had become a Christian. Two

> former cell mates of mine who had been released testified that I had lived a sincere Christian life for the two months that they had been incarcerated with me. Then Major R. B. Curry spoke, said he had visited me twice while I was in jail and was convinced that I was a sincere believer in Jesus Christ. . . .
>
> Judge Watkins looked at me and said, "Because of the testimony of these witnesses, I sentence you to one hour in the custody of the United States Marshal and I suspend that." Then he added, "This is a red letter day in the history of Greenwood when lives are changed for good within our prison system." That was the exact headline of the newspaper.
>
> Many years later, I spoke at the First Baptist Church of Anderson. After the close of the Sunday morning service, who should invite me to his home for lunch but Judge Watkins, a member of that church. Sitting around the table, he told me that he had used my story in many a courtroom when he sat at the trial of young men. When lunch was over, he gave me $20 and told me to buy some books and remember him every time I read them.

For a full account of the Jay/Hagan/Lieberman story, see appendix A. Doubtless many members other than those mentioned here also remember Eddie Lieberman with respect and affection.

The minute book for 1942 begins with a bang in the form of a resolution against "the sale and consumption of intoxicating liquors" in South Carolina, citing both the evils flowing from such sale and consumption as well as the fact that South Carolina voters in a 1940 election had endorsed prohibition by a majority of nearly 60,000 votes. This work is not an appropriate venue to retell the story of the country's preoccupation with Prohibition, a matter that reached the rarefied heights of a constitutional amendment in 1920 only to crash and burn thirteen years later when the unenforceability of such a law was finally acknowledged by Congress and the first Roosevelt administration. Still, the difficulty was that a church could hardly respond unfavorably to a resolution condemning drinking whenever it arose, particularly when concern for the "religious, moral, and material welfare" of the population was invoked. And perhaps everyone realized by the early 1940s that while such a resolution might enjoy a long shelf life, it actually meant very little in practical terms.

A most interesting coda to the $75 Million Campaign, which had ended in 1924, appears in a stray church bulletin from 1942. Southern Baptists were being solicited again, this time in a campaign called the Hundred Thousand Dollar Club which was designed to wipe out the indebtedness of agencies of the Southern Baptist Convention—Home and Foreign Missions, three theological seminaries, and the Baptist Hospital. The movement had begun eight years earlier; during that time more than $1.5 million had been paid to reduce the debts. The article explained the dilemma:

> [T]hese debts were made at a time of great emergency. With perfectly good faith in our brethren that they would pay the $92,000,000 they subscribed during the 75 Million Campaign, the leaders of our boards and institutions projected their work on this basis, making due allowances for shrinkage. But when the financial crash came and our receipts suddenly dropped to a mere pittance, it was impossible to withdraw the missionaries and reduce the work sufficiently overnight. Just as soon as possible our boards and institutions did adjust their budgets to the new conditions, but in the meantime a huge debt had piled up.
>
> Furthermore, they are our debts.
>
> The agencies of the Southern Baptist Convention are our agencies, the Boards and institutions are ours, their victories and achievements are ours, their assets—$25,878,746.49—are ours, and their debts are ours.

Dr. Charles Sims resigned in early 1943 to go to work for the state Baptist board as field secretary. The minutes of the church conference reflect a certain shock at the announcement, even to the point of a motion urging the church to take a week before acting on the resignation and appointing a committee to investigate in the meantime. A more prudent view was presented by another member who knew Sims's mind was made up and who urged the church simply to accept the situation and wish the pastor well in his new work. A huge pulpit committee of twenty-two men and six women was summarily organized and charged with the duty of securing a pastor. Evidently the members were able not only to work together but also with great dispatch, for by mid-June they were ready to make their report to a conference called in special session to hear it. The pulpit committee, jointly with the finance committee, recommended that the church call the Reverend James A. Bowers of Darlington at a salary of thirty-six hundred dollars per year, plus a home and the services of a secretary. The motion passed unanimously.

Dr. James A. Bowers, pastor 1943–1977.

The tentative budget for 1944 appears in the minute book pasted on a sheet all its own. Clearly the church had continued its progress on the business front. The budget is divided into several categories with individual item subdivisions under each. Local needs were obviously growing while expenditures for missions and benevolences remained at the seven thousand dollar level, and for the first time the church set up an investment fund earmarked "for future building improvement." That item, budgeted at five thousand dollars, appears to be made up of expected revenue over and above actual expenses. If anyone were listening, and surely many were, Greenwood's First Baptist Church was beginning to make the first tentative noises about a new building.

About this time the church began the practice of pasting copies of regular bulletins in the official record, though every now and then the clerk would still record handwritten notices of elections, ordinations, and other special events as they occurred. This practice ensured that

Partial view of the kitchen in the church on North Main, surely one good reason for a building program.

information on a variety of topics, from Sunday school attendance to notices of members' surgical procedures, was safeguarded for posterity. One particularly poignant reminder of the facts of American life in 1944 appears at the end of the bulletin for May 14:

> On the day the news is heard that the invasion has begun the churches of the city will be open for prayer and meditation. Sometime during the day the citizens are asked to go to their own church or to some other that is more convenient for a few minutes of private prayer. At the close of that day there will be services conducted in various places throughout the city which will be more formal periods of prayer. It is not sufficient, however, to wait for that day to begin our prayers. In anticipation, let each one of us be much in prayer that God's will may be done in this conflict.

There seems to be a growing emphasis on young people and their activities during this period. Some of this can probably be explained by the times. World War II might have been the last so-called "popular war," but it still meant the untimely death of many young Americans on foreign soil and the commensurate realization of the importance of nurturing a new generation of citizens and church members. In addition, one of the charges the pulpit committee had stressed when seeking a new pastor was that he would be expected to work with the young people of the church. Accordingly, the church would on occasion welcome as special guests to the worship service Sunday schoolers and others of similar age attending as a group. The bulletin would mention these events, assuring the youngsters that the church valued them highly and pledging its "time and counsel" to help as they grew to adult wisdom and responsibility. Regular membership also grew to new highs during the mid-1940s: a report in September 1944 set the total at 1,204, with a Sunday school enrollment of 876. Collections, too, were quite healthy; the bulletin records that gifts for all causes that year totaled nearly $24,000.

The tentative budget for 1945 broke down the various categories into percentages, with some interesting and revealing results. Expenditures in the "Personnel" category, for example,

A group of girl scouts and RAs meeting in the North Main building, 1940s. Ruth Markham and Flonnie Marbert are shown far left.

An interior view of the 1897 church, 1940s.

exceeded by only .2 percent the amount slated for "Missions and Benevolences," and the two categories taken together accounted for just over half the church budget. The most significant change was a 100 percent increase over the previous year in the "Investment Fund" category earmarked for future building improvements. The church's operating expenses and local church education totaled a little over 16 percent of budgeted funds. Priorities for 1945 could not have been more clear—a new building was definitely just over the horizon. One reason for the optimistic projection can be found in the financial report for the previous year which was featured in the bulletin for January 7, 1945. The 1944 budget had been oversubscribed by some $4,100, an increase of nearly 18 percent. Whether this evidence of financial health can be attributed to a booming wartime economy or simply a renewed dedication to the church and its program is impossible to determine and probably does not matter greatly in any case. It is enough to say that the First Baptist Church had clearly become a mature and stable component of the Greenwood community by the mid-1940s. Still, the pastor evidently found it expedient to remind his flock that the church's mission must always be its primary consideration: "Let's be sure," he wrote, "that 1945 will be our best year yet financially. To do this . . . it must also be our best year spiritually."

Judging from the cut-and-pasted snippets from the church bulletin that by this time had become the norm in the official minute book, the pastor was quite skilled in getting his points across to the flock. Little jogs about attendance, the "good spirit" prevailing during worship services, names and addresses of new members, and comments on financial stewardship appear on every page during this period, and Bowers was always careful to mix words of praise with those of admonition; surely not every pastor would use the term "spiritual history" as he did in describing a memorable Sunday in April 1945, nor the heading "Echoes from last Sunday" when reporting dry statistics of attendance and offering.

The deacons were ready by September to act upon the recommendation of the finance committee that the church get serious about a building program. Evidently leaders believed the congregation had outgrown the quarters it had occupied on the fringe of downtown Greenwood for nearly fifty years. The resolution was specific and comprehensive:

> The Finance Committee recommends to the Board of Deacons that the Church proceed with plans to acquire a new site for a new church and educational building; that the present property be sold; the Church build a new church building and education building on the new property—all of the foregoing to be begun when, in the opinion of the church, building and property prices are reasonable and when not less than $100,000.00 in cash is in hand.

This motion was evidently viewed as putting the cart before the horse and was subsequently revised in order to clarify priorities and commit the church even more firmly to its basic task of raising funds for a new building. R. B. Curry, with the knowledge and approval of the finance committee, took the floor and moved

> that this church proceed with plans to raise funds to be used for the construction of a new Church and Sunday School Building; that as soon as the sum of $100,000.00 is in hand, the Finance Committee, with the approval of the Board of Deacons, present to the Church its recommendations in regard to plans for the Building Program.

The vote was an impressive 207 for and 15 against the motion. A month or so later the church adopted another record budget of nearly $39,000, an increase of more than 29 percent over the previous year. Clearly the church saw itself as accepting the challenge of an ambitious building program.

As further evidence of the level of commitment, a new committee of nine members, three of them women, was appointed to study the all-important question of location for the proposed new physical plant. A report by the end of the year was anticipated, but the committee's first and only report, recorded in the bulletin for December 15, was limited merely to its finding that the current site was not satisfactory for the proposed building, nothing more. Oddly enough, a blurb in February called for a whole new committee, of five members this time, whose charge would be the same as the first—to study the question of site selection. The notice called this "the natural outgrowth of the action . . . when the church approved the change in the location of our new church building." The new committee, when it was named in July, was composed of five prominent businessmen: L. B. Adams, J. W. Bradford, R. B. Curry, E. W. Milford, and Fred Smith. These five took on the project in their characteristically efficient fashion, though they promised to listen to suggestions from any interested church member. No women were named this time.

While nothing in the official record supports the idea that all was not smooth sailing in the matter of the building program, several people remember this period as one of serious disagreement among longtime members. The problem was not concern about the financial obligation the church would incur, as might have been expected, but rather with strong sentimental attachment to everything about the current building, especially its memorial stained glass windows with their reminders of family solidarity and pride.

The Baraca Class, c. 1944. R. B. Curry (front row second from left) taught this class from 1920–1945. Seated next to Curry are Sara Culbertson, pianist, and her father, Arthur, song leader.

Boykin Curry remembers that those who could not seem to reconcile themselves with the idea of a new home for First Baptist Church acted as though its current environs were holy ground, and he remembers one member who vowed never to darken the door of any new structure. As far as Curry remembers, he never did.

A giant step came for the music ministry when Dr. and Mrs. A. Elbert Adams brought their letter from South Main to First Baptist in February 1946. The deacons lost no time offering Adams the post of organist. Edgar Davis had served as both organist and choir director for several years by this time; his new title of director of music probably suited him very well indeed, and the church became ever more noted for the quality of its music program as the years passed.

Sunday moring service with James A. Bowers in the pulpit, 1940s.

Another healthy budget was adopted for 1947; the building fund this time was set at $25,000, an amount of nearly half the total. Salaries, too, were beginning to inch upward, as was the size of the church's paid staff. In addition to the pastor's annual salary, which had advanced to $4,800, an increase of 20 percent over the previous year, the budget contained slots for a full-time education director, a secretary and a janitor, as well as an allowance for part-time pay for the music director and organist and a small stipend for the treasurer and clerk. Membership totaled 1,249, a net gain of 31 during the year 1946.

Bowers left in July for an international conference of the Baptist Alliance to be held in Denmark. Obviously the church had defrayed his expenses, a gesture for which he expressed deep appreciation as he prepared for the trip to Copenhagen. This trip marks the first time the Greenwood church had sent a delegate to a Baptist meeting across the sea. While the pastor was not particularly forthcoming about the content of the conference, at least in published statements, he was notably effusive in his remarks as recorded in the bulletin of September 14, 1947. What are we to make of the desire "to be back among these excellent people" that the pastor noted had "grown intensely during the past few weeks"? While he was willing to describe the journey to Denmark as pleasant and profitable, Bowers's trip seems chiefly to have brought the realization of the depth of love he felt for the people of the church and intensified the desire to make a "contribution to the ongoing of the kingdom of God, and the development of the spiritual life of this city." A reader more than fifty years later can still feel the earnest sincerity of this man's declaration of pure joy to be home again in the midst of his flock.

Once again the church outdid itself in oversubscribing the 1947 budget by nearly one thousand dollars, a budget that the bulletin describes as "the largest . . . in the history of our church by far." There is an almost palpable energy contained in bulletin entries of this period, probably a reflection of the energetic young pastor's dedication to and pleasure in his work. And as evidence of the church's financial health at this point, the bulletin noted in April 1948 a recommendation that the church purchase a new organ from the Shantz (later spelled Schantz) Organ Company, "as specified by the organ committee," for the sum of $14,581, "*which sum is to be paid out of funds on hand*" [emphasis added]. While support was not quite unanimous—two people spoke against the resolution—the motion to purchase an instrument to be installed in the old building, and possibly moved to the new one, carried easily. The new organ was played for the first time ten months later. The bulletin for February 13, 1949, noted that the installation had been inspected by Dr. Adams and pronounced satisfactory only the week before, and the pastor and trustees had formally accepted the instrument on behalf of the church. Typically, Bowers praised everyone involved, including the organ company, for their fine spirit, cooperation, and cordial relations during the entire project. Two sentences in the announcement are typical of Bowers's style: "We are sure that it [the organ] will add greatly to the worshipful nature of our services," and "Let us pray that this, too, shall add to our ability and desire to magnify the name of our God."

The Easter Sunday bulletin of 1947 contains the following paragraph:

> We wish to take this opportunity to thank all of those who have had a part in providing the funds for the purchase of an automobile for Miss Clifford Barratt to be used in her missionary work in China. The total amount of this fund is now $2,354.31, which is a sufficient amount to purchase the car and ship it to her at her mission station in China. We sincerely appreciate the generosity of her friends, not only in Greenwood, but in various places throughout the South who have heard of this campaign and have contributed to it. There have been certain difficulties to arise in getting the car to its destination, but the money has been deposited and will be used as soon as possible. 'Tis hoped that the difficulties will be cleared out of the way in the next few weeks so that the car can be on its way. . . .

An article entitled "Automobile for Miss Barratt" in the *Baptist Courier* of February 13, 1947, under the byline of Gerald H. Smart, reads:

> Several weeks ago Miss Clifford Barratt left Greenwood to return to China to resume her work as missionary there. It will be recalled that Clifford Barratt had been serving as a missionary for many years prior to the outbreak of war with Japan. She was interned for many months in a guarded camp but was finally given a passport back to America and returned on the *Gripsholm* during the war. She has since that time been residing in Greenwood with her family, awaiting opportunity to return to China and her beloved life-work among the Chinese.
>
> Within the past year Protestants have reopened their missionary activities in the war-ridden areas of the Orient, and Miss Barratt is again at her post of service.
>
> Though Miss Barratt never complained of her limited resources and modestly asked for only the minimum needs, friends have learned that she served a wide area and covered this territory on a bicycle,

riding 30 to 40 miles to reach her objectives. It is not in the bounds of reason to ask or expect her to continue to carry on her work under present conditions with only a bicycle for transportation.

Being exceedingly grateful for many other gifts and expressions of kindness she has stated to someone that she did not have the courage to ask for a car though secretly she has greatly longed for one, that she might, not only more efficiently carry on her present activities, but greatly extend the area and possibilities of her usefulness.

To this end a Clifford Barratt automobile fund has been established in the county, and subscriptions to this fund are earnestly solicited so that posthaste an automobile may be forwarded to her. The board has agreed to send the car out from San Francisco port, and arrangements have been entered into to buy a car on the west coast, for immediate shipment.

Some $1,500 or $1,750 will be needed for the undertaking. Since not even the pastors of our smallest churches here at home are willing to carry on without a car, it seems asking too much of Clifford Barratt to undertake her important and widely scattered field of activities on a bicycle. No doubt friends of Miss Barratt and those interested in Christianizing the Orient will get this little matter out of the way in a few days.

This country is greatly disturbed over conditions in China, and not lessened by the report of General Marshall just now returning to the states from a mission to that country. Also General MacArthur has recently stated that the one hope over there is the ideology of democracy, which ideology must be based simply on the ideals and teachings of Christianity. We Americans can best prevent future conflict and complications with foreign nations by bringing their philosophy, their moral and ethical standings in line with our own.

If you are interested in this work and wish to help Miss Barratt, our own county representative in the promotion of Christianity in China,

> you may send any check or contribution to Mrs. Alma C. Gibbons, acting as chairman of a group from the missionary societies of the Abbeville Association. Associated with Mrs. Gibbons are: Mrs. R. E. Seymour, President of First Baptist WMU, Mrs. J. P. Abney, President of South Main WMU, Miss Maude Pratt, Member, Business Woman's Circle, First Baptist Church, Mrs. Horace Free, Secretary, South Main Baptist Church.

Miss Barratt added her own note to this lovely story when she put together her autobiography many years later:

> Funds for this car were raised but because of the fighting in China, I was never able to get it into China. However, when I had been in Formosa (Taiwan) for two years and was at home on furlough in 1952, the funds being available, I bought a nice 1952 Chevrolet 4 door car. I had the use of the car during my year of furlough. Then my nephew, William John Park, took it to Charleston, SC, and shipped it for me to Chi Lung, Taiwan.
>
> The money the friends provided was sufficient to pay for the car, the transportation and the duty and I had the use of it until my retirement in 1963.[9]

The ordination of the Reverend Robert E. Seymour Jr., was a special event of the summer of 1948. Seymour, now the retired pastor of the Olin T. Binkley Memorial Baptist Church of Chapel Hill, is a Greenwood native; he was raised in a house that still stands on Grace Street, just across from the church. In his book *Whites Only: A Pastor's Retrospective on Signs of the New South,*[10] dedicated to five congregations, one of them First Baptist Greenwood, Seymour recounts his own rather curious reaction to the ordination service. "I draw a complete blank," he writes, adding that family illness might have been one cause of this strange "failure of memory." Another might have been what he believed was an "understandable anxiety" on the part of the pastor to convene an ordination council of local clergy because of his divinity degree from Yale University! If that sounds strange to readers in the late 1990s, they need only remind themselves that in 1948 southerners were still a long way from recognizing the emergence of social issues such as civil rights for black citizens, including desegregation and a whole new way of life that lay dead ahead. Seymour left the South after college and naval service to enter Yale Divinity School for training as a Navy chaplain. There the young man found himself questioning everything about his southern upbringing, at least where racial matters were concerned, and there he was able to put into perspective aspects of southern culture he had never been willing to scrutinize closely. The result was inevitable: Seymour became sensitized to the race issue in a way that would never leave him. Furthermore, he admitted that he could not keep quiet about what he termed his "unpopular views." One aspect of those views involved his childhood church:

> My stand against segregation also threatened First Baptist Church whose favorite son would no doubt soon ask to be ordained there. My parents understood the congregation's ambivalence toward me but resented that I was seldom asked to supply the pulpit. They suspected that this was due to anxiety about what I might say regarding the racial issue. The anxiety was well founded.

The Reverend Mr. Seymour might well have been absolutely correct in these assumptions, but if he was, no evidence to that effect can be discerned in the official records of the church. The report of the examining presbytery praises Seymour for responding "clearly, humbly, and intelligently" to questions regarding his conversion, call, and preparation. And the answers he gave to questions of faith and doctrine were pronounced "quite satisfactory." The bulletin's account contains phrases such as "real joy" and "happy privilege" and commends Seymour for his "deep spirituality" and "understanding of the Scriptures." Seymour came back the following year to deliver the charge at an ordination ceremony for new deacons. Nor was this the only time he participated in an ordination service at First Baptist. His name appears again and again in the records of his home church, and he filled the pulpit numerous times during Jim Bowers's pastorate. Seymour also

The Robert Seymour Sunbeam Band, 1949. Back row left to right: Verena Monroe, Elma Montjoy, Elizabeth Gravlee (Moss), Robert Seymour, Ray Young, Mary Frances Long, unidentified, and Rena Bailey.

appeared as an honored guest at the 125th anniversary celebration in 1995.

A bulletin entry in September 1948 recalls a public health issue that, thankfully, no longer strikes fear in the hearts of parents. Polio was considered a summer-onset disease, one that threatened young people in alarming numbers with death or long-term paralysis, and before the development of a successful polio vaccine a number of precautions were undertaken to protect children from this scourge. One sentence in the bulletin reads: "The Sunday School also took a turn for the better, with the return of several children who had been out in recent weeks due to the ban that had been imposed on the gathering of children under sixteen years of age."

For some reason the church budget for 1948 does not appear in the official record, but the budget had contained provision for the new full-time position of educational director the year before. The search process must have taken some time; the first mention of filling this position appears as an announcement in the bulletin for November 28,

1948, introducing Miss Elizabeth Gravlee who was to begin her duties as of January 1, 1949. Gravlee, now Elizabeth Moss, remains a very active and loyal church and chancel choir member nearly fifty years later. Actually, her first job lasted only a little over two years, until her marriage in the spring of 1951, since southern women of that era chose more often than not to give up any idea of careers outside the home when they married; still, it is reassuring to note that Gravlee's devotion to the church's music program was unaffected by her marriage. Her contribution to the music ministry dates from the very beginning of her involvement with the church. In addition, though she was a native of Alabama and had worked in North Carolina, Gravlee chose to adopt Greenwood as her home. She was married to Edward Moss at First Baptist Church. Her successor as educational director was Harriett Littlejohn, a Greer native who came to Greenwood from the Baptist church of Wallace, North Carolina.

The big news in the spring of 1949 was the report of the building site committee to the board of deacons. As announced in the bulletin for May 8, the site chosen was about four acres on Grace Street just next to Edgewood Cemetery. While both the committee and the deacons were unanimous in recommending the property, it remained for the church to hear and vote on the proposal in official conference

Beginners Sunday School Class in the old building. Standing, left to right: Mrs. S. W. Page, Tweedie Ann Durst (Devlin), and Mrs. Joe Benjamin.

assembled. Accordingly, a letter of invitation to a conference was mailed on May 11, exactly two weeks before the appointed time, along with a detailed diagram of the location. The idea was to hear the report of the committee, discuss it thoroughly, and then to act upon the recommendation. Members were urged to consider the site "seriously and objectively" with a view to the future and to pray for guidance in making a decision.

The question was presented by J. W. Bradford Jr., who spoke for the committee and offered a resolution recommending an option on three adjoining lots which, taken together, would provide a suitable area for the proposed building project, including possible future expansion. The combined asking price for all three lots came to $17,950; the motion gained a second. Though discussion revealed that the church had raised only about three-quarters of the amount previously determined to be needed before an actual building campaign could be undertaken, 172 members stood to be counted in favor of the committee's work. With no overt opposition recorded, the vote was considered unanimous. The site committee, having discharged its single duty, was dissolved on the spot.

The bulletin for May 29 described the location as "one of the loveliest building sites in town," as indeed it must have been, with paved streets on all sides and nestled between a thriving residential section and one of Greenwood's most important early cemeteries. A little blurb in the bulletin a few weeks later gives an idea of the euphoria of the moment:

> The new lot purchased by our church (to which the deeds have been obtained) has been cleared off and now our people can see what a lovely lot it is. Many will be surprised to see what a beautiful site it is now. Drive by and see it. Stop your car and get out and walk up on it. See what a lovely view it commands. You will be delighted with its beauty and with the location. It is far nicer than most folk realized.

Meanwhile, the church continued its steady forward progress. The Abbeville Association letter in the fall of 1949 showed membership of 1,222, with 946 on the Sunday school rolls and 307 in the Women's Missionary Society, total gifts of nearly $57,000 for the most recent

New lot on Grace Street purchased 1949.

year, and church property valued at about $85,000. The budget for 1950 totaled $58,445, an increase of more than $3,000 over the previous year. One way to put these figures in the proper perspective is to note that the pastor's salary that year was $6,300. The clerk added a few lines to the budget entry that seem to indicate disagreement over the budget as presented, but the attempted insurrection went nowhere and the question passed on a standing vote. The pastor's note took pains to congratulate the church on its continued financial progress and tied it firmly to "previous spiritual progress." In a prophetic vein Bowers added, "It thrills us to realize the potential power of our church when we finally reach the peak of our spiritual growth."

The next step in the building project was the naming of a committee whose charge it was to *select*, but not to *employ*, an architect to draw plans for the structure. This committee was quite small in actual number—only four members—but very large in prestige and know-how. Two women, Martha Bishop and Angelle Adams, were selected to join Elbert Adams and Horace Brinson for this most important part of the preparations. The committee's work began in late October 1949, and the group was ready with its report in a surprisingly short time, especially when one considers the amount of work involved. Presented in January 1950, the report is a densely worded two-page document setting forth in detail the committee's findings and concluding with a paragraph entitled "The Recommendation." A genuine pleasure to read because of its clarity and organization, the document is in reality a sort of unfolding of the committee's deliberate approach, its conscientious and methodical examination of churches—either completed or in progress—in a number of cities, and the steps it took to seek out only firms that specialized in church architecture in order to make a selection to lay before the church. In the all-important matter of finding the right firm, the committee had sought help from the American Institute of Architecture (AIA), which in turn directed them to the Interdenominational Bureau of Architecture, a group that existed for the sole purpose of brokering church-building contracts across the country. The director of this bureau actually visited Greenwood to view the site and analyze the church's particular characteristics as they related to projections of building design and layout. Details of this visit were carefully laid out in the report. So thorough was the committee's work, in fact, that the clerk's laconic entry, "Show of hands in voting to accept—none voting to oppose—therefore recorded as unanimous," must have seemed almost anticlimactic at the time.

Thanks to the committee's work, the church now had the name of an actual architectural firm, Harold E. Wagoner of Philadelphia, on which to pin its hopes for the perfect design of a new home for the First Baptist Church of Greenwood, South Carolina. The committee had unhesitatingly named Wagoner as the "correct choice" and had invited him to Greenwood for a mutual closer look. When Wagoner visited to meet personally with the committee, he evidently made a favorable impression on everyone he met. The committee learned that his work included Baptist churches in South Carolina and Washington, D.C., as well as a church at Davidson College and both Presbyterian and Lutheran edifices in Atlanta. A specialist in the field for more than twenty years and an ecumenist as well, at least in his work, Wagoner must have seemed the ideal choice to a church that was beginning to realize its huge potential as a positive force in the community. The committee assured the church also that Wagoner could hardly have been more highly regarded by those for whom he had worked in Florence, Atlanta, and Washington, reporting that he had been found sincere, cooperative, and intensely interested in every project. No criticism of the gentleman whatever, either personally or professionally, could be discerned; on the contrary, he "met every requirement and measured up to the exacting demands of each church and of each committee with whom he had dealt." His fees, the committee noted almost as an afterthought, would be those set forth as standard by the AIA.

The next step was the creation of an advisory board from which various committees would be selected to, in the words of the newsletter, "take care of certain necessary phases of the work," among them finances, promotion, and various elements of the building project itself. Some thirty-five regular members, plus six who would serve *ex officio*, made up the advisory group, and two more were added a short time later. It hardly seems necessary to note that this move also gained the unanimous approval of the church. The first group of committees was up and running by the middle of May.

Even as the church gathered its resources for an all-out effort to provide a totally new and much larger physical plant, there was steady progress in other areas of church life as well. Bulletins for the spring and summer months of 1950 are studded with notices of new members, both youngsters from established families who made their own professions of faith and newcomers to Greenwood who brought letters or requested baptism. The bulletin noted that seventeen were baptized on one July Sunday alone, with six others to follow "in the near future." It is actually possible to trace the growth and development of Greenwood's business section in large part simply by scanning the notices of new families who joined the Baptist church during this period.

A special "extra edition" of the newsletter was required to record the first of the various building committee reports to the advisory board in June. One paragraph in the introductory section is so compelling and so characteristic of what might be termed the "spirit" behind the building project that it deserves quoting in full:

> One of the most pleasing factors in the development of the program thus far has been the careful thought and the vast amount of time and work that have been given by the members of each committee to the building project. There has been no guesswork. Nothing has been taken for granted. Diligent research and earnest prayer seem to have been the practice of each member of the various committees.

A sort of summing up of this early work reveals that a sanctuary seating 1,000 and a chapel with a capacity of 150 had been determined adequate, while the Sunday school recommended facilities to accommodate about 1,100 persons from birth to old age (described tactfully as adults "above 25 years of age"). The group from seventeen to twenty-four years old, characterized as the young people's department, was being considered separately for the first time, and other departments which had been, according to the report, "severely cramped" were finally to be provided adequate accommodations with room to grow. It is easy to see in these early reports the careful planning that went into the physical appearance of the church today, facilities that current members might seem at times to take for granted. Perhaps it was something of that sort that prompted Bowers to include a little box on the front page of the newsletter with the words: "We take pride in remembering what our grandparents achieved here. Will our grandchildren be proud of what we do?"

The church continued its tradition of unanimity with only one nomination required to fill an entire slate of officers in late September 1950. Eight deacons were elected also to serve staggered terms of two or four years. The pastor took the opportunity to remind all those named to a church office at any level that their election was not to be viewed as a tribute to themselves personally but as an opportunity for service and responsibility to the church. His conclusion was a nice touch: "What there is of honor in a church office comes as the result of a job well done."

The inevitable announcement of a fund-raising drive for the new building came in early December 1950 as part of the projected budget for 1951. As usual, Bowers was tactful and upbeat in presenting both the budget and the new campaign as opportunities for spiritual growth. Every category of the proposed budget showed an increase, some larger than others, as a reflection of the ever-rising costs of operation, with the result that the regular bottom line stood nearly 7.5 percent higher than the year before. When the separate line item "Special Building Fund Drive" was added in, that percentage rose to a sobering 178.5 percent. There was no attempt to disguise the fact that the church would be taking on a monumental obligation in adopting the 1951 budget, but Bowers knew exactly how to deal with any second thoughts individual members might be indulging. "This is the campaign for which we have all been waiting and hoping," he wrote, "and let us not forget the purpose: it is entirely for God's glory and the advancement of His Kingdom. Let this purpose and God's blessings to you be the measure of your pledge."

Exactly one week later Bowers was able to report that the preceding Sunday would "stand in the history of this church as one of its noblest days" when the largest budget ever was passed "without dissenting voice." For the next five years the church's single most significant goal would be to bring to fruition the plan set in motion seven years earlier with a proposed investment fund earmarked for future building improvement as part of the budget for 1944. In a sense the church's progress in this important sphere might be viewed as a microcosm of the postwar building boom so evident throughout the United States. It is not too much to say that neither the church nor the country would ever be the same again.

CHAPTER FIVE

Maturity

(1951–1967)

At the beginning of 1951 the church reported its membership at 1,229. It also moved into preparations for a spring revival featuring the services of the Reverend D. H. Daniel, a seminary classmate of Bowers as well as his traveling companion to the meeting of the Baptist World Alliance four years earlier. Daniel was at that time pastor of the First Baptist Church of Hendersonville, North Carolina. Revivals in 1951 meant both morning and evening services for virtually an entire week, and members were urged to clear their calendars and allow "nothing to interfere with . . . attendance." The preparations must have been thorough, and if a column in the church newsletter for April 19 is any indication, the church's efforts were well rewarded. Bowers termed the revival the most successful the church had ever held and pronounced himself and everyone else "amazed" at the "great spiritual blessing" the week had brought. Nor was he remiss in tossing bouquets to the flock. One especially charming compliment to the organist, Elbert Adams, deserves quoting in full: "Dr. Adams displayed again his remarkable way of 'carrying' a service with the introduction of hymns and the interludes that provide such possibility-laden moments for meditation." Among the immediate results of the revival that spring were nineteen new members, including the new director of religious education, Harriett Littlejohn, who had come by letter from the Baptist church in Wallace, North Carolina.

As preparations for the building program began to pick up steam in several directions at once, the church found itself involved in some novel financing arrangements, among them converting a gift of a city lot into cash. This was done by granting a sixty-day option to Southern Bell Telephone and Telegraph Company to purchase the lot at the price of $3,750. Naturally, this transaction required meetings and lawyers and resolutions and documents, but the church was well equipped by this time to deal with virtually any business deal through its trustees, and the disposition of the parcel on Rush Street (Avenue) donated by L. B. Adams sailed through without a hitch. At the same business meeting the church voted to sponsor a local student, John Cann, to study for the ministry at Furman University. These two actions, which might on the surface seem rather far removed from each other, actually serve as a neat illustration of a modern church's role in modern life—two sides of the same coin, so to speak.

When the fund-raising drive for the new building kicked off with a workers' dinner at the Oregon Hotel on June 28, 1951, the combined clout of the speakers alone, regardless of what they had to say, could have guaranteed what Bowers termed an "outstanding meeting." Prominent businessmen such as E. W. Milford, R. B. Curry, and Jim Burns spoke to the seventy-five assembled workers, providing both helpful hints (called "technical instruction") and lofty inspirational messages (the need for "faith and diligence") to kick off a campaign to raise the amount of $329,225 in a period of thirty months. Pledges of more than $100,000, representing gifts from about sixty members, were already in hand, but six hundred more prospects remained to be contacted, and the pastor left no doubt that he believed the church was more than equal to the task. A special edition of the newsletter was mailed to the membership a few days later. Under the heading "What Is My Share in the Building Fund?" a detailed listing—or perhaps a schedule—of gifts appeared. This schedule was divided into twenty categories by size of gift, and the number of projected donors in each category was shown in another column. This method computed to 662 pledges totaling the magic $329,000 goal. Members were expected to find their own places on the grid, make their pledges, and complete the gift process by the end of 1953.

Meanwhile, the decade of the 1950s began to unfold. In December 1951 the church passed a resolution protesting the naming of a U.S. ambassador to the Vatican on the grounds that such an appointment would be in direct opposition to the Constitution's guarantee of religious freedom and the separation of church and state. One of the arguments in the resolution, that the Vatican could not logically be both a state and a church at the same time, must have provided an interesting talking point for those members of the congregation who wished to debate the issue.

Although the 108-acre city state, nearly half of which consists of the Vatican Gardens, was granted its independence and sovereignty by the Italian government in 1929, its head was then, and still is, undoubtedly the pope, and all unmovable property within it is owned by the Holy See, defined as the bishopric of the pope himself. Still, the Vatican City had its own coinage, postal system, radio station, and newspaper even then, and the fact that it sent and received official representatives to and from other countries is a matter of record dating from the fourth century. Modern versions of such representation have evolved in various ways; some, for example, are specifically instructed to deal with the pope in his capacity of civil ruler alone. Until 1950 the presence of the United States rested in a personal representative of the president to the pope, with the privileges but not the title of ambassador. Evidently the government was attempting to regularize that arrangement in 1951. No one seems to remember the action that prompted the resolution, but speculation would have to be that Protestant churches, at least in South Carolina, did what they could to oppose the move. A little research supports that speculation. *The Encyclopedia of U.S. Foreign Relations* settles the matter in a very few words: "President Harry S. Truman, *bowing to Protestant opposition*, abandoned his plan to appoint General Mark Clark as ambassador to the Vatican" [emphasis added].[1] The first Roman Catholic president, John F. Kennedy, as well as all the others from Truman through Carter, apparently made no move to further Truman's plan, or had no success if they did; it remained for President Ronald Reagan to elevate the representation of the United States to embassy status in 1984 and name William Wilson as the first ambassador. "Domestic opposition was muted," wrote David Alvarez, "suggesting that religious passions had finally given way to national interest as the principal determinant of U.S.–Vatican relations."

As for the 1951 candidate for the post, World War II hero General Mark Wayne Clark, South Carolina was destined to hear more from this gentleman. Though Clark never held the title of ambassador to the Vatican, he did find something to do in Korea where another war (though President Truman liked to call it a "police action") had erupted in 1950. He was named commander in chief of the United Nations Command and in that capacity signed a military armistice with the North Korean Army and the Chinese People's Volunteers in Korea in 1953. He was chosen president of The Citadel, the military college of South Carolina, and served in that capacity from 1954 to retirement in 1965. Regular army generals are often famous for their homelessness—many people will remember that General Douglas MacArthur lived his last years in the Waldorf Astoria Hotel in New York—but Clark found his special place in Charleston where he was a much beloved figure until his death just before his eighty-eighth birthday in 1984. He is buried on the grounds of the military college near a building that bears his name.

There appears to be a gap of a whole year in the minute book for this period. One page covers the above-mentioned Vatican resolution and the adoption of the 1952 budget, while the next contains a four-page report of the building advisory board which was presented on November 2, 1952. The gap turns out to be a false alarm, since routine 1951 and 1952 business details resume a few pages later. The board report itself is another masterpiece of detail from which we learn that the architect's four trips to Greenwood and numerous committee meetings had resulted in a great many actual decisions. First was the determination to divide the project into two phases, the so-called "unit plan" of construction used by most larger churches whereby both the timing and the financing of large building projects could be broken down into more handleable segments. The first unit would consist of everything but the sanctuary of today, called "future church" on the floor plan.

Another decision was the building material of Sutton stone which, according to the report, was both reasonably priced and an attractive material about halfway between regular granite and crab orchard stone, "colorful but not brilliant," in the words of the report. Further, the structure was planned to take full advantage of its sloping lot, which on the Grace Street side would give the appearance of a one-story building and on the North Street side a full two stories, with each room on the ground floor having the advantage of natural light. While the report used the term "temporary church" to refer to the sanctuary/fellowship hall, the board was quick to note that "temporary" referred in no sense to the type of construction but only to the time lag between two phases of building. The space was termed, in fact, "far more practical and attractive" than the present sanctuary, particularly in its arrangement.

One important feature of the proposed plan was that additional wings could be conveniently and easily constructed at any one of several points without detracting from the beauty of the building. Thus was the probability of future growth nicely anticipated and accommodated by the alert planners. The report concluded that the best available estimate of cost of the first unit would be $450,000, an amount that appeared quite possible to raise so that the church would incur no indebtedness, at least for its first phase. The beginning of construction was projected as March or April of 1953, and a period of at least eighteen months was anticipated for completion. Once again there was neither discussion nor opposition, and the recommendations contained in the report were unanimously passed.

Perhaps it is not surprising that the church seemed to feel the need for a bit of retrenchment in its operating budget as an offset to the rather sobering financial obligation the new building represented. Whatever the reason, the 1953 budget was exactly ten dollars less than that for 1952; Bowers called it a "slight change," which might almost qualify as a large understatement or even a nod to petty cash. The category of "Building Expense" bore the brunt of this tiny budget reduction, quite naturally when one considers that new building projects always tend to drive out old building maintenance costs; "Operating Expenses" moved up slightly. The church discovered the hard way that its budget for 1953 was a little too modest when the 1954 edition had to be increased by nearly three thousand dollars. Bowers explained the increase with the wry comment, "[I]t was found that we required more funds to operate properly than we had estimated."

The church newsletter for September 6, 1951, contains notice of a special program for the church's annual day of prayer for state missions. The program would be based on "the work of the Negroes in the local community" and would feature the president of the missionary organization and one young person from each of Greenwood's black Baptist churches: Tabernacle, Macedonia, Morris Chapel, and Walker's Mission. There is no hint that this meeting was in any way unusual; indeed, the notice seems as normal and routine as that describing "family night" directly above it. Still, it brings up questions, particularly in view of Robert Seymour's misgivings about the church's racial attitudes as lately as 1948, only three years earlier. Ms. Laura Boyd, proprietor of Boyd's Tailor Shop, was ready with some answers. A lifelong Baptist, she remembers excellent relations between her church, Morris Chapel, whose pastor at the time was the Reverend H. B. Mitchell, and First Baptist Church. The unifying theme between the two churches was young people's work, notably Vacation Bible School and the Young People's Christian Assembly held each summer at Benedict College in Columbia. Boyd remembers that First Baptist would sponsor youngsters from the black churches to attend the assembly and invite them to report on the experience as part of a missions program after their return.

Boyd also recalls integrated Bible School sessions that would rotate from church to church during the summers. She believes, in fact, that this voluntary and pleasant practice came to an end only when integration became a question of law and force and publicity. The Reverend Mitchell, according to Boyd, filled the pulpit at First Baptist on more than one occasion. The assumption is that this was a reciprocal arrangement.

The church's third director of religious education was the first man to be named to the position. Miss Littlejohn had left after two years for the usual reason—that is, marriage—and in that more innocent and less politically correct time Bowers could actually put in writing, as he did in the newsletter for February 26, 1953, "We felt that it was better this time to secure the services of a man." He might also have considered it advantageous that Keith Fowler was a Greenwood native, married to a Greenwood girl, and a part-time student at Lander working toward his undergraduate degree.

C. Y. Thomason (1901–1994), Greenwood contractor whose bid was accepted for both Phase One and Phase Two of the building program, 1954–1971.

The first edition of the newsletter to feature an architect's drawing of "our proposed building" was that of December 10, 1953. It is significant to note that a stylized drawing of the entire building, or some part thereof, has been featured prominently in church publications since that time. Whether these drawings were ever officially accepted as logos has not been determined.

Eight contracting firms, two of them from Greenwood, submitted bids on the building project. When those bids were opened on March 19 the result was a carefully worded recommendation from the advisory board that the church enter into a contract with the C. Y. Thomason Company of Greenwood to construct the first unit of the building "at a price of approximately $473,667.00 . . ." The use of the word *approximately* was explained with the line that last-minute checks would need to be made before an actual contract was signed, and those checks might cause a very slight variance in the final figures. The recommendation was adopted.

A groundbreaking ceremony was held on Sunday afternoon, April 4, 1954. More than 350 men and women attended the 5 P.M. program; special guests included 15 men and women who were members of the church when it moved to its North Main location from the original Cambridge Street site in 1897. Additional honorees were daughters of two former ministers and those members who had joined prior to the dedication of the current building. The pastor pronounced the ceremony a success and church leaders "greatly pleased" with the excellent attendance.

Work on the building had progressed sufficiently by the middle of August that members could be urged to "go by to see what is being done." The architect's representative had made several site visits by that time and noted his own satisfaction with the level of activity. Concrete walls were poured, bricklaying was underway, and the exterior stonework had reached to window level and would be resumed as soon as window frames could be set in place. Two months later, however, a worried note can be discerned amid the glowing reports. "All of this costs money," admonished the pastor, "Do what you can now. It will be much easier to do it before the building is complete." Members must have responded satisfactorily, since a report in the March 10 newsletter revealed actual expenditures of more than $270,000, an amount that included the lot and the new organ and

Groundbreaking Ceremony, April 4, 1954. Left to right: Elbert Adams, Alma Johnson, Mrs. W. C. Strawhorn, Jack Wilburn, Paul Burgess, Jim Bowers, Keith Fowler, L. B. Adams, C. J. Brabham, and Cooper Sanders.

represented well over half the total projected cost. Even though members had done, in the words of the pastor, "real well," they could not rest on their laurels. Another $190,000 beyond what he called "present assets" would be necessary to finish the building and pay for related equipment. The last sentence of the building report is revealing: "Let us give by the week, by the month, at every opportunity, sacrificially and gladly so that we who have begun a great work shall be able to finish it with honor and with the approval of all who have witnessed this tremendous task."

Another ceremony, this time the laying of the cornerstone, was held on May 19, 1955. Members and guests were invited to tour the still unfinished building which had been under construction at that

Special guests, groundbreaking. Seated left to right: Mrs. E. D. Andrews, Mrs. J. M. Marshall, Mrs. W. L. McLeod, Mrs. A. J. Davis, Mrs. L. Z. Gunter, Mrs. J. G. Mattison, and Mr. and Mrs. M. A. Jones. Standing left to right: Mrs. W. C. Strawhorn, Mrs. Sims Andrews, Lee Beaudrot, "Pet" Andrews, Joe Beaudrot, and Jones Benjamin.

Mrs. W. C. Strawhorn and Dr. Bowers pose beside the newly laid cornerstone, May 19, 1955.

point a little over a year and was expected to be ready for occupancy by October. The pastor's remarks on that occasion were centered around the Latin phrase inscribed on the cornerstone—*Deo Gloria*—which means in English "to the glory of God." Bowers called the ceremony a "glorious moment" in the history of the church and deemed it perhaps the finest in his own tenure as pastor.

The church lost its third director of religious education, Keith Fowler, when he was ordained to the gospel ministry by West Side Baptist Church and left both West Side and First Baptist to enroll in the seminary in New Orleans. Beverly Johnson came to work in September in a clerical capacity but also took on other work with young people as time went on.

The church voted to place its real property on the market; that is, it would first advertise an intent to sell and then ask for sealed bids from those interested. This action was not to last, as subsequent events would show.

While the builders did not quite meet the October target for occupancy, the church was able to plan its 1955 Thanksgiving Day service for the temporary sanctuary which would, the pastor assured members, be heated for the occasion. Less than a month later the newsletter featured a full-page plea for funds to complete building-related projects so that the church would not be forced to incur additional debt. The church took the unusual step of extending its fiscal year by two weeks to allow a little more time for members to come to terms with the needs that remained. As Bowers put it: "There is air-conditioning to pay for. There is landscaping to be done, drives and walks to be laid. There is furniture to buy. These things all take money. . . ." These items, plus "an amount to be paid the contractor and the architect," required $60,000 in new money, and that money needed to be counted in the last month of the year so that December 1955 could be called "The Month for Success" in the great building program the church had undertaken. The pastor waxed eloquent when he wrote: "It is now our time and our privilege to provide for ourselves and our children what others have so generously provided for us."

The next newsletter called December, a little prematurely perhaps, "The Month of Victory." Unfortunately, contributions fell short, and the pastor was forced to report in the newsletter for January 12 that the amount received was just over $42,000, or 70 percent of the goal. Still, Bowers saw this as "very gratifying" evidence of the support of the rank-and-file membership. "[Y]ou have tried to do your part," he wrote, "and that is what counts." As always, Bowers knew precisely how to chide and when to praise. He also was able to report on two highly significant milestones for the church. One record had in fact already been set—fiscal year 1955 marked the first time that church members' contributions in the final weeks of a year amounted to more than $35,000. The second record to fall, if $500 could be raised by the following Sunday, would be that of total gifts for one year. The previous high was $110,020, and only $500 would push the total for 1955 beyond that figure. Receipts through January 15 totaled $110,422.

Of course no one was really surprised when the final work on the new building dragged on and on into 1956. The chapel organ, evidently a new instrument, was installed in February, and installation of the church organ was to begin immediately thereafter. Landscaping, too, began in late winter/early spring. But the first part of the building to be occupied, the church offices and pastor's study, were not ready until June. A lovely description of the furnishings and other decorating details appears in the newsletter for June 21, as does the notice of final inspection by the architect preparatory to offering the finished product for acceptance by the church. "It is a real joy to be in offices that were designed for office use," wrote the grateful pastor. Carpet, draperies, accessories, and all the furniture represented gifts from individuals or families. The building itself was "accepted as virtually complete" the same week. Another happy note in the bulletin was the announcement that Caulie Gunnells and Virginia Burns, both of Greenwood, would be the first to marry in the new sanctuary. The wedding, according to Bowers, "was beautiful in every respect."

The new building seems to have been the impetus for other changes in the way the church did business. For example, the heavy minute books were abandoned, and the weekly newsletter became both the official record of church business and its chief method of communication with members. Since a cut-and-paste system from newsletter to minute book had been in use for some time, the change actually made a great deal of sense. It also illustrated the level of autonomy and leadership vested by Baptist churches in their pastors. The "Bowers" stamp was in evidence on all fronts, not least where items in the newsletter were concerned. A wonderful example of this is shown in the description of Youth Week in the spring of 1956. The pastor not only devoted the entire back page of the newsletter to this event, no doubt so that he could recognize, by name, every single participant, but he also returned to the subject the next week when he devoted the first column of the front page to the same event. This time his emphasis was on the reactions of adults and the motivation of the young people involved. "It was for them no performance," he wrote, "they were seeking to express the religious feeling that was theirs."

But not every item in the newsletter was as positive as those praising Youth Week. The spring of 1956 must have reminded many people of a popular novel of the day entitled *The Rains Came*. Visitors to the unfinished building had to be begged not to track mud on new tile and flooring, curb and gutter work progressed very slowly due to weather delays, and drives and walkways remained unfinished far longer than anticipated. All that was bad enough, but the "furniture situation" almost caused a rift in the carefully laid building plans. Bowers wrote in the April 19 issue that the anticipated delivery date, after several extensions, was then set as the middle of June.

> We were quite surprised recently to hear some one comment that they had heard that the furniture was not ordered until last December. We do not know how a rumor like this would get started or how it could continue to live for the furniture was ordered in April of 1955.

These two deceptively mild-sounding sentences actually cover what must have been a very high level of frustration on the part of the pastor. Not only was the furniture manufacturer's schedule causing problems, but church members at home were indulging in speculation that held the potential of further complicating an already complex and far-reaching building program. Clearly, Bowers decided he needed to address the issue head on. Calling the work "highly specialized" and reminding readers that "delicate carving is slow," the pastor closed the door on griping with a thud: "But let us not feel that the delay has been locally caused. It has not." He expressed what must have been every loyal member's feeling that in spite of everything the new church would be worth waiting for.

The furniture question dragged on through a visit from the architect in May, when the pastor expressed the hope that Wagoner might be able to bring definite information about the pews, to Bowers's own visit to the contractor while he was in New York at a meeting of the National Tuberculosis Association. He went on to Philadelphia where he was able to spend a day with the architect as well as visit the manufacturer working on the pews and other chancel furniture. At long last he was able to report that the first load of furniture, including the communion table, would arrive in Greenwood in about a week. A June delivery would mean the end of an eighteen-month period of anticipating what it would be like to have brand-new furniture. We do not know whether the pastor's hopes were realized, even in part, since the newsletter of July 5 continues the lament over the elusive pews and pulpit furniture. August 1 was set as the new general moving date, about six weeks after the pastor and staff moved into their new suite of offices.

The great day finally came on August 5, 1956. It must have been a special pleasure for the pastor to write in the newsletter, "[A]fter that date any announcement of a church meeting will refer to the new church unless otherwise stated." The accompanying drawings show the building floor plan as well as a parking lot that looks very much like that in use today. Members were also reminded that entrance to the main floor was from the front of the building, while the ground floor opened to the back. Bus transportation was to be provided to help members adjust to the new commute. This service would last nearly ten years; it was suspended in favor of taxi service in January 1966 at a saving of about 50 percent.

A business meeting held after the worship service that Sunday morning revealed that the Greenwood County and City Library was interested in purchasing the church property on Main Street and Bailey Circle for the amount of $40,000. By accepting this offer the church would be rescinding an earlier motion to seek sealed bids for the sale. But the price was right, and the library project seemed to church officials a particularly suitable and appropriate use of the property. A motion to accept the proposal, however, hit a snag when four church members (representing a larger group) expressed the desire to keep the property for church use. The support they sought resulted only in the church's allowing a thirty-day option for this group to purchase the property for $40,000, an extremely unlikely prospect. If the option were not exercised, the library would be offered the opportunity. The group officially released its option during the thirty-day period, and the library board geared up immediately to accept the deal.

The services on dedication Sunday, except perhaps for the business matter described above, must have been impressive indeed, from the Sunday school hour when attendance ran nearly 40 percent above the usual number, to the worship service with crowds filling every corner and spilling over into hallways and chapel, to a full house for Training Union, all the way to yet another large attendance at the evening worship service. Interspersed with formal services were building tours and an open house for more than one thousand people.

A master plan for landscaping the church property was prepared about the time the first phase of the building was completed. Everyone knew the plan was just that, a goal, in the words of the pastor, "toward which we will work for years to come," but it was possible to make a start by early February 1957 when some trees were

The new chapel, viewed from the rear of the building, c. 1956.

planted in a move designed to enhance the appearance of the building. Other plantings would be undertaken from time to time as funds became available. Most people would probably agree that the pastor's prediction, "We will eventually have a very beautiful site," has been borne out to the letter.

At a business meeting in September the church was brought up to date on its financial standing. The new building with all its accoutrements represented assets valued at approximately $690,000. When the smoke cleared from the flurry of final payments here and there, as well as the sale of the old building, the church would be left with bonded indebtedness of $185,000, much less, according to the pastor, than that of most churches in similar circumstances.

The first baptismal service in the new building was held in September, and the first communion service followed the next month. In Bowers's view the new facility would bring an added dimension of spirituality to both of these important rituals. He called the baptism service in the chapel an "impressive moment" and remarked upon the sense of intimacy afforded by the new surroundings. Communion, "long . . . one of the outstanding moments in the life of our church," would be even more thrilling because the "beauty of the sanctuary and the arrangement of the communion table, together with the atmosphere" would contribute to "a deeply spiritual observation" of the ritual. He urged members to prepare themselves prayerfully for "this high hour."

As the last quarter of the church year began, the pastor was forced to remind members that their pattern of giving had not changed sufficiently to cover the new level of financial commitment the church had undertaken. "We had hoped that it [the income of the church for the year] would be much larger," he wrote, urging members to increase their contributions so that the church's "full dream" might be realized.

In the meantime, church groups lost no time making use of the fine kitchen facilities in the new building, but no one was prepared for the number of dishes—covered and otherwise—left at the church after a lunch or dinner function. After several gentle reminders in the newsletter, the pastor issued a two-paragraph plea under the heading TOO MANY DISHES! "If you left a dish or some dishes last week, please stop by the kitchen and get them soon," he begged. It seems that a group of five hundred Baptist students were scheduled to be entertained in early November, but the kitchen cabinets and counters had become so cluttered with pieces of forgotten kitchenware that meal preparation would be nearly impossible. This is an interesting reversal: it has become commonplace in our day for institutions to be concerned about keeping up with their own property; First Baptist Church had a problem with accumulating other people's!

According to church records, the first performance of Handel's *Messiah* had been presented in 1954; by 1956 the oratorio had become a routine expectation of the Christmas season. Full credit belongs to choir director Edgar Davis and organist Elbert Adams for setting this grand tradition in motion. These two, along with outstanding Greenwood soloists Ann Hutto and Evelyn Martin, were joined that year by Furman University's DuPre Rhame and a tenor named George

Bradley in a performance under the sponsorship of the Greenwood Chapter of the American Guild of Organists. Another example of the quality of musical programs connected in one way or another with First Baptist Church was a recital of sacred music by the world famous Virgil Fox in February 1957. Organist at Riverside Church in New York City at the time, Fox had been voted the most popular organist in the country in the first poll of this kind ever taken, and he was selected to represent the United States at the First International Congress for Church Music. Having Virgil Fox in Greenwood represented quite a coup in 1957 for both the organists' guild and the church.

The pastor made another appeal for funds in a column entitled "Your Financial Program" in the newsletter for December 13. The reason for his concern was that the church found itself carrying not one, but two, notes with separate lending institutions as a result of the building program, and paying on both at once presented what he called "pressure" and "complications." Even though the debts were local and no one was agitating for payment, the pastor obviously wanted to liquidate these obligations as rapidly as possible. Perhaps he was already dreaming of the new sanctuary and the completion of the architect's original plan. Even so, the eventful year 1956 ended with a Christmas Eve program, Student Night on the Sunday after Christmas, and the pastor's pleas that members guard against what he called "an almost pathetic drop in . . . attendance" after the holidays.

The pastor's greeting to his flock as 1957 began was a reminder that the much-used term *Happy New Year* was meaningless unless it was understood to carry the message that the happiness, success, and prosperity of any year depended upon people's willingness to follow Christ's leadership into fellowship and service. The program of church activities seemed to grow and expand with the fine new facilities, and the newsletter took on an ever more diversified focus. Church leaders reported renewed interest in both Sunday school and Training Union, while adult groups held study courses at the church, fellowship evenings at each others' homes, and regularly chipped in with new money to furnish and equip the various classrooms and other spaces in the new building. The pastor was lavish with praise: "It is amazing that such beauty has been achieved," he wrote, "We are proud of every classroom in our building." Bowers made sure also that the church continued its policy of involvement in the wider Greenwood community. The newsletter of January 24, for example, contains reference to the continuing education program sponsored during that period by Lander College. The Education Center offered a number of short courses of broad appeal, as well as activity programs ranging from ceramics classes to square dance instruction. Bowers recommended particularly a class dealing with the Book of Job, taught by the Reverend Allen W. Joslin.

The year 1957 was also notable for the first mention of the Bethea Baptist Home, at that time a fairly new concept of retirement living. The idea has gained broad acceptance over the years, and decades of experience have resulted in a number of tried and true practices now standard in the field. Every idea has a beginning, however, and Jim Bowers became involved on the governing board nearly ten years after the original plan for a Baptist facility for the aging was conceived. Joe King describes that event as a resolution from the Fairfield Association to the state convention as early as 1949. The convention's response, naturally, was to name a committee to study the matter and report at the next regular session. A gift of $100,000 and a plot of land from Dr. Percy A. Bethea in 1951 was enough to ensure the name of the proposed facility, as well as its location in Darlington County, and by the end of 1953 the general board had drafted a constitution and elected the first trustees to oversee the new enterprise. More land was purchased and the Bethea Home project moved ahead rapidly over the next four years; by the time Bowers joined the board, the convention had authorized a half-million dollar loan for construction. Six hundred people attended the groundbreaking ceremonies in June 1958, and the first residents were received two years later. Most South Carolina Baptists are familiar with at least the name of their denomination's first venture into assisted living facilities for senior citizens.

The young people of the church showed their affection for the pastor in 1957 with an imaginative surprise birthday party based on the television show *This Is Your Life*. A birthday cake with fourteen candles marked Bowers's tenure in Greenwood, and a program of both lighthearted reminiscences and serious tribute demonstrated that pastor and people shared a mutual regard. One episode involving a hat and a contract made clear that the young people hoped Bowers would stay for the "rest of his natural life."

The pastor noted "with real regret" the demolition of the old church building on North Main Street in the newsletter of March 14; he also devoted a couple of paragraphs to the matter of the memorial windows that had meant so much when the building was erected sixty years before. Since these windows had been the source of some factional disputes when the new building plans were broached, Bowers's words might hold special significance for some members today:

> A few people have asked about the possibility of getting the memorial windows from the old church which had been given in memory of some member of their family. These windows will be available to the families of those in whose memory they were placed there.
>
> We have not learned the exact time that these windows will be removed but will keep you informed about it. The windows will be removed from the building and placed outside. Those who wish to get them will please notify the church office of their desire and will make arrangements for the removal of the window from the church yard. Those in charge of the project will set the time when the windows can be obtained and the final date they will be held.

The last paragraph of this column seems to be a call to the church to, in today's parlance, "move on":

> We do honor to the building that served us so well for so long. In it we had many wonderful experiences. It is not only a landmark in the city, it is a spiritual memory within the soul. As the building has been replaced by a more modern, efficient building, may the work we do surpass that which we have done in the past. This is our challenge and opportunity. May God empower us to accomplish it.

In May the pastor reported in detail on the church's indebtedness: the $185,000 debt announced at the close of the building program consisted of a shortfall of $150,000 on the structure itself, as well as $35,000 the church had borrowed locally to complete the installation of air-conditioning. The sum of $19,000 had already been paid on the latter amount, which was secured by open notes with two Greenwood banks, and a payment of $17,500 would fall due on the larger debt as of June 1. The pastor wanted members to understand that the total indebtedness would be reduced significantly—to only $156,000—if the payment date could be met. It hardly seems necessary to add that the church was able to meet its commitment, even though the payment "practically exhausted . . . operating funds." A balance sheet dated May 31 revealed assets of just under $700,000.

A budget for 1957 was finally offered at a business meeting in August. Evidently there had been a delay in preparation to allow time for church leaders to adjust to a whole new universe of planning, projections, and other details of a financial operation that, in keeping with other aspects of church life, was becoming ever more sophisticated. Also, as the pastor pointed out, the church had actually been operating well above its budgeted level for several years, and the new budget simply showed revenue and expenditures that conformed more nearly to reality. Still, it must have been a little shocking to face a bottom line some 53 percent higher than that of the previous year. The pastor's soothing words reminded members that this was "the sort of budget a church like ours should have." Another milestone was surely reached in 1957 when Greenwood's First Baptist Church adopted its first six-figure budget of just under $104,000. The pastor's salary stood at $6,900 that year, and the total payroll, including fringe benefits (such as they were at the time), was less than $30,000, or about 25 percent of the total budget. By way of contrast, it is interesting to note that debt service represented nearly 40 percent of expenditures the church expected to make that year.[2]

The pastor took formal notice of the first anniversary of moving into the new building in the newsletter of August 1. Among the more significant results of the expanded facilities were greatly increased attendance at all services, particularly Sunday school and Training Union, as well as a commensurate increase in financial receipts. Bowers did not forget to add, however, that his greatest joy was the "fact that we seem to have grown in spirit and in effectiveness" as well.

When the town of Greenwood celebrated its centennial in 1957 the church was called upon to participate. More specifically, the centennial committee wanted a religious service to kick off the week-long festivities and called upon the Greenwood Ministers' Association to plan the occasion. "We feel that this is most fitting," wrote the pastor in the newsletter for September 12; indeed, he added, "It would be totally unfitting to omit such an emphasis from the celebration." Accordingly, plans for the service included an outdoor gathering at the American Legion stadium (which had to be changed to Greenwood High School when the weather refused to cooperate), a music program featuring an interchurch choir with organ accompaniment in the capable hands of Edgar Davis and Elbert Adams, Bowers as master of ceremonies, and a special address by Wallace Fridy, a Methodist preacher from Columbia who had strong Greenwood connections. The pastor's critique in the next newsletter noted attendance of more than a thousand people and called the service "a fitting and significant beginning for the centennial week."

A formal Bible study group was begun in the fall of 1957, evidently the first time such a program was proposed for adult churchwide participation. "[T]his is the kind of program that many of us need," wrote the pastor. "Every one of us should be, yea must be, better informed" about the Bible. Two classes were offered: the first, to be taught by Bowers, covered the Book of Acts and was called "The Church in Action," while the other, called "The Life of Christ," was taken from the Gospels and taught by the new minister of education, Edwin Ellis. Bible study groups in one form or another have been a regular part of the church program ever since.

A new committee was created to help with the all-important task of finding workers for the various church organizations, particularly the Sunday school and Training Union. Among the most intriguing provisions of the church leadership committee was that exactly two of its six members (33 percent) had to be women. The group would be appointed by the deacons and meet at least monthly. Its primary charge was to bring to the church all nominations and recommendations for leadership positions in Sunday school and Training Union, and all other organizations as well, save only the board of deacons and committees pertaining to it.

A men's brotherhood club was formed about the same time; its kickoff was a steak supper "with Wells Henderson in charge of steaks!" About seventy men paid $1.50 for a ticket and submitted to "a brief business meeting." In true American style, the group immediately elected a whole slate of officers, all the way down to a third vice president. Wilson Henderson was named the first president. Still another innovation that year was a change in family night; twice a month the regular Wednesday night schedule of organizational meetings, choir practice, youth activities, and prayer services was expanded to include an early supper for family groups beforehand. Bowers called these evenings "delightful" and noted a feeling of fellowship that was "quite pronounced." Family nights continue in the church calendar of weekly events. Actually, the whole idea of a calendar itself took hold about this time. A three-week period in late November and early December showed only four days when no church-related event was scheduled.

Another banner year ended with every expectation that the church would meet its financial obligations, provided December's collections surpassed those of the previous year by only $3,000. The debt had been reduced significantly; in fact, there was a distinct possibility that the new year would begin with outstanding indebtedness of only $140,000. The pastor could hardly conceal his pleasure at the notion of tackling the second phase of the building plan:

> The annual accomplishments over the past ten or eleven years give basis for yet another hope. It is that we shall be able to remove all indebtedness much sooner than we had thought and will soon be in position to begin our plan for our much needed sanctuary. This is a wonderful hope! But if we neglect our duty, it will turn out to be nothing more than a pipe dream.

Another large budget, this time totaling $107,600, was adopted in the last days of 1957 for the following year.

A Boy Scout troop was organized at the church in early 1958 under the leadership of the minister of education and scoutmasters Dr. George Parsons and Al Reid. The church also sponsored a Brownie troop of the Girl Scouts, led by Mrs. W. R. (Ruth) Dunn, Mrs. Tom (Ann) Walker, and Mrs. Robert (Margaret) Ray. The pastor urged the Brownies to "continue to strive toward the development of a character that will exhibit the helpful power of womanhood." We are left to wonder exactly what advice the boys received, but it is probably safe to assume it did not contain the words *helpful power*. The church also fielded a team for the YMCA-sponsored church softball league. Strict rules governed the league's activities: either Sunday school or church membership was a requirement of each team member; another was that players had to attend at least two Sundays out of each month to retain eligibility. Six other Greenwood churches also fielded teams (South Main Baptist had two: the Reds and the Greens), and an active schedule was posted for the 1958 season.

Two weeks before a mortgage payment of $12,000 fell due and without sufficient funds on hand to meet it, the pastor revealed some rather hard truths to the membership. It seems that sixty-five member families had made no contribution at all to the church in 1957, and an additional ninety-four families had given twenty-six dollars or less during the year. Translating families to individual members meant that 475 people, or well over 30 percent of the church membership, were not participating significantly in the business life of the church. This was dismal news indeed, especially in view of the fact that the church owed about $140,000 at the time *and* had visions of completing an ambitious building program in the foreseeable future. Even so, there seemed no real expectation of an embarrassing default, and Bowers probably knew very well from past experience that the payment would be made on time. Only three days before the due date, he brought up the matter once again to report a shortfall of at least $3,000 if the debt payment and other first-of-the-month obligations were to be met. No one will be surprised to learn that a loan payment of $11,998.91 was made on time, though the church was forced to sell some stock shares this time to make it happen. The treasury might have been pretty well depleted, as the pastor put it, but the church's debt dropped to $130,000.

The second anniversary of moving into the new church quarters inspired Bowers to reminisce about the "days of discouragement and doubt but . . . many more days of satisfaction and assurance" that had led up to what he called "this wonder among us." Reminding members that a building in itself must never be considered an ultimate goal, Bowers pointed to increased efficiency, interest, cooperation, and a renewed spirit within the congregation, all of which he was confident the new church had inspired. He also promised to work with ever more diligence and confidence to win the lost, develop character, and produce what he called "soul growth" in everyone. Once again the pastor proposed a challenge: "Why not," he wrote, "begin 1959 with only $100,000 indebtedness? That would require only $30,000 paid on the building the remainder of this year. With your help we can do this. Wouldn't it be wonderful? It can be done!"

Clearly the church had a most enthusiastic cheerleader in James A. Bowers. Actually, the pastor must have noticed this tendency in himself when he spoke of the danger of something he called "spiritual pride in his people" and pronounced himself "constantly on guard against it." Even so, Bowers could not resist praising the excellent work of the many and varied church organizations. He gave credit at the highest level to both the music and worship programs, calling them the best of any church he knew. In fact, he faulted the church only in that members were "perhaps too careless about sincerely inviting others to participate with us in our spiritually beneficial programs and in sharing with them the experiences and the joy that come to us as we work together in the church." He closed a positively lyrical column in the newsletter for August 14, 1958, with the words, "You will understand that this is by no means boasting."

Bowers spent his fifteenth anniversary as pastor of Greenwood's First Baptist Church in Dallas, Texas, where he filled the pulpit of a very large church, Park Cities Baptist. This church had issued three invitations previously, and the pastor had to be urged by his deacons to accept when he was asked a fourth time. He called his experience there "a pleasant one" and rated his audience as "unusually large"; still, Bowers confessed that the congratulatory telegrams from Greenwood people marking the anniversary made him happiest of all. No false note creeps into Bowers's assurances of his devotion to his flock and to the work of the church.

The statistical report in the associational letter set membership at 1,242 in the fall of 1958. Sunday school attendance averaged 568 and Training Union, 100. Twenty percent of the total contributions of nearly $105,000 went to missions that year, and the church physical plant was again valued at $690,000.

Church members were reminded of another budget crunch in the offing with four lines in the newsletter of November 20, 1958. Those lines speak for themselves:

THERE REMAIN ONLY SIX SUNDAYS IN 1958
OUR BUDGET FOR 1958 IS $107,300
OUR CONTRIBUTIONS TO DATE FOR 1958 ARE $77,300
TO MEET OUR BUDGET, $30,000 WILL BE REQUIRED IN THESE SIX SUNDAYS

The proposed budget for 1959 inched upward to $108,635.

As the new year got under way the pastor, or someone else, found room in the newsletter to report a growing, and quite unintended, feature of church life, a lost and found department. In a last ditch effort to find their owners, "innumerable accessories and twenty seven Bibles" were placed on a table in the main corridor before being given (except for the Bibles) to the Salvation Army or some other charitable group.

A notice in the newsletter of February 5, 1959, reveals that Mr. and Mrs. R. B. Curry Sr., had made a gift to the church of three chancel windows for the chapel. Bowers called these windows "new, modern and very lovely stained glass," and surely no one who has seen them will disagree with that assessment. The windows were being made at the time the announcement appeared; installation was expected later in the year, "sometime around Easter."

While the subject of windows had undoubtedly been discussed many times by church leaders, architects, and builders—surely no single item is more important in church design and construction—this notice was the first to introduce the subject to the membership. Everyone is surely aware of the possibilities of stained glass windows beyond the obvious fact that they contribute to the sheer beauty of buildings, most particularly churches. Windows also allow such lovely gift opportunities that churches often seem to treat the subject with particular care. First Baptist is really no exception to this rule, except that the pastor and others seem to have adopted a rather chilly attitude toward the memorial windows in the building on North Main Street. Many members no doubt recall with varying degrees of emotion the fact that no one seems to have had the slightest interest in finding a home for those windows somewhere in the new building.

Though the making of stained glass is an ancient craft, it attained the status of high art only when it became an adjunct of church architecture in northern Europe early in the Christian era. Glassmaking itself had developed many centuries earlier—both Egyptian and Roman civilization contained many examples, as did that of the Arab culture of the Near East—but it remained for Christianity of France, England, Germany, and the Netherlands, where "a transcendent religious impulse" arose, to put "the miraculous vibrant aspects of colored glass" to appropriate use, particularly in the wave of church and cathedral building that was well under way by the eleventh and twelfth centuries.[3]

The pastor's two-paragraph description of the three-part prayer window in the new chapel stresses elements of both a very old art and a very new execution:

> The windows are entirely new in concept of design and fabrication. The glass is a blaze of lovely color, deep and sufficiently opaque to keep out all glare. The lead of the windows forms lovely miniature figures that give almost the appearance of statuary. These figures are done in gold leaf and silver leaf. The effect is magnificent, both day and night.
>
> These windows are to be the "Prayer Windows" of the chapel. The center window has the head of the Christ in the center with the heads of the disciples grouped about. It is the Christ teaching his disciples to pray. The left window has scenes of Old Testament prayer and the right has scenes of New Testament prayer.

Amazingly, these windows were made and installed at a cost of only four thousand dollars. Six additional windows, all traditional stained glass but of different and less expensive construction, were planned to complete the design of the chapel. These side windows were offered to the congregation as giving opportunities. The pastor pointed out their practicality in eliminating glare, as well as the beauty and symbolism the windows would add to the worship space. The only odd note in the announcement of the chapel windows is the emphasis on the words *new* and *modern*. On the other hand, this may have been a portent; these words were destined to take on a whole new meaning when the windows in the permanent sanctuary were executed.

When installation was completed and the windows revealed for the first time in all their glory, the reaction must have been everything the pastor had hoped. He called them "truly works of art" and remarked on their different appearance by day and at night. The announcement that three side windows at a cost of six hundred dollars each had been promised by three church families was another indication of the desire to enhance the beauty of the chapel. Two more were pledged soon afterward. All six side windows were installed in the summer of 1960 and the five donors were recognized in the newsletter for July 21. Resident members who donated windows were Mr. and Mrs. W. A. Lomax, the Horace Brinsons, Elbert and Margaret Adams, and the William L. Jays. Mrs. John H. Cheatham of Griffin, Georgia, whose membership status was not mentioned, was the fifth donor. The side windows were meant to complement those in the chancel, and the symbolism of the entire installation reflected the activities to which the chapel was devoted—praise, baptism, teaching, preaching, and the Lord's Supper. All the chapel windows were the work of the Willet Studios of Philadelphia. Yet another donor later provided special outdoor lighting for the chapel flèche (spire) and the windows so that their full beauty could be appreciated at night.

Continuing what seemed to be almost a preoccupation with windows, blinds (or more accurately, shutters) for the sanctuary windows were installed in the summer of 1959 and proved a very nice way to commemorate the third anniversary of the room's occupancy. The gift of a member couple who evidently wished to remain anonymous, these shutters must have made a tremendous difference indeed, both in the appearance of the sanctuary as well as in the efficiency of its heating and cooling systems. It is easy to believe with the pastor that the addition had "worked wonders" with the place of worship, especially in the heat of a South Carolina summer.

Bowers's latent interest in the world of drama began to emerge in early 1959. The first indication was the announcement that a religious play, *Simon the Leper*, would be part of the Easter program, and the newsletter revealed the very next week that Bowers had accepted the lead in the Greenwood Little Theatre's production of *The Passing of the Third Floor Back*, scheduled for a March opening. The item is titled "Since the Man is Away . . ." and ends with "We are certainly pleased that Mr. Bowers has added to his busy schedule his participation in this program. We are not quite sure that he would approve this article if he were here, but since he is away . . . ." Bowers was in New York at a board meeting of the National Tuberculosis Association, another of his many interests. The Little Theatre play would not be Bowers's last venture on the stage. No further mention of *Simon* was found, but *Passing* rated a line in the newsletter of March 12 when the pastor indicated that the play seemed to have "the impact of several sermons."

First Baptist Church joined with others of the Abbeville Association to constitute Woodfields Baptist Mission into a full-fledged Southern Baptist church in August 1959, though West Side Baptist had assumed the most direct responsibility for overseeing the mission's activities. The organizational meeting was an occasion for recognizing the growth of the denomination in Greenwood. "The work has prospered out there and the prospects for the future seem good," wrote the pastor.

The year 1959 was noteworthy in that the debt was mentioned hardly at all. Possibly this was a deliberate move on the part of the pastor and church leaders; only one column was devoted to the subject about midyear, and in that column the pastor urged, "Let us not get accustomed to the debt so that it no longer becomes an incentive and challenge." This sounds very much like a general warning against complacency, and a paragraph in the newsletter of September 10 is almost equally offhanded: "It may be of interest to know that our church was established in 1870 and that our present property is valued at $690,000. We have an indebtedness of $111,500."

With that background, a column entitled "A Look at Our Finances" in the newsletter for October 8 takes on even more significance for its evenness of tone coupled with a serious underlying message. The column begins with a priceless sentence: "As one reviews the work of our church, there are many things that amaze one," followed by the reminder that the church's financial support was based solely on the desire of members to give and not on a system of assessments or pledges. A totally laissez-faire attitude prevailed and had done so since the first fund-raising drive was launched to get the building program under way. Especially in view of this phenomenon, Bowers pointed out, "We need to take voluntary stock of our contributions at times, *since there is no demand that we do so*" [emphasis added]. A few paragraphs later, referring to the current reality, the pastor wrote, "The debt is real and it must be dealt with. We hope in a few weeks to have that debt down to the $100,000 mark overall." A column entitled "The Year's End" in the November 25 newsletter reiterates the desire to decrease the debt, but sets $90,000 as the goal. A copy of the budget for 1960 is not among the papers for the prior year, nor are we able to learn whether the debt was reduced to Bowers's satisfaction by the end of the very eventful year 1959.

The very first edition of the newsletter for 1960, dated January 7, contains the information that 1959 was the best year ever in terms of financial contributions. More than $125,000 flowed into the church coffers, and the pastor, as always, was ready with a response as he wrote: "We now set out on a new year's effort with confidence, assurance and faith. Best of all, we rejoice to contemplate the future."

The first half of the year, judging from routine newsletter items, was a busy and productive time for First Baptist Church. A full program offering something for everyone unfolded every week; exceptions were made only for special events such as organists guild programs or similar community-wide projects, as well as the suspension of Sunday night services every August. First Baptist also continued to hold fast its reputation as a progressive, even liberal, church as the decade of the sixties opened. On the other hand, married women were still designated by their husbands' Christian and surnames, no doubt because the iron bands of etiquette were still in place. Men were, however, occasionally pressed into service as nursery helpers, and they could always be counted on to make up any deficit in the Lottie Moon and Annie Armstrong offerings from the ladies of the Woman's Missionary Union (WMU).

By midyear the inevitable rumblings about the need for additional space began. One wonders if the opening sentence of the first article in the June 9 newsletter—"The deacons have been giving a great deal of thought lately to the need . . . for additional facilities"—was 100 percent accurate, or if the deacons' thoughts had perhaps been guided by the expert leadership skills of Jim Bowers. Perhaps he was even able to make them *think* the subject was their idea. Whatever the nuances behind the announcement, the deacons not only appointed two separate committees to study the church's needs but also adopted a plan submitted by the finance committee to pay off the debt remaining on the building. The plan was to designate the second Sunday of each month as "debt retirement Sunday," and the goal was to raise about $70,000 from gifts over and above contributions for the regular church budget. "With more effort and the full cooperation of all," the pastor wrote, "we can do this." More than $600 was collected on the first special offering day in what Bowers termed a "quiet beginning." It seems that some Sunday school classes had plans of their own for that Sunday's offering, and a few individuals were unaware of the drive.

A new note appeared in the August 11 newsletter when the matter of debt retirement Sundays was addressed again. Suddenly there seemed to be great concern over where to put all the people who wanted to be a part of the church's activities: "It would be tragic if we do not provide places for those who want to worship in our church," the pastor wrote, but "we cannot make this provision until we have fulfilled our obligation on our present building." Church members were reminded that they had "a tremendous responsibility to make a place for all who want to worship with us." This novel notion could not have failed to strike a chord with the congregation; surely no Baptist could resist the idea that lack of space alone was denying access to hordes of potential members! As for actual numbers, these were revealed in the association letter for 1959. Membership totaled 1,286, only 200 of whom were nonresident. Ninety-eight new members were received during the year, balanced by 61 removed by death or transfer, for a net gain of 37. Sunday school enrollment was nearly as large, but Training Union had suffered a decline to less than 200 members. Attendance at both averaged a little over 50 percent. Other church organizations appeared reasonably vigorous, and revenue and disbursement figures showed that the church continued to operate in the black.

The church called a new minister of education in 1960 to replace W. E. Ellis, who chose to return to graduate school and high school teaching in Columbia after three years in Greenwood. There must have been concern about finding exactly the right person for the job. Boykin Curry remembers calling a number of his Furman classmates for help in locating candidates; a friend of Curry's in Rock Hill, in fact, recommended W. C. (Bill) Treadwell Jr., who was associated with the Oakland Baptist Church there. At least in part on the strength of that recommendation, the church extended a call to the young man.

Treadwell made a point of visiting on a Wednesday night when he was able to see the church in action on a number of fronts, and he posted his answer to the call within a week: "The Wednesday that I was privileged to spend with you was most helpful in enabling me to reach a decision . . . I shall be with you on Monday, November 14, 1960." After a welcoming service the following Sunday evening, Treadwell plunged in. A message in the newsletter of December 1 spelled out his priorities and philosophy rather succinctly: "We need to know each other," he wrote, and he was clearly determined to work toward what he called "a living atmosphere of love motivated fellowship . . . molding us into growing Christians." He stressed the value of "precious people" over mere numbers and promised to be "honest about our expectations of each other." Most people agree that Bill Treadwell lived up to this early expression of his goals. Among his first innovations was an "after church fellowship," a thinly-disguised excuse for social gatherings of high school student groups in people's homes. The idea was to extend the organized youth programs for another hour, both to build camaraderie and provide safe and wholesome entertainment for young people in search of "something to do in Greenwood." Host families were asked to provide light refreshments and direct two party games; they were assured that the groups would be well chaperoned, well mannered, and stay no more than an hour.

By the beginning of his third month on the job, the new minister had hammered out a total program of Christian education for the year. Treadwell called it a "serious work" that demanded "complete freedom to speak and think" as the various groups worked in Christian fellowship toward a common goal. He called the attitude he hoped to develop "intelligent enthusiasm." The program he envisioned consisted of a general philosophical statement and one setting forth a series of goals. Three additional columns spelled out the "how-tos" for Sunday school,

Training Union, and all other nonworship service programs. The goals statement pointed out that the church needed to find a balance, since its concept of worship was at that point far ahead of its educational program. Treadwell clearly grasped early on the eternal dichotomy between the church as a community service institution and its role in individual and corporate worship. He also brought great energy to the task of building a strong program for young people. Evidently he was popular from the first, but his outspokenness was bound to cause problems for him sooner or later.

A budget of $124,390 was proposed for 1961, an increase of about $5,600 over the previous year. At the same time the pastor reminded members that contributions were behind those for 1959 by about $2,000 and urged extra effort over the four Sundays in December to remove this deficit. "We cannot let this continue," he cautioned, "We were really hoping to remove our debt this year." The new budget, adopted without a dissenting vote the next Sunday, contained an increase in the pastor's salary to $8,500. He expressed his appreciation in a note in the newsletter, even as he referred to the "humbling effect" of the raise.

Though the Baptist denomination cherishes the independent stance of its separate churches above all else, it is also true that a certain openness and simplicity has gradually become associated with worship services in Baptist churches. Similarly, many artifacts of Christianity such as statuary, paintings, candles, stations of the cross, holy water fonts, censers, crucifixes, screens, robes, and hangings of all descriptions so abundantly evident in high-church Protestant and Roman Catholic churches, are viewed by many Baptists as "trappings" at best and dangerously close to graven images and idolatry at worst. It must have surprised some members of Greenwood's First Baptist Church one Sunday in early 1961 to find colorful fabric hangings on the lectern and pulpit of the chancel. The minister took the trouble to discuss the significance of these antependia, which were the gift of an interested member, in the newsletter of January 26. "Their purpose is to add a bit of color to the chancel and enhance its beauty," he wrote, adding that the symbolism of such items was a means of reminding worshipers of certain important truths. Actually bookmarks, the hanging on the left, for example, showed three nails, the crown of thorns, and a cross to evoke images of the Crucifixion, while the piece to the right pictured a lamp representing both truth and the Holy Spirit, along with a shepherd's cross.

The pulpit hangings were concerned with the Christ of the Resurrection: a palm wreath and a crown symbolized victory, while the Greek letters *chi* and *rho* stood for an abbreviation of the name of Christ. Bowers was careful to note that the hangings and their symbolism were not liturgical, by which he meant prescribed rites pertaining to public worship, but were to serve only as reminders that the church's life was the result of Jesus Christ's atoning death. He added that similar pieces would soon be placed in the chapel.

The format of the newsletter for February 23 deserves a quick mention for its originality and style. Because this newsletter is so very different from the usual, surely it must be an example of Treadwell's work. In addition to an intriguing paragraph describing the by-products of Christian growth as (1) healthy curiosity, (2) intellectual honesty, and (3) willingness to understand new ideas, the entire back page is a series of pseudo "gossip" items, complete with clever cartoons, about the various activities scheduled for the coming week. At the bottom is the line: "In the opinion of the editor, this is legitimate gossip material for our members this week!" A few issues later, the question of editorship is resolved when Treadwell signed an item asking for feedback on the newsletter. The item is headed, "Have You Read This Far?"

The minister of education was also making a name for himself in other parts of the state. One April newsletter documents a Treadwell appearance of some sort in Clemson, Aiken, Myrtle Beach, and Columbia, as well as frequent sessions with the Baptist Student Union at Lander. In addition, he was following through on his commitment to upgrade the educational arm of the church. Suddenly new classes in Bible study were formed, and the adult Training Union undertook group discussion on such dangerous subjects as "difficult Baptist beliefs" as a means of stimulating their thinking on a variety of topics. Nor were Sunday school class presidents, teachers, and other workers overlooked in this churchwide revitalization effort: a prospective workers class was formed for adults "willing to spend five months in concentrated methods, administration and Bible study" to prepare for Sunday school leadership positions. Treadwell's hand was evident in all these innovations; more and more newsletter items contained the line, "Please call Bill at the office if you need . . ."

So successful were these new-ventures that Treadwell was invited to talk about them at a regional pastors' conference in North Carolina during January 1962. Noting that the invitation itself was a signal honor, an item in the newsletter indicated that a number of attendees had expressed the desire to visit First Baptist to see its educational program in operation. Treadwell's popularity and influence extended to the larger community as well; he was named "Young Man of the Year" by the Greenwood Jaycees in 1963, and Lander hired him as an adjunct professor, beginning with the school year 1963–1964.

By midyear 1961, the pastor was forced to admit that about $65,000 of the church debt was still outstanding. "Frankly," he wrote, "we have neglected this item for the past few months. This ought not to be." He urged members to make their contributions before taking their vacations. An item called "A quick financial look" in the July 27 newsletter makes no mention of the debt but laments that contributions for the first half of the year were well under half the budgeted obligations for the same period. The giving pattern was then, and to some extent still is, typical of First Baptist Church. A number of members, for their own reasons, have always preferred to make their gifts near the end of the year.

The budget for 1962 continued to climb, and even the pastor used words such as *significant* and *challenging* when he presented the figures in the November 30, 1961, newsletter. The bottom line of $130,280 actually represented an increase of less than 5 percent over the previous year, but that budget still stood some $35,000 short in receipts. The pastor reminded members also that the indebtedness could be completely paid by the end of 1961 if members would come up with only $6,000 more in receipts than those of the previous December. Appeals were still being made in the newsletter for December 28 as a most successful year in terms of numbers, spirit, and financial strength came to a close.

As usual the books were kept open for the first two weeks of the new year to allow members extra time for contributions that would be counted in the previous year's receipts. Also as usual, the pastor was able by the middle of January to report that receipts had exceeded budgeted revenue by $1,500. As good as this was, Bowers confessed that he had allowed himself to hope for $10,000 extra to erase the debt. As impatient as he was for the church to pay off its mortgage (so that it would be free to embark on further financial ventures), Bowers could state confidently, "[W]e know you will do that in the next few weeks."

And the pastor was right! The title of the lead article in the newsletter of February 1 said it all in just three words: "Church Reaches Goal." Bowers was ecstatic; "It is a noble thing you have achieved," he wrote, and he called the Sunday the goal was reached "one of [the church's] greatest days of victory." Actually, receipts were sufficient to meet all obligations and allow a bit of reserve to apply to the all-important sanctuary fund. Everyone understood that the completion of the building plan would be the primary focus of the next few years, but in the meantime the church conducted what Bowers called a "most significant service" when it publicly burned a facsimile of the mortgage and announced itself not only free of debt but also possessed of real property assets valued in excess of $700,000. Bowers commended members on a remarkable achievement.

A brief business meeting was scheduled for March 18 in order to authorize the deacons to move forward on the building plan for the sanctuary. A committee consisting of four members, plus the ministers and chairman of the board of deacons, was named to select an architect.

The church undertook an experiment of sorts about this time when it changed its Sunday evening services to a formal vespers program. Starting the evening schedule at 5:00 P.M. was meant to enable the various organizations to complete their programs and still allow time for family togetherness after church services. It seems a number of churches that tried the new format had reported increased attendance and a renewed spiritual atmosphere when Sunday evenings were a little less rushed. The plan went into effect in April 1962, and the pastor pronounced it "tremendously successful" less than a month later, particularly in attendance numbers. Worship

The church burns a facsimile of the mortgage on Phase One of the building project, 1962. Left to right: Paul Burgess, Bill Bradford, John C. Young, Caroline Beaver, Dr. Bowers, Bill Treadwell, and Elbert Adams.

service participants immediately increased more than 100 percent and the seminar/Training Union attendance soared by a full 60 percent. The pastor believed also that the needs of more people were being met. Even though these startling increases did not hold in the long run, church officials pronounced themselves "quite pleased" with the vespers program as 1962 wore on.

Given the ever growing emphasis on its education program, surely it is not surprising to find the church becoming more and more active in community enterprises of various kinds. Boy and Girl Scouts, Greenwood Little Theatre, and YMCA-sponsored sports groups have already been mentioned, but church interest branched out even more in the early 1960s. Week after week the newsletter carried items linking the church with various groups, among them the local chapter of the National Secretaries Association, the Salvation

Army building fund drive, and even the Greenwood chapter of the Jaycees. Many times members of these groups would attend services en masse and be recognized for "their civic concern and . . . sensible leadership."

The church staff grew and changed also in the summer of 1962. In addition to a summer youth worker, college student Buddy Puckett who had worked the previous summer as an intern and who was hired as early as February, the church named Sue Waldrop to the new position of educational assistant, an appointment that was to last only a year as this young woman moved on to marriage and subsequent relocation with her new husband to Easley. She had moved to Greenwood from Rock Hill and a job with the Baptist Student Union at Winthrop.

Waldrop was the replacement for Joyce Foxworth Williams whose tenure dated from 1958 and who was to return to employment at the church more than once. At the specific request of the pastor, Williams juggled raising a family with part-time work as bookkeeper for two years, filled in from time to time after that, and returned to the church office full time in the 1980s. She retired in 1991, ending a career spanning more than thirty years. Williams's long association with the business side of the church's operations—she also served as clerk for a number of years—make her insights particularly valuable. She points out, for example, that the church's most significant growth spurts can be traced to the immediate post-World War II period and the late fifties and early sixties, after Chemstrand (later Monsanto, now Solutia) came to town. She also points to any number of church families who had moved to Greenwood as a result of the expansion of the area's industrial base.

Even as the church celebrated six full years in its "new" building, everybody's thoughts were occupied with completing the overall building plan conceived nearly twenty years earlier in the first flush of post-World War II optimism. The same pastor still served, with a message that had changed little, if at all, over the years. Clearly he believed his church was equal to any task its members set themselves, and he had never wavered: "By following our original plan," he wrote, "we shall be able to secure additional space as we provide our adequate sanctuary. . . . Let us . . . make the building plans and dreams a reality."

Surely no one was surprised when the search committee reported its choice of Harold Wagoner of Philadelphia to complete the plan he had originally conceived when the education complex was designed. Wagoner's initial visit was scheduled for late September.

The messages at year's end 1962 were not much different from those of other years. There was the usual flurry of holiday activity combined with a rather sobering Thanksgiving meditation that questioned the growing indifference among Americans, many of whom were enjoying material blessings beyond their dreams but were still ignorant of the reality and power of God. The church seemed busier than ever with a burgeoning program of activity and the beginnings of a new and heavy financial commitment for the coming years. In addition, federal regulations had been put in place that demanded the church close its books on December 31, thus ending a neat little tax loophole church members had enjoyed for many years. A proposed budget totaling $143,840 was presented for adoption in early 1963. Its bottom line represented the largest increase since 1956.

The pastor greeted his flock in early 1963 with three paragraphs of praise and gratitude for their achievements over the years, including unprecedented growth in membership and attendance as well as a record of giving in 1962 that had exceeded the budget by more than $8,000. "Your interest, your love, your dedicated loyalty and your consecration have enabled God to work wonderfully through you," he wrote. Unfortunately, however, members seemed to want nothing more than to rest on their laurels after achieving this superb giving record. The pastor noted nervously on February 14 that receipts for the new year would be seriously short if January's experience were any indication. Collections were under those of the previous year by $13,000.

The first issue of the newsletter also contained information on a new phase of adult Christian education—a series of seminars focusing on the workaday business world and the role of Christian ethics therein. Several businessmen from across the state, as well as a number from Greenwood, were invited to bring messages from their own experience in an ongoing program with the straightforward title, "Christ and Business in Greenwood."

Still another organization called Round Table was mentioned for the first time in early 1963. This group, which might have been an outgrowth of WMU emphasis on mission study, invited anyone interested in reading good books to meet in the church parlor for discussion, not only of the works themselves, but also of the means of purchasing new books and circulating those already owned by the group. This sounds very much like the beginnings of a church library, but Gertrude Sanders remembers the group simply as a missionary circle whose members were particularly interested in reading. She recalls that two roundtable groups—one that met mornings and the other afternoons—eventually evolved into circles named for Louise Bowers and Joann Gray. She also recalls that the strong emphasis on reading lasted only a year or two.

The church received preliminary drawings for the new sanctuary from the architect in October 1963. The pastor pronounced himself "a bit surprised" at the scope of Wagoner's imagination, which had evidently ranged a bit further than the committee was prepared to consider. Some "cutting down" was accomplished the first week, so that it appeared the project could be brought within reach of the church's resources without too much alteration. Even so, it was clear that a minimum of $100,000, more than twice the amount available, would be needed before breaking ground could be considered.

There were no surprises in the financial picture for 1964; indeed, the budget was virtually identical to that of the previous year, and as usual it was adopted unanimously. Still, giving for 1963 continued to be somewhat problematic. Receipts were short by $50,000 as late as November 30, but the pastor indicated no particular concern. "We know we can [meet the budget] with your help," he wrote. Actually, the budget was not to be met this time, and 1963 ended with the church still about $9,000 short of projected receipts. At the same time the pastor announced that an additional $45,000 had been placed in the building fund (which means the shortage did not come from that particular line item),[4] bringing its total to $83,000 and the new sanctuary that much closer to reality.

The congregation's Christmas gift to the pastor in 1963 was a brand new Buick with, as he put it, "all sorts of accessories, including air-conditioning." It is interesting to note that air-conditioning in our cars was viewed as an *accessory* rather than a *necessity* as late as the 1960s.[5] Bowers pronounced the gift "unbelievable" and praised the thought and love that had prompted it. Though no mention was made of Bowers's tenure at First Baptist, possibly the gift was also meant to commemorate his twenty years in the pulpit.

The church seems to have tried to meet the challenge of the 1960s head-on. Perhaps it is only in retrospect that this particular decade seems so significant, but there is no question that a number of issues were seething just below the seemingly placid surface of American life during this period. The assassination of President Kennedy in November 1963 impacted everyone and set off practically an epidemic of shocking violence nationwide, yet not a single mention of this seminal event made the newsletter. President Lyndon Johnson was in the process of committing more and more American troops to the no-win situation of a land war in Asia, the struggle for civil rights was moving toward its long and bloody public phase, and college students throughout the country were flexing the muscles of rebellion against authority—any authority. American life was about to change forever, and a miserably unpopular war would be the catalyst of that change. There is some evidence that First Baptist Church stepped up its activities program during this period; more and varied opportunities for study and learning seemed a healthy contrast to any number of beach trips, cookouts, banquets, and ball games. Lander history professor Dr. Joe Stukes joined the church's seminar staff, bringing provocative lectures to crowds that soon overflowed meeting rooms. His broad topic of "Christianity and Politics," with diverse subtopics ranging from the implications of NATO to the Peace Corps and civil rights, found eager audiences at First Baptist Church as the 1960s wore on.

Among the new programs and activities that flourished in church life during this period was the growing emphasis on camp experience for youth and children. First Baptist had sponsored a few sporadic efforts in this area before Bill Treadwell joined the staff, but he was quick to see the value of a structured program and under his leadership camping activity grew rapidly. Treadwell possessed a rare talent for the entire camp concept. He was totally comfortable with young people and equally adept at enlisting other adults as chaperones and camp leaders. The sense of camaraderie among the young people who embraced the camp experience was directly traceable to Treadwell's enthusiastic involvement.

The full-fledged camping program actually grew out of boat trips Treadwell organized. He and Bill Allred, Bob Barmore, and Vernon Moore began taking boys on boating excursions. Pleased with the way the time together seemed to create a certain group consciousness among the men and boys, Treadwell determined to expand the effort to involve more youth in varied outdoor pursuits. Accordingly, he moved in 1961 to set up a camp program for all young people at an Episcopal campsite at Black Mountain, North Carolina, called "In the Oaks." The purpose of the program was threefold: to build a sense of community among the youth themselves, to increase rapport between adults and young people, and to provide children and youth the tools and experiences with which to make spiritual teaching a guide for everyday life.

In the Oaks remains a symbol for the camping program at First Baptist. The main house on the grounds had a Great Hall for group gatherings, a gym floor for basketball and square dancing, an indoor pool and bowling lanes, and a basement that made an ideal haunted house. Other sites were used as well—Bonclarken Assembly in Flat Rock, Hilton Head, Jekyll Island off the Georgia coast, Blowing Rock, the Garden City Chapel in Myrtle Beach, Furman University, and the YMCA Camp at Black Mountain, but it seems clear that those who went to In the Oaks think first of that special location.

In the beginning separate weeks were scheduled for junior high and senior high youth and for children (known at the time as Juniors), but several times the groups were combined. Perhaps the highlight of the entire program came in 1969 when more than 185 students, counselors, and staff (including several people from the First Baptist Church of Jefferson, Georgia) attended Youth Camp at Jekyll Island, Georgia. Jim Bowers served as camp pastor, Bill Treadwell directed the senior and junior high divisions, and Charlotte Washington led the junior campers (children in grades four through six). The counselors—most of them parents of campers—recruited for this week must have enjoyed themselves thoroughly; they would remain active in the program for years to come. Counselors and workers whose names appeared in the report of the experience were Tom and Barbara Chandler, Cliff and Rose Fagan, Judy Cheek, Jeannie and Julie Jay, Dixie and Tom Walker, W. D. Wilburn, Lou Treadwell, Melvin and Joyce Poole, Judy Powell, Wiley and Peggy Price, Bill and

Evelyn Allred, Buddy and Mary Hamrick, and Kathryn Moore. Jean (Mrs. Tom) Wood, Donna Byrd, and Peggy Hamrick and her brother Jack, who did double duty as camp bugler, were in charge of music, while Cliff Fagan and Louise Bowers helped with drama. Cooks were Janelle Anderson, Rebecca Wilburn, Dixie Walker, Mrs. Bob Patrick, Mrs. Claude Burnett, Ann Ella Dorn, and A. D. Davis.

The camping program was never meant to be an end in itself, but rather was undertaken as a direct ministry for the mutual benefit of the church and its young people. A great many significant and permanent changes in programming for youth came directly from the camping experiences of the 1960s. The music program was enhanced by campfire singalongs, time spent in camping activities contributed to the development of leadership qualities within the youth group, and roundtables such as the "Encounter Group" and other specific ministries at home could be easily traced to provocative ideas raised and discussed in camp gatherings. Clearly the camp program was largely responsible for the remarkable cohesion among the young people during this period; the general membership gradually came to realize the importance of time set apart to nurture its children and youth.

This period also seems to have been the high-water mark of the church's music ministry. Almost an embarrassment of riches in the form of choir directors and potential music makers existed: Mary Moore led the beginner music activity, while Ann Arrington, Margery Lightsey, Jean Wood, and Edgar Davis directed full-fledged choirs called, respectively, the primary training, the carol, chapel, and adult choirs. Some met for rehearsal on Sundays, others on Wednesdays, but all seem to have been vital components of education and worship services alike. As always, the pastor was generous in praising the church's music program, especially its longtime organist, Dr. Elbert Adams.

The late 1950s and early 1960s marked a transition period for the church in any number of areas. The music ministry is a particularly good example of the sort of change from the days when a few seats at the front of the church were set aside for the "best singers" in the congregation. A notice entitled "Our Appreciation" in the newsletter of May 22, 1958, set the stage with the question: "Did you know, for example, that two members, J. L. Beaudrot and G. E. Bannister, have been singing in our choir for more than 55 years?" The article added that no one else even approached that record. By the time these two tenors resigned (a better word would probably be *retired*) from the choir three years later, their combined service totaled about 125 years.

Only one activity outranked Sunday morning church services for Beaudrot and Bannister, and that not very often. Edgar Davis remembers that their absence meant most often a funeral at which the services of Greenwood's most famous male quartet were required. These two men, along with J. T. Stogner and T. J. Rollins, usually performed together, though others (including eventually a few women) filled in from time to time. A Beaudrot family history calls the group the Greenwood Quartet, though no one believes it ever officially adopted that name. The quartet was so well-known for its work at funerals that one bereaved widow told the director the only thing she *knew* she wanted at her husband's funeral was music by the Blyth Quartet. Wayne Gantt reports that he purposely failed to correct the lady's impression that Blyth Funeral Home and the quartet were connected.

Edgar Davis recalls the group with a particular fondness, since he too was called upon to fill in for a missing member now and then. No one remembers how long the quartet flourished, but everyone remembers the group itself; Beaudrot, Bannister, Stogner, and whoever the fourth member happened to be at any given time,[6] were simply fixtures in town and county life for many years. Their specialty was, of course, hymns, and they could perform equally well a cappella or with instrumental accompaniment. A comment from the newsletter of September 7, 1961, acknowledges Beaudrot's and Bannister's choir service but could be applied equally to their work with the quartet: "Their spirit, their ability, their faithfulness have meant more than any of us could ever calculate." It is necessary that the record show that both men were ordained deacons, and Bannister's service also included more than twenty years as church treasurer. Both were honored for all they had meant to the church in a service of recognition held on September 14, 1961.

By the last quarter of 1964 the goal of a $100,000 building fund had mysteriously grown by a full 50 percent: "We need $150,000 in our building fund by December 31. . . . It is imperative that our contributions keep pace with our building plans," reads a blurb in the newsletter for October 15.

The annual association letter contained the most complete statistical update carried in the newsletter in several years. Since the church seems to have been in a particularly flourishing state at this time, perhaps selected excerpts from that letter would help to round out the picture:

> Members received during the year—95 (41 by baptism)
> Members lost during the year—59 (15 by death)
> Present membership—1369 (216 non-resident)
> Sunday School enrollment—1265, average attendance 588
> Training Union enrollment—207, average attendance 148
> Vacation Bible School enrollment—332
> WMU enrollment—546
> Value of church property—$711,000
> Total receipts through church—$135,134

After consultation with the architect during one of his regular trips to the Northeast, Bowers brought the latest information on the design for the sanctuary. It seems that a few "basic decisions" remained for the committee to make before the architect's conception could be brought before the church. Bowers noted somewhat ironically that the problems were the usual ones of design and cost, particularly cost. The building would have to be large to meet the church's burgeoning needs and, as he pointed out, "large buildings are expensive." By December 10, the pastor was clearly optimistic that the year's financial goals would be met and the building fund reach the magic total of $150,000 by the end of the month. Meanwhile, a new budget, itself totaling nearly the same amount, was proposed for the church's consideration. The newsletter dated December 31 announced receipts totaling nearly $3,000 in excess of the 1964 budget; the pastor also noted that the proposed budget for 1965 had been approved without a murmur.

The first mention of finance in 1965 was the happy report in the first newsletter that the church had exceeded its goal for contributions the previous year by nearly $10,000. Bowers was probably correct when he termed this record "a clear indication of . . . genuine interest in the church and in its program," and he must have felt new confidence that his dream of completing the building program was nearing reality. "We must keep up our good work," he wrote, "so that 1965 will be even greater."

The same issue carried the announcement of a new educational venture: a six-week series of classes especially designed for adult laypeople interested in an in-depth study of biblical subjects. Four well-known professors, three from South Carolina colleges and one from the Baptist seminary in Buenos Aires, Argentina,[7] made up the faculty. The Greenwood Community College in Biblical Studies was an interdenominational endeavor—the instructors represented four Protestant denominations—and was open to anyone, regardless of race, creed, or nationality. Though the series was not officially a church program, the deacons had given their blessing to the project and provided space for classes. Since the cost was a nominal $7.50 per two-hour course, clearly no one was receiving a financial windfall from this venture. Apparently it was simply what the deacons called it—a "Christian community witness"—a ministry, as it were, that the pastor believed could turn out to be "a privileged blessing." An announcement two weeks later that Dr. Joseph Stukes would serve as dean of this endeavor hints at a connection with Lander College's continuing education program, since Stukes was a member of the college faculty. The series opened with more than 150 adults in attendance. An item in the newsletter termed the school "a good example of bi-racial cooperation on a high and meaningful plane" and pronounced the church "justifiably pleased" with its participation. The program continued for several years.

Still another nod toward ecumenism was the invitation to an open house and Good Will Sunday at the local Catholic church that appeared in the newsletter for February 21. Featured would be both tours of the new building and celebration of the "English Mass," as the non-Latin version of the service was then called. The last sentence of the announcement, "Those who are interested are invited to attend this program," while not exactly a ringing endorsement, is nevertheless interesting since Southern Baptists have never been noted for their support of Roman Catholic institutions.

When Bowers was notified that Furman University would award him the Doctor of Divinity degree at its spring commencement in

1965 he was quick to share the moment with the congregation. "This is as much an honor to you as it is to me," he wrote, and added, "your challenge and encouragement . . . have enabled me to grow, if grow I have." As though in response to assuming a new level of professionalism, Bowers began addressing a number of seemingly small matters in brief newsletter items. One was the warning that being known as a "friendly church" might not be a good thing, if that friendliness were merely a superficial covering for selfish motives among its members. He let it be known that he preferred *compassion* and *concern* to *friendly* as terms descriptive of his church. Another was the criticism that churches in America had become little more than country clubs. The warning this time was that the church was to be viewed as a redemptive society, not an association of those who considered their own salvation of prime importance. The goal is not to "get saved," but rather to be "part of the body of Christ whose function is to redeem, to impart the religious truth and spirit that bring life," he wrote.

People began referring delightedly to the pastor as Dr. Bowers immediately following the awards ceremony at Furman, and the honoree addressed the question of his new title in a lighthearted article called "A Thorny Problem" in the newsletter of June 10:

> Life becomes complicated as one grows older! Added to other complications is the question, "What do we call Mr. Bowers?" Many have asked in fun, "Do I have to call you Doctor?" In the same vein the answer has been, "Just once." But seriously, your pastor is the same man he was before, only a bit humbled by Furman's action and your gracious comments about it. My preference is that you follow your preference. What you have called me before was no problem to you or to me. It must not be now. The important thing is our relationship, not the title.

Bill Treadwell chose the newsletter of September 23 to report on the status of the education program he had hammered out within a few months of his arrival in the fall of 1960. After five years of hands-on experience he could say with confidence, "We no longer are experimenting. We are sure of some things." From the record, there is no question that the church's education program at that point met the definition of the words Treadwell used to describe it: *dynamic* and *creative* it certainly was, and also quite effective if the many references in the weekly newsletter are any indication. Treadwell was ready to move toward enhancing the impact of the education program by involving more of the membership as leaders and workers. To that end he proposed a five-day churchmanship institute during which both a specialized clinic and a general lecture would be offered each night. The goal was to get across the message that each member occupied a special place in the life and work of the church above and beyond his own individual spiritual concerns.

Actually, the emphasis on churchmanship at this particular time seems to have been an example of inspired leadership much like the idea of corporate worship spelled out in the church's current publications. The practical ramifications of the idea, of course, included recruiting and training the sizable cadre of volunteer workers necessary to carry on the ever expanding education program of the church. According to the evaluation forms, the first churchmanship institute was a rousing success, and everyone believed it should join the church calendar as an annual event. Though no actual attendance figures were reported in the newsletter, one statement seems to sum up the general response of participants: "I think it does us good to meet together, to check ourselves, to learn new and better methods, and to receive inspiration." In an amusing juxtaposition, the very next item announced the retirement of two church workers. Obviously Bernice Penn and Bill Brabham had decided that their combined total of more than fifty years of teaching in the junior department of the Sunday school entitled them to a rest.

The second annual institute might have been a little more low-key, but it too was evidently quite effective. Dr. Theron Price of Furman delivered a series of lectures every Sunday afternoon in September 1966; the in-house clinics were also well attended.

As part of a report on special gifts beyond regular contributions, the pastor reported a balance in the building fund of nearly $175,000. Calling the spirit of the church "as refreshing as an oasis," Bowers speculated that the fund would reach $225,000 by the end of the year. The proposed budget for 1966 totaled $169,150, an increase of about

13 percent over the previous year, and contained a line item of $50,000 for the building fund.

Both Bowers and Treadwell attended a special seminar sponsored by the Louisville seminary for active pastors and ministers of education as 1965 drew to a close. Entitled "The Church in the Modern World," this seminar stressed pastoral counseling, an area that would grow in importance as the church continued to find its place in a changing American society.

The new year began with the exciting news that the 1965 budget had been oversubscribed by about $19,000 once the interest and dividends from invested building funds were added in. "You are to be congratulated," the pastor wrote, but he added a kicker with the words, "Let's begin now to exceed our 1966 budget!"

The church decided to create a new position—an associate in children's education—early in 1966. The expectation was that this person would be a young woman, not ordained but seminary trained, and preferably experienced in work with children from nursery level up. Seven areas of responsibility were specifically spelled out, but salary references were left vague ("commensurate with her training and experience"). The first applicant for this position, Mississippi native Charlotte Washington, was offered the job in May 1966 and reported for work in July. A recent seminary graduate with a master's degree in religious education, she accepted a salary of forty-five hundred dollars and fringe benefits.

When Bowers returned from his annual sojourn in the Northeast, he brought with him an update from the architect in Philadelphia. A few revisions to the preliminary plans had been made, he wrote, and "some fascinating suggestions about the communion table" discussed. Bowers promised an early report from the building committee after they had digested the new information.

First Baptist was recognized in a rather significant way when it received one of only ten invitations to an important conference sponsored by the Southern Baptist Theological Seminary in Louisville. Those churches chosen to participate were asked to send their pastor, the minister of education, and a strategic layman to join with their counterparts in deliberating possibly the most vital question of the twentieth century: how to make the Christian church relevant to a "man-centered, science-centered, materialistic age." Tom Wood was chosen for the layman's seat and assigned the job of reporting to the adult seminar group soon after his return.

No formal assessment of the conference made the newsletter, but a notice in the March 17 issue calling for at least twelve new workers might have been a direct result of its impact. The same article warned that at least thirty-eight new Sunday school teachers would be needed for youth classes as soon as the new building was ready, and the education minister wanted a training period of six months to a full year to prepare these workers for their tasks. Clearly these "training opportunities" were to be taken quite seriously. Treadwell's rhetoric very nearly carried him away as he described the situation:

> It is time for [Sunday school] class loyalty that grows into a confident pride that is expressed in the warm satisfaction of belonging to an adult class with depth enough and spirit enough to produce fine Christian adults and then to send them into a service mission on the firing lines of youth. [!!]

Nor was the seminary's renewal conference the only such movement within the denomination at that time. The results of another so-called "grass roots study" were reported in the *Baptist Standard* and reprinted in the newsletter of May 19. It seems that forty-one study groups affiliated with the Southern Baptist Convention had undertaken a two-year look at the work of the convention and proposed a number of changes for Baptist institutions in the decade beginning in 1970. The newsletter outlined eight key points from that study, all of which dealt with emerging social issues of the day, such as alcoholism and drug abuse, sex education, the needs of handicapped citizens, delinquency, church and state matters, health and education, interdenominational issues, divorce, and so on. Of particular interest is the fact that this remarkable document mentions the issue of race relations not at all. Still, the study could easily have been subtitled "The Baptist Denomination in Modern America." To paraphrase the words of Bob Dylan, "The times, they were a'changin'."

As 1966 wore on it became obvious that work on the new building had hit a snag of some sort. Bowers made a trip to Philadelphia in

May for the express purpose of discussing building plans with the architect, but nothing of substance appeared in the newsletter as week followed week into the summer. Finally, the matter was addressed in an item entitled "You Have Been Asking." The pastor was probably being intentionally vague when he wrote that "many things" had delayed the project, the most recent being "several problems of design" that had to be ironed out with the architect. He did express the belief that the change under way at that point would be the last, and the artists' concept when it finally emerged would be the one presented to the church for approval. A visit from Wagoner himself soon followed. The architect's visit in August might have been a little low-key—the words *interesting* and *profitable* were applied to his meeting with the building committee—but at least he came, and that alone was enough to reassure the church that the project was alive and well.

A special gift from "an anonymous friend" made possible the purchase of a twenty-five-bell carillon for the planned tower of the new building. By an odd twist of fate dating from 1939, the order for the instrument could be, and was, placed with the van Bergen Bell Foundry of Greenwood. The name had been a fixture in the town since the arrival of H. T. van Bergen, whom James C. Self recruited, along with the carillon his company exhibited at the New York World's Fair in 1939. Self had a particularly good reason for this interest: he was building a new church in his model mill village in South Greenwood and naming it to honor his mother. So thorough and so enthusiastic was he in this venture that he persuaded the bell-founder to accompany his product to make sure the installation in the tower he had personally designed was perfect.

Self must have made an offer van Bergen could not refuse, and Greenwood thereby gained a new family and a new business. The escalating war in Europe at that time must have been a factor as well; van Bergen was probably relieved on some level to be able to emigrate with his family from his native Holland about the time Hitler's armies were marching through the low countries. At any rate, he made Greenwood his home for the next forty years and practiced the fine art of casting, tuning, installing, and maintaining carillon bells until old age and ill health forced him to close the business in 1980.

The bells in the church tower would range from 44 to 3,200 pounds with diameters from 12 inches to 4 feet, 3 inches. Three would be large enough to be used as "church bells" in addition to their place in the carillon. Bowers was surely speaking for the entire membership when he wrote, "We shall enjoy [the instrument] for many years to come."

An architect's drawing of the new sanctuary, along with a rough floor plan, was included when the newsletter for November 10 was mailed to members. Unfortunately that drawing did not stay with the file copies and cannot be described here. Members were asked to study the plan and be prepared to vote on November 20. The vote, as usual, proved to be unanimous, and the architect was instructed to move on to large scale drawings. A period of six months was estimated to complete this work so that construction bids could be solicited. Members were reminded that the church needed to raise as much money as possible during this period. "The more we have in hand," the pastor wrote, "the less we have to borrow." Another sizable budget was proposed for the new year; the bottom line of $172,300 contained an item of $50,000 for the building fund. The minister termed 1966 "an excellent year in every way."

The church continued its resolute march toward meeting its financial obligations and completing its building program by oversubscribing the budget again in 1966. The first report in early January of the new year showed total revenue of $185,000 and an increase in assets to more than $737,000.

Though the subject of a full-fledged kindergarten ministry for the community at large was not mentioned in the long list of duties spelled out for the new children's worker, it came up during her first year on the job. Charlotte Washington, in fact, wrote the progress report detailing the work of a kindergarten committee that appeared in the newsletter of February 9. While not exactly lukewarm in tone, neither was the report wildly enthusiastic about the idea. Clearly the committee was at that point nowhere near ready to recommend that the church undertake such a venture at all, and definitely not in the coming fall. Parents were advised to enroll their children in one of the existing kindergarten programs rather than count on the church to take favorable action right away. But the subject came up again in a couple of interim reports during the year, with the result that by October the leadership had made the first moves toward entering the kindergarten ministry, probably by the fall of 1968.

The Mother's Day message in 1967 was another portent of things to come. The pastor noted what he saw as a "marked improvement in the observance of this day in our churches" from the time when it meant little more than "sweet sentimentality" that often led to feelings of remorse and guilt. Women's opportunities to influence society were improving, he mused in the newsletter, and the best way to honor them was to cheer them on their way to new and challenging service opportunities and new levels of responsibility. In the same vein, a commentator recently observed that the woman who worked for an official day to honor mothers, Anna Jarvis of Philadelphia, lived to regret it when Mother's Day in the United States degenerated into a sort of "Hallmark moment." Bowers saw that danger also and made his position known.

Other rumbles that year included a convention-sponsored study task force to deliberate on the "present situation of our colleges and seminaries and to project a program and philosophy for the future." Higher education, whether church-connected or not, was feeling the pressures and strains of the times, not only from the rising secularism of society in general, but also from anything that smacked of restraint, authority, and most of all the concept of *in loco parentis* as an institutional role.

While the pastor's visit to the architect in late May resulted in "not a great many new facts," Bowers was treated to "an interpretation of the building and the philosophy behind it," as well as assurances that it would be "a delightful building, though not an extravagant one." If he expected plans and specifications to go with the philosophy and assurances, he was disappointed. Those, it seemed, would not be forthcoming before the first of August. Still, if that schedule held, Bowers could visualize at least a start on the building before bad weather set in. The visit, he wrote, had been "truly exciting."

This timing was still on when the pastor made his next report in the middle of July, but the money question was looming large once again. Construction costs were high in 1967, and the architect had warned Bowers not to expect low bids. The word *low* was relative in any case, since the building was never understood to be a venture in economy. "We shall need much money in the next few months," the pastor warned. The $280,000 in the building fund suddenly seemed too little; Bowers wanted to make it $300,000 by the time bids were let. "What could you do about that?" he wondered in print, and he also asked members to begin thinking in terms of memorial gifts. An organ came to mind immediately, as well as chancel furniture and sanctuary windows.

The church approved a number of recommendations from the building planning committee, most of which had to do with the formalities of bidding and communications with the architect, in late September. By the middle of October invitations to bid had been mailed to twelve area contractors. Bids were to be received by the middle of November and a contract determined within an additional thirty days. As events intensified, so did the pastor's efforts to ensure that the church would not find itself facing a crushing load of debt after the new sanctuary was completed. The building fund at that point totaled about $290,000, and Bowers was convinced that with concentrated effort members could easily increase that to, say, $350,000 within the two months of the year remaining. Some people apparently believed the church should launch a full-fledged building campaign, while others viewed with pride the results of the policy of voluntary giving then in place. "What do you think?" the pastor asked in the newsletter. Then, in a remarkable short paragraph he probably answered his own question:

> At least, let us start now to make contributions to our building fund that will show our enthusiasm and interest in this project. We are all aware of our need for these new facilities. We all know that building costs are exceedingly high. But we all know, also, that our church meets every challenge presented to it. Let's amaze everyone with how well we finance our new project.

The newsletter for November 22 contains a three-line paragraph that begins, "Many meetings concerning our building are being held," and ends with the sentence, "Yes, the bids were high!" A few more details, this time including the phrase, "considerably higher than we were expecting," appeared the next week, and a week after that came the announcement of "a most important business meeting" on December 13, a Wednesday night. Both a proposed budget for 1968 (in a new format) and a discussion of the building proposal appear in the same issue.

Briefly, the budget, which the finance committee termed "challenging," primarily because the building program was incorporated within it rather than treated as a separate issue, represented an increase of about 30 percent over the previous year, but only 20 percent over actual receipts. That increase was deemed "well below the amount usually sought by churches during construction."

As for the building proposal, the low bid of $907,000 had once again been submitted by C. Y. Thomason Construction Company of Greenwood and covered the sanctuary alone, excluding "the garden wall and the stained glass windows." The plan was to borrow no more than $600,000 from local financial institutions on a fifteen-year note. That amount of debt was considered well within safe limits for the church and its potential liquidation about equal to the experience of the preceding fifteen years during which the church had built its assets to above the $1 million mark and still met its obligations in operating costs and missions activity. The report is clearly written, unambiguous, and nicely detailed, and the new budget format allowed comparison from one year to the next. The most significant difference, of course, was in the line item "Building Fund," which jumped from $50,000 to $100,000 in anticipation of a sort of "pay as you go" plan for building extras such as windows, carpeting, furniture, etc. over the next two years. The votes that day not only approved both budget and building without a dissenting voice, but First Baptist Church also elected to establish a brand new program: a kindergarten ministry for the Greenwood community to open the following year. The pastor noted that the two-year building project meant that a new sanctuary would be dedicated during the church's centennial year, 1970.

CHAPTER SIX

New Directions

(1968–1978)

The new year got under way with another groundbreaking ceremony when a large group gathered on the first Sunday of 1968 to watch church officials turn over the symbolic spadeful of earth at the site of the new sanctuary. In addition to the ministers and deacon chairman Ernest Norwood, those who participated were Tom Wood, chairman of the building planning committee; L. B. Adams, finance committee chairman; Gertrude Sanders, WMU president; Leland Stoddard, trustee chairman; and C. Y. Thomason Sr. and Jr., building contractors. Norwood, himself the great-grandson of two charter members, paid special tribute to those in attendance whose ancestors had been among the church's original members. As Bowers put it, "It was truly an exciting time . . . a great day in our church." He called for faith, courage, and most of all, wisdom as the work progressed.

When the finance committee made its report for the year just ended, members learned that the church had reached a new milestone: for the first time in history, its revenue had topped the $200,000 mark, exceeding the budget by $28,000.[1] The building fund balance was very healthy as well at $340,000.

Plans for the kindergarten program scheduled to open in the fall moved ahead in the early months of 1968. Workers were recruited, space needs determined, and a statement of philosophy and purpose hammered out as the year unfolded. The determination to serve both four- and five-year-olds was made early; the plan was to open enrollment to the children of members by February 15 and to others in the community after April 1. Jo Ann (Burgess) Stevenson was named the first director, but pregnancy forced her to withdraw her name only a few months later. She was replaced by Barbara Byrd Chandler, whose winning personality and years of teaching experience made her an ideal candidate for the position.

As the foundations of the new sanctuary were being laid with, in Bowers's words, the sort of "precise exactness" upon which the "shape, strength, and precision" of the entire building depended, the church was also beginning to look, no doubt somewhat uncomfortably, at emerging social issues in the community at large. The focus in February was on the race question, specifically exploring how Christians might learn to face and deal with their own prejudices. In addition to their own leaders, church members heard from Dr. John Murdoch, chairman of the Greenwood Human Relations Committee, who spoke about the racial climate and attitudes in Greenwood, and Circuit Judge Francis Nicholson, whose topic was law and behavior. These programs were presented as part of the series entitled "Tangled World," an in-depth study of vital issues of the day. Other speakers and topics were Mayor John Nave, who took on the subject of the church and local politics, and Congressman Bryan Dorn, who spoke on international affairs. One session even dipped a tentative toe in the waters of civil disobedience, then among the most disturbing signs of the times.

Another interesting and possibly revealing venture undertaken in early 1968 was a merger of the church's RA (Royal Ambassador) program and the Boy Scouts of America. The two organizations actually were more alike than they were different, but local leaders were convinced that the outdoor emphasis of the Scouts was more appealing, and possibly more meaningful, than the RA's mission-centered program as sponsored by the Baptist conventions. The church moved slowly and deliberately, "with much study and conversation," toward merging the two groups into one, a full-fledged Boy Scout troop sponsored by the church and with a program of religious emphasis under the God and Country Award that was already part of the Boy Scout program. Evidently nobody objected to this commonsense move.

In a similar vein, the church reprinted a section from the report on the state's first conference on early childhood education as a preliminary to the kindergarten ministry then in the planning stage. Fourteen benefits of a sound program were listed in the newsletter, all of them pertinent to the church's first venture into a whole new area. At the same time the church was working with Main Street Methodist and First Presbyterian churches to bring a learning program to four- and five-year-olds living in the Town House Apartments[2] complex within the city limits. The plan through the summer months was to provide instruction for two hours on Mondays, Wednesdays, and Fridays to a target group of about a hundred youngsters, none of whom could be expected to be part of the kindergarten enrollment.

With the coming of spring, the steel for the framework of the new building began to arrive at the site. Most of the work accomplished to that point seemed to be hidden, and the pastor was delighted that the steelwork would finally give people something to look at. And look they did as the weeks passed. By the middle of May, an outline of the building's ultimate shape could be discerned. Expenditures, too, were accelerating rapidly, and the pastor felt it necessary to remind members that a larger increase over the previous year's revenues would be necessary to keep pace with the contractor's invoices. The goal this time was something of a negative: not to have to rely on borrowed money before September 1.

The church celebrated the twenty-fifth anniversary of Bowers's pastorate on September 1, 1968, by, in the words of the deacon chairman, "rededicating ourselves to the successful achievement of the various organizations of the church with which each of us is associated." As further evidence of its love and appreciation, the church presented the Bowerses with a silver service meant to symbolize the quality of the services the pastor had rendered to the church. Chairman Ernest Norwood pointed out that his tenure, longer than that of any previous minister, had amounted to more than a quarter of the church's existence. He also referred to the date of Bowers's appointment as "the most important date in the history of the church," a singular compliment indeed.

Even as the church officially recognized this significant moment, it was also forced to take notice of the war in Vietnam and its effects on the home front. The newsletter regularly listed a "serviceman of the week," and a group called the waiting wives club (those whose husbands were serving in Vietnam) was formed. One of the projects of this club was to collect supplies for civilian refugee groups in the war zone. Study groups, too, tried to understand both the war and the increasing resistance to it. Clearly, the issues were no longer black and white; even so, it is probably safe to state that no one was prepared for the far-reaching changes in American society the war would produce.

And still the walls of the new building rose, stone by large stone, around its steel framework. A note in the newsletter of August 28 describes the work site: "The stone masons will begin work in full force next Tuesday. One mason is here now and the familiar ring of the chisel is constant." Another physical change in the landscape came when a large play area was fenced off on the back lawn. Inside the fence were a playhouse and other equipment meant primarily for the new kindergarten but also to be used by other church groups. All was in readiness for the orientation and open house set for August 30, followed by a regular schedule of early childhood classes beginning on September 3. Only nineteen children enrolled the first year, which meant the program had to be subsidized by the church, but everyone believed the school would grow to be self-supporting (except for equipment expense) within two or three years. The first year ended on a happy note with an open house for families and friends of the students. Bill Treadwell praised the work and spirit of the program in the newsletter of June 4, 1969. Even so, the church decided it needed a special committee to study the advisability of continuing the kindergarten ministry.

The business session held in November covered two important topics: the regular budget proposed for 1969 and the matter of equipping the new building, the latter a question that was looming ever larger as the building progressed. The budget itself held no surprises—indeed, it projected an increase of less than 2 percent—but the building extras were another matter entirely. It seems that a number of items previously thought suitable for the new sanctuary were finally deemed (by someone) either improper or inadequate. Still, the various committees had agreed to honor the original estimate of $200,000 to cover such things as windows, a new organ and pianos, carpeting, sound and other equipment, furniture, and landscaping. It remained to be seen, of course, whether this limitation could be met while providing for the needs of a large and growing church program.

Two interesting asides to the building activity occurred during the last half of 1968 when the chief architect, Harold Wagoner, was elected a Fellow of the American Institute of Architects, and Dr. Bowers was invited to speak to the American Society for Church Architecture on the influence of modern theology on church architecture. These events were surely proof, if such proof were needed, of the position of First Baptist Church in the mainstream of American life, at least where churches and their architecture were concerned.

The pastor's message to his flock as the new year began was a call to accept the challenges inherent in every new beginning. He urged members to expand their interests, to discover some new area of life and learn about it, to seek out new people and try to understand them. He also suggested trying for maximums rather than minimums in church life, attending worship services with expectation rather than as a duty, and most of all, giving, not as if gifts were dues, obligations and debts, but rather to provide a program of which each giver could feel an integral part.

The first mention of stained glass windows for the new sanctuary appeared in the newsletter of January 22. Evidently decisions regarding style, type, and manufacturer had been made much earlier, since the notice revealed that the contract had been let the previous month. The supplier was Willet, the same company that had made the chapel windows, but the differences in the two styles could hardly have been more marked. These would be created through a relatively new process called "faceted glass windows" consisting of bits of glass of varying color, size, and thickness set in an epoxy that would blend in color with other building materials. There would be twenty so-called "aisle windows," ten pairs along either side of the nave, and seventy-two clerestory windows along the top of the building just under the roof line. The aisle windows would contain symbols depicting the parables, while the others were meant merely to add their color and shape to the overall design of the building. Both types were offered as memorial opportunities, the larger for $1,350 each and the others, $250. One, in memory of Clayton Beaudrot, had already been subscribed. Another was purchased by the Robert Seymour family in memory of Mr. and Mrs. J. W. Sproles.

The cornerstone for the new building was laid on March 30, Palm Sunday, with the entire congregation looking on. The pastor pronounced it "a great occasion." As for the construction itself, Bowers was able to report in early April that preparation for the plaster work was nearly complete. In addition, the bells for the carillon tower were delivered from the foundry. "Things are moving," he wrote, "and it is exciting to see the progress." Contributions, alas, were not faring nearly so well. First quarter receipts were about three thousand dollars *below* the previous year, when they needed to be considerably above that figure.

The window lumieres (an architect's word for a small-scale replica of a stained glass window drawn on paper) arrived in April for final approval. It is hard not to wonder if anyone was taken aback at the time by what they saw. Even though the design follows the Gothic model of a pointed arch, albeit in a somewhat narrow and elongated form, there is nothing remotely traditional about these windows. Thoroughly modern in materials, conception and execution, they describe the parables on one side and miracles on the other in images not readily discernible as pictures. The images are almost like 3-D puzzles in that a form will emerge, but only after a certain intense scrutiny. The colors, on the other hand, are as vibrant and intense as any lover of stained glass could wish, and the shape and height of the windows do serve to emphasize the soaring sweep of the sanctuary.

That "sweep" was evident also in a progress report a few months later when the pastor noted that the sanctuary area was "so full of scaffolding one [could] hardly tell what [was] going on up above." Considering the amount of detailed work in the finished structure, that statement is hardly surprising. It is also interesting, and not at all surprising, that a safety warning had to be issued in October about children climbing in and around the building on the scaffolding, on stairs without rails, and most of all, in an almost irresistible tower where ladders leaned invitingly against walls. The warning was meant primarily for children nine to twelve years old. It seems that the unfinished building was in danger of becoming, in legal terms, an "attractive nuisance." Stonemasons estimated that their work would be completed sometime in August; but as for an overall completion date, the answer was always simply, "We do not know at this time." Memorial gifts, while unsolicited as such, were being made all the time, among them a communion table and a pulpit Bible.

In spite of questions raised in certain quarters about the feasibility of continuing the kindergarten program, the ad hoc committee appointed to study the question brought a positive report. According to the newsletter of July 23, the committee's recommendation to continue the program was based as much on the church's public commitments to pupils, parents, and the community as on any hope that the venture might become a break-even proposition financially. The recommendation covered only the year 1969–1970 during which time the standing committee would review the situation. Thus the program gained a one-year reprieve. But two years was to be it for the kindergarten. Citing a lack of need, and noting also a lack of interest on the part of church parents, the deacons accepted the recommendation of the kindergarten committee not to offer the program for the school year 1970–1971. Committee members also suggested that they restudy the question at least every two years so as to be ready to respond when and if the situation changed.

The bombshell of Bill Treadwell's resignation fell in the late summer of 1969. The third paragraph of his open letter to the church set forth the reasons for this difficult decision:

> As many of you know, it has been my conviction for some time that I should travel down some other roads of ministry. The smaller church has long had its appeal, and graduate work in the related fields of education has been a dream often discussed.

Treadwell left to become pastor of the First Baptist Church in Jefferson, Georgia, eventually to enter graduate school at the University of Georgia. There may be a between-the-lines message in the paragraph that followed in the same newsletter; if so, it is too faint to discern at the remove of nearly thirty years. Certainly Treadwell had been the most visible of the church's various associate ministers, and by far the most influential, but whether he had managed to offend in some way is impossible to determine from the record. The following paragraph is entirely bland:

> The entire congregation will be surprised, we are sure, by the letter from Bill Treadwell that appears elsewhere in the newsletter. We will be commenting on this later but must say we regret to lose Bill, but feel that he must be free to follow what he believes to be God's will for his life. The church will act formally on his letter next Sunday morning in a very brief called business meeting at the worship hour.

The all-church picnic that year included a recognition of the Treadwell family and statements of appreciation for his nine years of service. And a declaration of faith, or manifesto, which obviously owed a great deal to the influence of Bill Treadwell, was read by Donna Byrd the following Sunday on behalf of the senior high young people of the church.

In the first ever dedication service for an infant, young Gregg, infant son of Mr. and Mrs. Kenneth Jennings, was the honoree at a small service held in the chapel in October 1969. The pastor made his position clear: "We feel that such services are significant and we encourage others to think in terms of services of dedication for their children." Baptists are notoriously opposed to infant baptism, but dedication services for families and their new offspring are routine and charming events at First Baptist Church today. This move was further evidence that the church felt comfortable breaking, or at least bending, tradition.

The association letter in 1969 showed membership of 1,324 with a Sunday school totaling 1,099 members and a Training Union/seminar group of 211. These figures are not awe inspiring; in fact, many show a sizable decrease from earlier years. Expenditures during this high profile year, however, were more than $500,000, much of which came from the building fund balance. A related item in the newsletter reveals the church's giving pattern by family unit. Nearly 18 percent of church families had made no contribution at all to the budget that year, while another 41 percent, the largest group, gave $100 or less. Only one family had contributed more than $3,000. It seems almost impossible to believe, but this pattern of support is not at all unusual in church and other charitable giving.

A unique and unexpected gift was announced in the newsletter of November 5. A special window designed for the south wall of the tower was donated personally by Crosby Willet, president of the Willet Studios. The gift was in honor of the architect, Harold Wagoner, and Jim Bowers; the window depicts the architect at his drawing board and the minister in the pulpit. Some say that if one looks closely a golf ball can be discerned as well.

The church lost its children's director when Charlotte Washington resigned in November in favor of a similar position at the First Baptist Church in Greenville.[3] Her three years had been full of productive activity, including a greatly expanded program of summer activity for children and also a full-fledged, if unfortunately short-lived, kindergarten.

The financial picture at the end of the year was not inspiring. Explaining that the church was some $42,000 short of its goal, Bowers assured members that operating expenses had been fully met; the shortfall was in the categories of special missions and building expense. But the very first newsletter of 1970 contained the good news that about $67,000 had been collected for budget items in the month of December, a circumstance that enabled the church to meet a full 94 percent of the largest budget it had ever adopted. In a coincidence not likely to be overlooked by the pastor, the church had exceeded its previous year's revenue by 8 percent, and the budget for 1970 was projected at 8 percent above that for 1969. No wonder he could write, "Your cooperation is truly fabulous."

It all started when a membership study group was appointed by the board of deacons to consider four questions: (1) Who shall be accepted? (2) What are the qualifications for membership? (3) What are our responsibilities? and (4) What shall we ask of a new member? Nineteen men and women of the church, whose ages ranged from twenty-five to eighty years, met weekly for about six months to hammer out their recommendations to the church based on the answers to these four questions. The first mention of this committee appeared in a newsletter in the month of March 1970, after its recommendations had been received and approved by the deacons. The fact that the committee's report was delivered in three sessions is in itself a strong indication of the seriousness of the issues. And the issues were indeed serious, reaching at once into two sacrosanct areas of southern religious life: race and the form of baptism. "There has been some misinformation about the report . . . ," the pastor wrote, doubtless in something of an understatement, but he was confident that a series of discussion sessions would soon set matters right with the membership.

The full report of the membership study committee, plus some background on its makeup and its deliberations, made up page 2 of the newsletter of March 11. Clearly the pastor recognized the potential for conflict contained in the committee's report and wanted to provide ample opportunity for questions and discussion among the members. It is probably significant that the report had not been adopted unanimously by the deacons; two had dissented, and the rest had felt the need to present the matter to the church in the form of seminars. Church leaders were equally clearly prepared to hold these forums "as needed or desired" until every member understood the ramifications of the proposal. "Read this report carefully," the pastor wrote, "*taking time to see what is really said*" [emphasis added].

What was really said in the membership study report amounted to a repudiation of not one, but two, popularly held positions at that time—one a southern custom of long standing, and the other as close to Baptist "dogma" as a dogma-free denomination can come. Not only was the church effectively ending its de facto "whites only" membership policy by stating its only criterion for membership to be "faith in Jesus Christ . . . and experience of God," but it was also proposing to end its insistence on baptism by immersion as a requirement for accepting members from other denominations. Baptist heresy indeed, and an open challenge to Southern Baptist institutions from the conventions to the local association. Response would not be long in coming, but in the interim, life went on, and the newsletter continued its policy of chatting about flowers in the sanctuary, members in the hospital, WMU meetings, and so on. Easter came and went; the church joined other community institutions in various activities; work continued on the building; and adult seminars were quietly scheduled and well attended as week followed week.

When members decided they were ready, the meetings were ended, and chairman Boykin Curry accepted commendations for the manner

The Reverend Jerry Keeney, Associate Minister, Pastoral Services and Youth, 1970–1975.

in which he had led the discussions. Another full page of the newsletter was devoted to answering questions about the proposed change in baptism requirements alone. The way was cleared for an up or down vote by the church on April 26, 1970. The vote would be by secret ballot; a sample, with explanations, was run in the newsletter of April 22.

The result of the vote probably surprised no one. The question that removed race as a criterion for membership passed by a margin of 58 percent to 42 percent, while the baptism question came in at a clear 60 percent to 40 percent split. A full quarter of voting members objected to the third question, which dealt with new member orientation. Immediately obvious was the fact that quite a strong minority had voted in opposition to all the proposed changes. Church leaders would need to proceed carefully to safeguard their hard-won victory and turn the holdouts to their way of thinking. Bowers put it this way: "[T]ogether we shall work to make our church strong and spiritual, so that it may be a source of strength and truth in our community, elevating the Christ to the best of our ability, which is our primary task."

In the meantime, a progress report on the new building seemed in order. The stonework was virtually complete, except for the crab orchard paving stone for the aisles, the chancel, the porches, and the steps. Painting was well along; the scaffolding was slowly coming down as work on the tower section was completed; and the slate roof was nearly finished. Such problems as remained were concerned primarily with furnishings. Contracts could not be let without sufficient funds in hand, and the giving pattern of members was such that the early months of a budget year allowed for very slim pickings. "This year," Bowers pleaded, "let's not wait so late to give generously."

Another item in a newsletter about this time concerned the church staff, or more accurately, the lack of church staff. Bowers had been the whole thing, in fact, since Treadwell's departure the previous September and Washington's only two months later. The personnel committee, however, had not been idle; two names were presented to the deacons as replacements. J. Russell Comer, of Greenville First Baptist Church, and Jerry Keeney, from Durham, North Carolina, were proposed as associate ministers in religious education and pastoral services and youth respectively. Both were fully qualified at the master's level, and both were family men. No one will be surprised to learn that, while Comer was to be paid exactly what Treadwell had earned, Keeney's salary would be a good deal more than Ms. Washington's. Both men accepted the church's call and reported for work in June, just in time to fill the pulpit in the pastor's absence.

The Reverend Russ Comer, Associate Minister, Religious Education, 1970–1978.

Though the newsletter took no notice until July, the reaction to the church's historic stand on membership requirements began as word filtered out even before the vote was taken. An article in the *Baptist Courier* of June 18 credited Bowers with the idea to dispense with what he called the dogmatic insistence on a single form of baptism for church members. Though he held to his own belief that only immersion was truly "biblical," Bowers also thought his church should not challenge the validity of other people's Christian experiences.

"We could become . . . a stumbling block rather than a help to those to whom we would minister," he said. According to the article, the Abbeville Association planned to appoint a committee to study the action and bring a report within two months "so that if the church's relationship to the association will be affected, we can . . . at least be aware of it before the fall meeting." First Baptist was the second largest church among the forty-four in the association,[4] and though the Greenwood church was the first in South Carolina to take this step, the action was not unheard of in other states. Three Charlotte churches had done the same thing, as had churches in both Arkansas and California, within the previous three years. The local association had withdrawn fellowship in all these cases, though the Southern Baptist Convention and state conventions continued to seat messengers sent from their congregations.

As it turned out the Abbeville Association was unmoved by the church's desire to remain a member. It had already heard from Boykin Curry at a session in May when he defended the church's action in a strong and clear position statement:

> We would like a few more minutes . . . to make some statements that we hope may enable you to understand our adoption of these recommendations. This will not be an effort to debate the issue or to change the mind of anyone. But we are most anxious that you understand our position before you vote on the proposal to exclude us from the fellowship of this Association.
>
> 1. This was not a decision that was made hastily or carelessly—the Committee studied these questions weekly for 6 months—the deacons then considered the report for several months—and the membership then considered these questions in seminars and study groups before making a final decision. We feel we have made the right decision.
> 2. We were not led into this position by our pastor. We asked Jim Bowers to attend our meetings because we respect his judgment but this was a *group* discussion and a *group* conclusion. We all agreed these sessions were a great experience for us because we learned to discuss controversial and highly emotional issues in a very frank and candid way without becoming personal or angry.

3. We are puzzled by the reaction of some of you to our decision. A statement, agreed to by a number of you, recognizes our right to take this position but warns if we exercise this right we shall be "excommunicated." How is this different from the father who tells his daughter she has the right to choose her own mate but that if he disapproves of her choice she will be disinherited? Frankly, this doesn't sound like Baptist Freedom to us.
4. Why this decision on baptism? There was only one reason for it—to eliminate families with a divided membership. More than ever before, young people are crossing denominational lines in selecting a life partner. In many cases, both husband and wife have *strong* feelings about their Christian experience and commitment. We propose to waive the requirement for immersion *only* when the individual does have such strong feelings and resents the requirement of immersion. We feel the united family is more important than the absolute requirements of this symbolic act. We do not think this is an "un-Baptist" or an "anti-Baptist" position. Really, we feel this is permitting someone, with whom we disagree, to enjoy a basic Baptist Freedom.
5. We are interested in noting that we have heard no criticism of our statement on race. To be quite honest with you, the racial issue caused more concern among us than the requirement on immersion. We hope it is correct to assume you are ahead of us on the race issue.
6. We think our action is in complete accord with the basic Baptist principle that each person has the *individual freedom* and the *individual responsibility* to interpret for himself the scriptures under the leadership of the Holy Spirit. We do not think any Baptist has the right or the duty to attempt to enforce conformity.
7. And finally—let me express again the sincere hope that you will not dismiss us from this Association because you disagree with us. For in disagreement, we need each other more than when we are in agreement. However, if you do decide to dismiss us, we will accept this decision although we do not feel we have "sinned."

But, in any event, we assure you of our continuing love and support.

When the pastor found time to respond to the uproar, he did so in a long article in the newsletter of July 8. "We did not intend such publicity," he wrote, but both the religious and the secular press had taken notice when the association committee was appointed, and the race was on. The pastor lamented that he had been grossly misquoted in some articles, though on the whole the reports had been accurate. The basis of contention seemed to be that some association members believed the church had no right to do what it had done. Others, however, agreed with First Baptist that the principle of local autonomy was every bit as important as the manner of receiving members. The biggest surprise for Bowers had been in the number of personal letters, telegrams, and telephone calls praising the church for its stand, calling it a "breath of fresh air," one that would surely foster more love, openness, and understanding among Christians. Only a very few opposed the move; one Colorado Baptist saw it as "a stumbling block to your fellow Baptists." Bowers ended the article in characteristically mild terms:

> We know that such issues are not decided by public reaction, but we do feel that you should know that the criticisms you may have heard are only one part of the reaction. Our purpose is not to antagonize or to gloat but to inform you of a widespread and spontaneous reaction.

Though the executive committee of the Abbeville Association adopted a statement by one member of the subcommittee appointed to study the church's recent action on baptism, that statement merely confirmed both the general Baptist position of immersion and the autonomy of local churches. It was not therefore accepted as a clear-cut policy decision. Besides, as Bowers pointed out, the association's constitution contained no provision for expelling a church, and such action would surely require a properly executed constitutional amendment. One paragraph in this article is so illustrative of the church's, or at least the pastor's, confidence and serenity regarding this issue that it deserves to be quoted in full:

> One other thing should be clarified. While there are many in the association who would like to take "punitive action" (which we

> assume, means excluding our church from the association) there are others who feel that we have this right and are seeking to prevent such drastic steps. We have no guess as to what the association will do. We only hope that all people, Baptists and others, will realize that being a Baptist entails far more than being immersed. We also hope that the fundamental tenet of the autonomy of the local church will be magnified. (We do not deny the autonomy of the association, either.)

Clearly there would be no backing down by the church. The ball was now in the association's court; the next move would be up to them.

Readers will have noticed by this time that the full furor in the ranks of South Carolina Baptists was all directed at the issue of the form of baptism recognized by local churches. The far more telling question of opening membership to people of "the other race" was mentioned not at all (except in Curry's statement to the association). The church did bring up a related issue, which it called the new "unitary system" in the public schools (the dreaded term *integration* was not used, probably as a nod to political correctness), once when it showed a documentary film the Greenville school system had produced on the subject, and again in September to commend the "smooth change" the Greenwood schools had achieved.

In a "surprise announcement" the membership learned from the newsletter of September 23 that the Mathews Foundation, part of the Self family network of philanthropies, wished to purchase pews and carpet for the main floor of the sanctuary. This was a boon indeed; the building committee had resigned itself for financial reasons to moving the pews from the old sanctuary to the new, at least temporarily. The gift of $35,000 would cover the full cost of both pews and carpeting, which meant that church funds would be freed for other expenses in connection with the new building. The pastor expressed his and the church's appreciation in a glowing paragraph, in the center of which was the sentence, "It [the gift] is all the more significant since it was entirely unsolicited." Still, the interest and generosity of the Self family in projects of this kind was well-known in Greenwood and elsewhere, and it is probably safe to assume that members of First Baptist were not at all surprised to learn of the foundation's largess.

As the last quarter of 1970 began, the pastor reminded members that the financial needs for the next three months would be the greatest in fourteen years. The building would be formally accepted as complete in a few weeks' time and upon final payment of about $50,000; the chancel furniture bill would total about $12,000; and the church had to meet a $4,300 monthly loan payment, all of this over and above its normal operating costs. When the pastor wrote, "We need your help," he could specify exactly how and why. He appealed for funds again in early December, but this time the tone was more urgent and the figures quoted lower than before; for example, the final payment would be $45,000 (perhaps there had been an interim payment of $5,000), and the chancel furniture came in at $11,000, not $12,000 as reported in October. The pastor also felt he needed to remind members that the amounts paid out for the building were *not* increases over the funds originally approved as some members apparently thought.

The Abbeville Association had made no official decision on the church's membership and baptism policy as late as October; indeed, a session of its centennial year fall meeting was scheduled for October 15 at First Baptist Church Greenwood. But the last sentence in the item announcing the meetings was ominous: "Very probably some will bring before the association the action taken by our church with regard to our new policy of receiving members from other denominations."

Exactly that happened on October 16 at the association meeting in Calhoun Falls when the group voted to withdraw fellowship from the Greenwood church. The twenty deacons and more than forty others who attended on behalf of the congregation were probably not at all surprised when the matter was brought up, but they surely expected a period of deliberation before the vote. Bowers chose to respond in the newsletter of October 21. He attempted, again, to clear up the misconception that the church had "done away with immersion" with these words:

> WE HAVE NOT DONE AWAY WITH IMMERSION as a church. All candidates who come on profession of faith will be immersed. Some who come from other denominations will be. Those, however, who have strong convictions about their Christian experience and baptism will not be required to be immersed. We will continue to contribute to

the Baptist causes of missions, education and benevolence as we have in the past. We will still avail ourselves of the services of the literature and materials of the Southern Baptist Convention.

As for the action that expelled the church, his response was strong and clear:

We feel the meeting on Friday night was completely out of order. The Executive Committee had studied the matter and stated that the constitution made no provision for action in regard to our church. If action was to be taken, it should be by amendment to the constitution. This would have required reading the amendments this year and acting on them next year. This report (and we believe the constitution) was ignored. We feel *Robert's Rules of Order* (the parliamentary manual for the body) was ignored. However, it was perfectly obvious that some 15 or 20 of the pastors were determined to accomplish this withdrawal by any means. This unofficial group of pastors had met on several occasions to plan how to do it. When their previously arranged motion to exclude us "on the spot" was presented, the moderator ruled it out of order, since it violated the constitution. He had informed the group previously that he would do this, which indicates that his decision was not on the spur of the moment, but well thought out. An appeal was made and his decision was overridden. We were excluded by two-thirds of one vote. One hundred fifty-three and one-third was required and the vote was 154–76.

We regret the spirit and the tactics of the meeting. We regret the action taken. However we must remember that THEIR DECISION does not mean that we are not Baptists. We are still the First Baptist Church of Greenwood and feel that we are more in line with the Baptist spirit and tradition than many who voted for expulsion.

In an unusual move, this time the pastor signed the item; the initials *JAB* appear at the end of the article.

The church's participation in South Carolina's tricentennial celebration in 1970 took the form of helping with the distribution of *Good News for Modern Man*, a translation of the New Testament in modern

English, which was to be given to every consenting person in the state. The church's share in this endeavor was to place at least 1,500 copies of the book in the hands of residents in a specific part of town. The expectation was that 16,000 copies would be distributed in Greenwood County alone.[5] More than fifty members volunteered for the church's share in the task, which the newsletter pronounced "most successful."

The pastor had hoped to be able to hold at least one service in the new sanctuary before the end of the year, but that turned out to be impossible. It seems the manufacturer had run into difficulty finding the right white oak for the pews, and the delivery date had to be changed to January. The carpet, however, was in the process of installation, and final odds and ends of work were being wrapped up. "We begin to realize," the pastor wrote, "how beautiful the building will be when complete."

The prospects for occupancy became much clearer in early 1971, and Bowers was able to use the word *definite* three times in the first couple of sentences of a progress report in the newsletter of January 6. "The pews," he wrote confidently, "will arrive on Monday and be installed next week." The organ company, too, was ready with a precise delivery date—February 22—which meant the instrument would surely be playable by Easter. And the deacons would decide when the first service could be scheduled.

Thanks in large part to the Mathews Foundation gift, receipts came to within five thousand dollars of the budget for 1970. The new budget, which actually proposed only a slight increase, would still require extra effort on the part of members because, as the pastor wrote, "We cannot count on outside gifts for next year." A copy of the proposed budget for 1971 was included in the records for that year. The bottom line was inching ever nearer the quarter million dollar mark, but the capital portion now contained only the items "debt retirement" and "equipment," the total of which was fully 10 percent below the amount entered under the old category of "Building Fund."

The date the deacons set for entering the new sanctuary was April 4, Palm Sunday. There is no real explanation for what seems to be a rather delayed entry. Perhaps the deacons felt it would be imprudent to use the facility before formally accepting it from the contractor; indeed, Bowers seemed to be allowing for the possibility that "a few exceptions" might still be on the table when the building was turned over at some point between February 17 and April 4. Even so, Palm Sunday must have seemed a particularly appropriate time, and many friends and former members were expected for the occasion. Never one to miss an opportunity, Bowers announced a few weeks later that members should make a point of recognizing and celebrating the "many varied experiences" connected with the temporary sanctuary which had served the church for nearly fifteen years. He promised a "most fitting time of worship together" in the old space for the last two Sundays before the move to new quarters. Who could resist his call for a large attendance and an "attitude of grateful memory" for all the temporary sanctuary[6] had meant to the church.

The comprehensive plan for Holy Week was revealed in the newsletter of March 24. Bowers's understated line, "Things are shaping up nicely" was quite inadequate to describe a week that was to begin with Palm Sunday services coupled with the dedication of the building. Dedication of the carillon would follow that afternoon, and Sunday night was reserved for dedication of the windows with Harold Wagoner and Crosby Willet as speakers. Civic night would be on Monday, while Tuesday services would feature other Greenwood churches. Dedication of the new organ would happen on Wednesday; a communion service would follow on Thursday; and Friday's services would stress denominational night with Dr. Harold Cole, executive secretary of the state Baptist convention, as speaker. The Reverend Wade Burton from Woodfields and Connie Maxwell's Dr. Sam Smith would also speak. Youth night would be on Saturday, and two services on Easter Sunday morning would bring a very special observance of Holy Week to conclusion.

Bowers held forth in his usual warm fashion in the newsletter of April 7, which fell in the middle of the week of celebration. One sentence was truly inspired: "We had thought the building was beautiful but the real beauty did not become apparent until it was filled with people." The same issue announced a number of memorial gifts the church had received for the new building. The pulpit Bible came from Mrs. James Bobo in memory of her husband, and Edgar Davis honored the memory of his parents with a gift of antependia (book marks and pulpit drop).[7] Members of the Bowers family gave a new

The Sanctuary, Phase Two completed, c. 1972.

robe and three sets of stoles for the ministers. New choir robes were made possible by a number of donors. In addition to expressing appreciation for these very visible items used in the worship service itself, the pastor did not overlook the hard work of the church staff and volunteer members who helped in more mundane ways. The whole church complex, old and new, received a sort of "spring cleaning" in preparation for crowds of visitors, and members also prepared and served refreshments at more than one after-service reception. "The list of things done is long—long," the pastor wrote, and "the people who have helped are many." He expressed in a charming turn of phrase "endless thanks" and called the words inadequate.

The Weston Chapel AME Church purchased the pews from the old sanctuary for five thousand dollars, a price that seemed to satisfy everybody. The church planned to refurbish the Great Hall as a multipurpose space—the chancel area would soon become a stage—but would start using it immediately. As a matter of fact, several youth activities were already scheduled for the room. But the term "Great Hall" was not destined to survive; by May the space was being called simply the (uncapitalized) fellowship hall, and a fund-raising drive to furnish it with folding tables, chairs, and recreational equipment was under way. The goal was two thousand dollars; about half of that amount was in hand by the end of the month. Minister of education Russ Comer explained many months later that his intention in naming the room was to remind young people of visits to a North Carolina retreat where one of the meeting spaces was called the Great Hall. When Comer learned that the name, in his words, "suggested too many things to other people," he readily agreed to the change. The assumption is that many members were put off by what they regarded as pretension.

The halfway point of the first year in the new sanctuary was clearly a mixed bag. The pastor cited roughly equal pluses and minuses when he assessed the church's position near the end of June 1971. One notable shortcoming was in budget revenue; only \$83,000—less than 35 percent—of the goal of \$238,000 had come in. Bowers blamed the shortfall on the summer slump that seemed to hit every year. A line from his August 11 message sums up the situation: "We operated very much in the red last month." The question of finance would plague the church all year. Perhaps it is not surprising that actually using the new building week after week was a bit less exciting than the anticipation before the fact. Members' giving habits might have suffered from a similar feeling of anticlimax after the urgency of meeting construction bills had subsided. Whatever the reasons, the pastor called 1971 "our most difficult year financially" and reported a budget shortfall of about $100,000 as late as November. Underscoring the note of concern was a letter from L. B. Adams, chairman of the finance committee, who urged members to give priority to the needs of the church so that "next year will be more comfortable."

Routine contributions to the budget might have been a little slow in 1971, but memorial gifts to pay for the new windows arrived with pleasing regularity. More than thirty donors, some of whom had given more than one of the small clerestory windows, were announced in August.[8] In addition, only five of the lancet (aisle) windows (defined as tall narrow windows set in lancet, or narrow pointed, arches) remained as memorial opportunities. As always, some donors preferred anonymity.

As the year wore on, it is revealing to note that the mission emphasis of the church centered more and more on needs within the Greenwood community where more and more facilities seemed to exist, among them the Taylor Nursing Home (now NHC Healthcare) on East Cambridge Avenue, the Methodist Home, the Anna Lewis Home in Ninety Six which became the Brewer Boarding Home, and Self Memorial Hospital. Most of the women's organizations named a mission action chairman through whom their activities could be coordinated for optimal effect. Beginning with visits to shut-ins, this type of ministry expanded greatly to include gifts of all types, as well as amenities for games, nature projects, and other activities to bring joy and pleasure to the residents and patients. Much of this activity was reported in the newsletter. The "Meals on Wheels" program, now an agency serving hundreds of county citizens with meal preparation and delivery, also had its beginnings during this period. A notice in the newsletter of March 29, 1972, sought clients, volunteers, and contributions to get this venture, which began as a ministry of the Greenwood Senior Center, off the ground. Another reminder of the way things were in the early 1970s was the notice that church women continued to fill "ditty bags" for servicemen overseas. Though no one talked much about it, at least in the church newsletter, Vietnam was still very much an issue in American life.

Still another activity, this time in the educational realm, was the churchmanship institute which featured a series of lectures by Greenwood's own Dr. Bob Seymour. His topic, the Four Faces of the Church—Worship, Education, Fellowship of Reconciliation, and Ministry—found eager audiences for four straight evenings in September 1971. Another seminar, this one on contemporary religious enthusiasts, provided insights into current religious expression, some of which must have been quite controversial. The pastor was careful to note that not all of these views were "endorsed by any manner of means." Still, he did hope that knowing what was being said and done in the name of religious practice would help members to understand better their own roles in the church. Readers will remember that the churchmanship institute and similar ventures had been inaugurated by Bill Treadwell as early as 1965.

Part-time secretary Rebecca Penn Wilburn smiles from her desk.

In a nod to Baptist history in South Carolina, the state Baptist Historical Society, of which Bowers was president, unveiled a permanent marker near the gravesite of the Reverend John Waller on Scotch Cross Road between Highway 25 and Ninety Six. Members were urged to attend the October 15 ceremony honoring the memory of an early Baptist pioneer. Waller, an ancestor of Greenwood County's first senator, C. A. C. Waller, had come to Greenwood in 1793 to escape persecution by the established church and civil authorities in Virginia. A tireless Baptist, Waller is credited with founding eighteen churches before coming to South Carolina where he would establish two more, Bethabara and Siloam. The Wallers were among Greenwood's most important early families in both the business and political spheres.

The pastor reported that the church had fifty-two additions to its membership during the association year just ended (October 1–September 30). Though the church was no longer affiliated with the Abbeville Association, the clerk continued to gather the usual statistics. The pastor called the increase in membership "a significant fact" since it was more than double the average increase for the last ten years. Four persons from other denominations had joined under the new baptism rule.

The pastor was still hoping for "a bit more" in the way of contributions toward the 1971 budget when he wrote his column in the newsletter of January 5, 1972. Though $52,000 had been collected in December alone, Bowers was not quite satisfied. "A few thousand more (three or four) would have put us in good shape," he wrote. The outlook seemed much less grim only a week later; contributions had eventually topped $218,000 in a year that many had viewed as the most critical ever. Bowers still sought what he termed "more balanced giving" so that the finance committee would no longer have to deal with "famine" in the first quarter giving way to "feast" in the fourth. He reminded members that debt meant periodic and regular payments, none of which could be delayed, as members evidently thought their contributions could be, until a more convenient time. When the official figures were released a week or two later, the finance committee, according to the pastor, was "delighted" with the report. Even more important than the record of giving was the fact that the last payment to the building contractor left the church with a single long-term obligation of about $542,000 amortized through local banks and savings and loan institutions. Bowers also noted that, unlike many others in similar situations, the Greenwood church had been able to increase its contribution to the cooperative program during its years of building. Its ranking at that time was forty-first in the state.

The church opened what it termed a "dialogue with the world of medicine" in early 1972 when member-physicians John Scott, Jack Parham, and Furman Daniel led seminar discussions on topics such as "Theology in Dialogue with Biology," "Theological Implications of Illness," and "Human Experimentation." Such an emphasis in the educational program of a church was surely on the cutting edge for the time; participants were provided an excellent opportunity to consider questions raised by the medical ethics movement which began with the advent of organ transplants in the late 1960s and continues unabated today. As a matter of fact, organ transplantation was the topic for Dr. Ronald Wise's seminar, and Wiley Price followed with a discussion on the prolongation of life. Roland McKinney weighed in with "The Moral Dilemma of the Medical Practice." Amazingly, Dr. Walter Bishop Jr. spoke on "Birth Control, Infertility and Abortion" more than a year before the Supreme Court addressed the abortion issue in the *Roe v. Wade* decision of 1973. Elbert Adams and Vernon Moore brought the dialogue to an end with "The Delivery of Medical Services" and "Toward a Theology of the Body" respectively.

During this period the church heard from assorted Peace Corps volunteers; the Reverend Jack Schreier described the work of alcoholic recovery at Faith Home and gave the church a wish list of needs at the home; the Howard Hanger Trio from Atlanta, whose "music . . . friends . . . poetry" program was billed as an "experience in joy," gave two performances (some people, it was said, found it an "experience in noise"); and church member Margaret Marks, who was also a member of the English faculty at Lander, led the church Acteens (grades 7–12) in a panel discussion entitled "Sounding Board." Clearly, First Baptist Church was "in the world" as it actually was in the early 1970s.

An item in the newsletter of March 22, 1972, contains the first mention of the gentleman who would become the church's fourteenth pastor in a few years. Dr. J. William Harris, at that time associate pastor of the First Baptist Church of Belton, accepted an invitation to speak at two Holy Week services. He was introduced to the Greenwood church with four brief staccato sentences:

> Dr. Harris is a native of Laurens and received his Doctor of Theology degree from the New Orleans Seminary. You will enjoy hearing Dr. Harris. He is a young man with a most pleasing personality and a keen insight. His message will be of value to each of us.[9]

Mrs. W. W. Benson gave the large chancel cross in the sanctuary as a memorial to her husband, who had died in 1959. Surely no single member of First Baptist Church was more loved and honored than "Major" Walter William Benson, a native of Travelers Rest who had come to Greenwood in 1915 to teach at Bailey Military Institute. A Citadel graduate with a degree in English, Benson's ties to a number of Greenwood institutions amounted virtually to a mutual admiration society for more than forty years. Benson left Bailey in 1924 to accept the job of principal of Greenwood High School, where he remained until his retirement in 1953.[10] The generous tribute to Benson concluded with a striking sentence: "[The cross] will inspire thousands of people through the years just as Major's personality and character inspired others during his lifetime." The flowers that day were given in Benson's memory as well.

Walter W. Benson (1885–1959). "Major" Benson came to Greenwood in 1915 to teach at Bailey Military Institute. He was principal of Greenwood High School, 1924–1953, and a faithful churchman and Sunday School teacher. A class was named in his honor, and the large chancel cross was given to the church in his memory.

The large cross truly is a thing of beauty, and many pronounced it at the time "the perfect finishing touch" for the sanctuary. Its design features symbols compatible with those on the lectern, the pulpit, and the communion table, as well as the end panels of the pews themselves. There is no hint that anyone was bothered by the use of the cross as part of the decor, even though such use is generally viewed as typical of Roman Catholic, and not Southern Baptist, churches. As evidence of the pastor's awareness that First Baptist might be considered somewhat out of the mainstream of generally accepted Southern Baptist belief and practices, it should be noted that he made a point of meeting with youth groups "to help interpret some of the symbols (carvings, stoles, pulpit cloths, colors, etc.) that enrich our worship."

In response to community need, but not without a touch of trauma, the church voted to allow the use of its facilities for a day care center under the auspices of GMAS Community Actions, Inc., a social service agency set up with federal funds that brought, among other activity, the Head Start Program to Greenwood. The primary thrust of the center was to provide child care services to three-, four-, and five-year-olds, children whose parents were either working or receiving job training between the hours of 7:00 A.M. and 6:00 P.M., Monday through Friday. The church would accept no payment except reimbursement for janitorial services and for any damages to the building and playground. No one knew exactly how many children would be served, but five rooms on the ground floor of the north wing were thought sufficient space to house the center. A six-month trial period was anticipated, with possible renewal of the contract for three sessions, or a total commitment of eighteen months. The last sentence of the recommendation of the committee of deacons who studied the matter is particularly interesting:

> It is the feeling of the committee that Christ works through us as His followers. We are men of responsibility. Even though with perhaps some fear and with caution, we would like to follow Christ into the community. It is our prayer that our purpose and our commitment reach as far into the community as we wish it to reach toward Heaven.

Within a month the center had a name—Child Development Center—and church members were being urged to take advantage of the program for their own family needs. The fee would be based on ability to pay, and the emphasis would be on educational development, not baby-sitting. More and more women were working outside the home; many church members must have breathed a sigh of relief at the prospect of dropping their youngsters off at their own church on the way to work.

The modest and retiring line, "We try to keep you informed as to our financial status from time to time," appears in the newsletter of

May 24, 1972. The second sentence, however, is just a bit more caustic: "The picture is not as lovely as we had hoped for at this time." In spite of repeated admonitions, members could not seem to adjust themselves to a pattern of giving steadily and evenly throughout the year. The pastor's frustration peeps through as he writes: "Our receipts are down a bit under this date last year. We go above for a while and then drop back for a while. At present, we are . . . behind last year." A few months later, the pastor called August "a very poor month." It must have been difficult for him to write, "We were financially embarrassed." September, fortunately, was better.

The church undertook the publication of its first pictorial directory in the summer of 1972. The newsletter called it "something new and different" and urged members to cooperate when they were called by a representative of the WMU to set up an appointment. The response was good; more than 325 families, well over 50 percent of the membership, had been photographed by the middle of July. The newsletter pronounced the level of enthusiasm among members "gratifying" and asked for help with layout. The directory was ready for distribution in the summer of 1973.

Church members were alerted to a challenge that could possibly arise at the November 1972 meeting of the South Carolina Baptist Convention. It seems that an amendment would be proposed to remove voting privileges from the twenty-five credentialed messengers representing the church. The reason, of course, was the baptismal policy adopted in 1970. Though the pastor managed, rather mildly, to call the issue "a difficult one," his real feelings obviously ran somewhat deeper. He wrote:

> We feel the right of the local church to act on its convictions is an equally important tenet of Baptists. We have been proud of the fact that our churches are independent and autonomous. Baptists have never had a creed which is to be imposed on churches. There are statements as to what a majority of Baptists believe, but such statements cannot be imposed upon churches. S. C. has never had a doctrinal statement to which churches must subscribe. We feel it is a dangerous precedent to set. Other creedal statements are sure to follow. We hope you will show your interest by attending this convention.

The budget for 1973 was adopted in the last days of the old year. Bowers called it "minimal," but its total of just under $240,000 must have made an impression, inching as it was toward the quarter million dollar mark. By way of comparison, the bottom line for 1963 was $143,840; the budget had increased by almost exactly two-thirds in ten years. And the pastor was still trying to come up with creative ways to stimulate giving. This time he wrote, "We are *so very close* to the end of 1972 . . . We are *so very far* from reaching our financial objective." The next week his message was a little more brusque: ". . . we must receive about $51,000 to meet our obligations. . . . We have 11 days to do it."

The day of reckoning arrived in early 1973. Notes at two Greenwood banks would soon fall due, and the $20,000 to pay them was not in hand nor in sight. There had been a 12 ½ percent shortfall in meeting the previous year's budgeted obligations, and there was nothing to do but ask for extra contributions to get out of the hole. The pastor observed that the church had often been tested in the past, but this challenge was the most urgent of all. "We have grown a little lax in the matter of our contributions," he wrote, adding that a constantly increasing budget had not triggered constantly increasing gifts. He reminded members that their church would take on new meaning if they made sure to contribute their fair share to its financial base. Members responded the very next Sunday with an offering nearly three times as large as the weekly budget requirements. "You responded beautifully," Bowers wrote, "We are sure more of you will respond next Sunday."

The church began taking a hard look at some of its long-standing policies, particularly in the matter of committee structure, as 1973 got under way. Among the "important and interesting innovations" put in place were as follows: (1) both men and women would be asked to serve on each committee, (2) at least one youth from the senior high division would be named, and (3) all committees would operate on a system of rotation. In retrospect, it is clear that the first step toward electing a female deacon was taken at this time.

There were, however, rumblings; nothing definite, but "rather frequent reports of 'unhappiness' and 'grumbling' in the church" had begun to worry both deacons and pastor. In true Baptist tradition, the deacons decided forthwith to name a committee "to study our problems and make recommendations for solving them." But the deacons did not stop there; a further motion urged that the committee be a carefully selected cross section of the church and that it "refrain from the possible temptation of 'witch-hunting' and/or 'whitewashing'" that would render its findings meaningless (or perhaps, just mean—the deacons had managed to hit on an interesting choice of words, to be sure). The committee of eleven women and seven men was formed soon afterward; Hazel Boyd chaired the group. The charge was to acknowledge needs that should be met, set priorities, and consider ways and means of enriching the fellowship among church members—in short, the committee was clearly expected to undertake an in-depth study of the entire church program. One of the first official acts of this committee was a survey designed to give members a chance to express their views on what the church should be and what place it should occupy in members' lives.

A most intriguing item appeared in the newsletter of April 25. Noting that "an honest ad for volunteers" in a church program might contain such phrases as "worthwhile organization of human but vague purposes . . . no experience necessary, but knowledge of everything helpful . . . no salary, but rewards depend upon . . . ," the article pointed out that more than five hundred leadership positions were required in the organizational life of the church. Statistically this meant that, on average, one person per church family needed to be part of the cadre of church leaders. No wonder the pastor asked for prayers for those responsible for enlisting volunteers.

Finances seem to have been less of a problem during 1973, even though the pastor was concerned that misunderstanding and misinformation were rife among the congregation. Though the church met its note payment of more than $13,000 in May, the pastor reminded members of what he called "the lean summer months" just ahead. He also pointed out that contributions of $26,800 by the end of June would place the budget at the halfway mark. "We can do this," he wrote. And "we" did; receipts for August alone were more than twice the previous year's, and the anticipated deficit for the year was only $1,550.

The church expressed its love and appreciation to the Bowerses for thirty years of service with a portrait of their grandchildren—

Bowers called it "a beautiful and unusual thought" as well as "a real masterpiece"—and a marble plaque for the narthex. He wrote, "I have told you before that I never dreamed of such a pastorate here or anywhere." The next newsletter featured an entire page of encomiums from friends and colleagues near and far testifying to the pastor's influence on their lives—officiating at family weddings and funerals, working together on association or convention business, during a morning on the golf course, and on Sundays in the pulpit. In summing up the many expressions of appreciation, Jerry Keeney characterized Bowers's thirty-year ministry in Greenwood with the two words *compassionate* and *capable*. Doubtless few members at the time would have disagreed with that assessment.

An item appeared in the newsletter of October 24, 1973, that seems at the same time to speak to the concerns of that day as well as hold out hope and faith for the future. Since no credit appears, the assumption is that the pastor wrote it. The message is appropriate for every age:

> So much is happening in our world to bring us sorrow and concern. Wars in the east and mid-east. Problems in our cities. Tragedies in our own community. The national situation is depressing to all of us, whatever our political alliances. The end result is a tendency toward depression if not despair. "Things are all shot." "You can't trust anybody," or at least, "I don't know who to trust." "I see no hope." But there is hope. The majority of the nations of the world are not at war. The vast majority of our citizenry has no police record. Most of the families of our nation, though they have their problems, are making a success of their marriage. And the majority of the youth they rear are not burning people or buildings, are not demonstrating against "the establishment," are not engaging in vandalism. True, there are enough broken homes, criminals, delinquents, vandals, to cause us concern; but there are enough who are a long way from this to keep us with hope and confidence in the future. And so with the church, and our church. Some do not seem to care, but hundreds do. Some may seem to be selfish, but hundreds want what is best for the church. Some few may have what seems to be a negative attitude, but most are positive and

> creative in outlook. But again, the real question is about me. Am I trustworthy? Am I a person of integrity? Am I seeking the best for the church? Am I giving my best to the church, the community and the nation? If I am, I can hope.

A budget for 1974—this one breaking the quarter million dollar barrier by $8,000—was presented in November, but the same newsletter brought the bad news that the previous year's budget had bogged down well below expectations. With only six Sundays to go before the end of the year, the budget shortfall topped $50,000, and the pastor was forced once again to resort to a cajoling "Let's all pitch in and do it." Still, the new budget was adopted as usual and, also as usual, no one suggested that it was time to move the church to a pledge system.

A guest sermon by the Reverend Bill Puckett reminded the pastor of the number of First Baptist members who had gone on to careers in one or another field of Christian service over the years. He mentioned four in successful pastorates, another with the foreign mission board in Argentina, and two women whose husbands were ministers. Two former members were engaged in evangelistic work, two were at the seminary, and two active in church music. Still others, he was sure, had derived at least part of their desire and incentive to serve humanity from their church association. He called the service they rendered every day "mission work at its highest," though he conceded it was not always recognized as such.

Presentation of Handel's *Messiah* resumed in 1973 after a hiatus of a few years attributed only, and somewhat mysteriously, to "certain difficulties." Edgar Davis and Elbert Adams were credited with reviving a long tradition, and a choir of nearly eighty people gathered with soloists from Greenwood and Greenville to perform the work for the first time in the new sanctuary, described as "a building wonderfully suited to such an ambitious and beautiful oratorio." The senior choir seemed to be chronically short of members during this period; the majority of the eighty voices for *Messiah* came from other churches or the community at large. Notices urging singers to join the choir of thirty to thirty-four members appeared regularly in the newsletter. Director Edgar Davis was seeking to expand the group to about fifty members, a size everyone considered optimal for the congregation and the sanctuary.

Though the choir might have had a bit of a problem in terms of *quantity*, there were no such concerns about its *quality*. Most people might not have come up with the phrase "crusadic determination" to describe the efforts of Edgar Davis and Elbert Adams, but members of the choir used exactly those words when they presented a clerestory window in honor of the two musicians. The dedication read, in part, "They have used their time and intellectual capacities to direct our energies constructively to preserve the quality of music for the personal enjoyment of every listener. Their character and work are stable, solid, responsible, and idealistic."

The music program had suffered a blow when Ann Arrington resigned in the summer of 1973 in favor of an appointment at First Presbyterian where the adult choir would be part of her responsibilities. Arrington's eleven-year tenure had meant a great deal to the youth, junior, and primary choirs at First Baptist, but whether her departure signaled any internal problems with the music program is unclear. Two people—Dr. Joe Hindman for the youth choir and Mrs. Ralph (Freida) Posey, who would work with the primary and junior groups—were hired to replace Arrington, but their tenure lasted only a few months. Jim and Jean Pruett, both of whom had seminary training and experience in church music, were hired as replacements for Hindman and Posey, but this arrangement was also short-lived. An item in a January 1976 newsletter names *three* directors—one for youth and junior, and one each for primary and beginner. One choir, the primary, was actually disbanded soon thereafter.

First Baptist joined other churches and community agencies in a relief effort for victims of a tornado that swept through the area on December 13. More than 350 families in Georgia and South Carolina lost their homes. The Little Mountain Road Community in Ninety Six was hardest hit, but Lake Shore Drive, Coronaca, and Cambridge Avenue Extension also suffered damage. A number of groups, including the Mennonite Disaster Service, pitched in to develop what they called a "recovery ministry."

When the financial picture for 1973 became clear early in the new year, nearly all the deficit noted in November had disappeared, leaving the church less than $2,000 shy of meeting its most ambitious budget ever. Individual contributions had soared $22,000 above the previous year, and total church income had increased by a whopping 17 percent. The pastor was careful to point out that no single large gift explained the banner year. "Individuals have made the difference," he wrote. The debt principal was also reduced to about $475,000.

The church study committee brought its report in January after a year of work on its assigned tasks. One deacon's comment upon reading the report was, "Let's not file this away and forget it." He might have been right on target, since the committee noted early in its report that "the church, by and large, has been relatively indifferent to the committee's existence and its assignment." Actually, however, this turned out to be a very good sign, since the committee's one broad and basic conclusion was that there appeared to be no major problem of discontent or dissatisfaction among the congregation. Still, the group made a number of very sensible recommendations focusing on music, format of the worship service, needs of children and senior citizens, curriculum, and communications concerns. It is probably true that a number of innovations still in place today came about as responses to this report.

The Child Development Center which had opened in 1972 moved to new quarters in the fall of 1974. The two-year experiment was pronounced "excellent" and "worthwhile" and "a valuable service rendered to many in our community"; even so, the church was clearly relieved at the change since the program had not been without problems. Janitorial services had been the most difficult to manage; the space could not be cleaned until after 6:00 P.M., and it was not easy to find or supervise cleaning personnel at that time of day. In addition, church activities had been affected by the loss of rooms used by the center. GMAS changed its name to GLEAMS when Edgefield and Laurens Counties signed on as part of the agency's territory, and the old Brewer Hospital became its headquarters after a brief time at Promised Land School.

The year 1974, which Bowers called "a fairly good year financially," drew to a quiet close. The church's program was intact, even growing since a radio ministry primarily for shut-ins started over WCRS in early December, and members seemed for the most part reasonably involved and content with their church activity. A new budget of just under $260,000 was adopted for 1975, even as the old budget was lagging by some $50,000 as December 31 approached. After pronouncing the annual deacons' dinner "a fitting close to a good year," the pastor added, "There is much to do and many checks to be written if we are to reach our budget goal for this year."

A disturbing notice in the newsletter regarding vandalism generally thought to be the work of young people, who might or might not have been from church families, turned out to be the forerunner of a much more serious problem. The newsletter of January 8, 1975, contains the following item:

> Most of you know that within the past year the church offices have been broken into several times. Money and office equipment have been stolen, files scattered, furniture destroyed. The deacons and trustees asked Mr. Comer to investigate an alarm system that would prevent recurrences of this. A very satisfactory system was located and has been installed. Because the system will be activated when the offices close in the afternoons, anyone entering the offices after hours must first notify a staff member to prevent setting off the alarm. We regret the need for this, but obviously it is necessary. . . .

The very next item also concerns money, but in a very different context. The pastor was able to report in January 1975 that 98 percent of the budget for 1974 was raised, which meant that members had managed to increase their giving pattern over the previous year by 6 percent. The 1975 budget would require increasing that amount by an additional 3 percent. The pastor as usual had no doubt his congregation was equal to the challenge. "This we can do and more," he wrote.

The church named its first building superintendent, C. J. Hendrix, in the spring of 1975, surely not a moment too soon in view of the amount of space, furnishings, and equipment the church had accumulated over the years. Hendrix seemed the ideal choice, having had experience with boilers and industrial air-conditioning. In addition, he was a carpenter and had spent time as a building contractor.

About the same time, the WMU took on a project to redo the church parlor, which had suffered from a lack of funds since it opened in 1956. The first estimate for redecorating came to about $6,000.00, which the women determined to raise on their own without interfering with the church budget. Director Olive Baxley pointed out that the original parlor fund of $115.00 had grown "with no special effort" to $1,475.00 in only a few weeks. She was confident that members, particularly older members, would take this project quickly to heart. "Let us hope that in a few months we will all be pleased with what has happened to our parlor," she wrote. Sure enough, when Ms. Baxley's WMU report was printed in the newsletter of June 18, the parlor fund stood at $6,196.50. The refurbished parlor held its open house later that year.

The church parlor after its first refurbishing, 1975.

The newsletter for May 14 opened with a letter from the chairman of the finance committee. This form of communication was evidently considered necessary to remind members of a banknote payment due in just two weeks. Less than half the funds needed in May had come in, and the letter was an attempt to spur members to give $14,000 over the next two Sundays. The chairman's letter also contained an update on the church's overall indebtedness: by the end of May, the outstanding debt would stand at just under $364,000, and the short-term banknotes had only two more years to run. The newsletter of two weeks later reported that while the banknote due that month was paid, other obligations had to be left hanging since contributions were about $4,000 under the goal.

Among the innovations that followed the church study committee's report was a full-fledged church library under the leadership of June Shaw, librarian. This project got under way early in 1975 with a request for the donation of a file cabinet and a typewriter. It is not clear whether anyone came up with these items, but we do know that by early summer the deacons had approved naming the library in memory of June and Curtis Shaw's young son Graham, who had died in 1972. The Shaws virtually donated the entire library—the newsletter reports they decorated the space and provided much of the equipment. The Graham Shaw Library, which opened officially on September 14, 1975, continues to operate as a very visible and valuable asset of the church. It now functions as a full-fledged media center.

Jerry Keeney resigned his position as minister to youth in the summer of 1975 in order to accept a pastorate in Missouri. His letter contained a sentence that surely brought a warm glow to every member's heart. Speaking for himself and his family Keeney wrote, "You have supported us, loved us, understood and accepted us in ways that have contributed immeasurably to our lives." Keeney's tenure lasted five years.

The pastor made a full-page pitch in October toward shoring up the church's financial picture. His main thrust was to pay off the balance remaining on the banknotes that came due twice a year. "These notes have held us down and kept us under a strain for the past four years," he wrote. The principal amount remaining was $25,000, a debt the pastor believed would be "easy enough to retire" if members would make a generous, extra contribution over their regular giving. He added that nothing would be more liberating than to free the church from that burden.

The big news of 1975 was the nomination of three women for the post of deacon. The names of Martha Bishop, Estelle Mauldin, and Frances Strawhorn appeared on the ballot alongside those of thirteen men. Women were included among the nominations at the request of the deacons themselves, who evidently had grown a little uncomfortable trying to maintain the fiction that women must not be placed in leadership (read: authority over men) positions in the church. This notion comes from the apostle Paul who wrote sometime ago to Timothy, "Personally, I don't allow women to teach nor do I ever put them in positions of authority over men. . . ." [11] If First Baptist Church had never "allowed women to teach" it is doubtful that its education program would have progressed very far; as for women-as-deacons, surely a church in its 105th year of existence had little to fear from naming a female deacon, particularly since women had been voting in state and national elections, among a great many other things, for the last fifty-five of those years. Martha Bishop was duly elected deacon, some say the first female in the state to serve in that capacity in a Southern Baptist church. She was promptly elected secretary, a post with which women identify much more often than with, say, chairman. Two women were elected the very next year, and females have routinely served on the board of deacons ever since.

A rather unusual notice appeared in the newsletter of May 12. Finance committee chairman Boykin Curry and Buddy Hamrick, deacon chairman, announced the suspension of worship services the following Sunday in favor of what they called "an important report and challenge to the membership." It must have been quite a session if the response described in the next newsletter is any indication. Opening with the sentence, "This surely must be one of the noblest churches I know," the pastor added that the challenge delivered the previous Sunday was simply to raise $50,000 over and above regular contributions by the end of May. "Would you believe that by Tuesday afternoon we had received $23,695? . . . we are sure we will receive the balance by May 31." In view of the remarkable response to that Sunday's appeal, a condensation of the report is reprinted here just as Curry wrote it:

For the past thirty years, money has seldom been mentioned during our Sunday morning service. For a long time now you have not been asked to sign a pledge card and few of you can remember when we last had an every member canvass. We just don't talk about money very often. I like it this way and I expect you do too. When Jim Bowers came to this church, he sold us on his philosophy of giving. He felt that we should not pressure members to give for if they were *really interested* in the church the money would just naturally come in. This is a beautiful concept and it has served us well over the years, but because we now have some financial problems, we are going to talk to you about money.

This decision to report to you on our financial situation and to initiate some action has the unanimous approval of the ten-member Finance Committee and the thirty-two-member Board of Deacons. To start at the beginning—this sanctuary with all that is in it had a total cost of $1,211,000. Prior to construction and during construction, donations and special gifts amounted to $611,000. We borrowed from the two savings and loans $500,000. That left a balance of $100,000. This $100,000 we borrowed from the two local banks. As of this morning, we owe the Savings & Loans $335,000. These are mortgages that are being amortized monthly by payments of $4,360. After five years, we still owe the banks $30,000 so the Finance Committee and the Board of Deacons recommend that we now make a special effort to pay off the banknotes.

We also need to make some repairs to our buildings. The tower of this sanctuary is leaking. It has been leaking since we first moved in and failure to make these necessary repairs will result in substantial damage to this building, and a higher cost of repairs at a later date. It is a long story as to why this tower is leaking, but it is leaking. I won't go into that this morning, but ask you to accept the recommendation of the Trustees who have carefully investigated this. The cost of the waterproofing of this tower is $11,000. The paving in the parking lot is 15 years old. It is full of holes, patches and cracks, and grass is growing through the pavement in many places. The surface is so rough it is dangerous for some of the elderly to walk across it. If it isn't sealed, resealed before the winter rains come we will have to replace the base. The trustees tell us of other minor repairs that are needed. You have noticed in some of the halls and rooms the tile is broken and loose. The kitchen needs a few improvements and the other building . . . after fifteen years, age, wear and tear just finally takes its toll. The total cost of all of these repairs is $20,000. These needs have been carefully analyzed by the Church Trustees and their recommendations have been carefully reviewed by the Finance Committee and they have been approved by the Board of Deacons. You may be assured that these repairs are needed. We, therefore, need to raise $50,000, $30,000 to pay the banknotes and $20,000 to make the repairs. Now, in the remaining time, I will try to anticipate some questions that may be running through your minds and answer them if I can. Some of you may be saying, We knew you were spending too much money on this building and we told you we were going to get into trouble; and to those of you who may be thinking that I say to you: I agree with you. I said the same thing seven years ago and some of you will remember I was quite vigorous and vocal in my opposition to the cost of this structure. I thought it a mistake seven years ago and I still think so. But friends, that's water over the dam. That's ancient history and there comes a time when even though you think somebody has made a mistake you just have to overlook it and forget it. . . .

There are times you think a mistake has been made and it is just best to pay for it and go on, and those of us who oppose the high cost of this construction I think are in a somewhat similar position so I say to you, "Let's join hands and forget the past," and let's help solve the problems of the present. This membership voted overwhelmingly to build this structure and that should have settled the matter. This is a democratic Baptist Fellowship and none of us would have it otherwise. So, to those of us who opposed I say, let's take an active part in this drive, let's ease this financial burden and I promise you it will be a blessing to you and it will be a blessing to this fellowship. And to those of you who voted "Yes" I would like to say we can't deposit anything in the bank and we can't pay anything on these notes except money. Now, a lot of nice talk, a lot of affirmative votes, and going along is all right on the surface but now the time has come to pay the debt. . . .

It hardly seems necessary to add that the goal was met.

With the church still shy of meeting its 1976 budget by some $65,000, its members voted to adopt a new budget of virtually the same amount for 1977. Debt service showed a dramatic drop which was offset by increases in missions activity and salaries. Finance chairman Curry hit on a novel notion, almost a questionnaire, which became the first page of the newsletter of December 8:

> 1–With only 3 weeks left the church is $56,750 short of meeting its budget.
> 2–If you have "done your part" this year—Thank you. *Read no further.*
> 3–If you *aren't sure* you have supported the church as you should—please consider these questions:
> —How much *have* I given in 1976?
> —What *percent* of family income is that?
> —Do I *resent* being asked to give money to the church? *Why*?
> —Do I feel this church *doesn't really* need my time or money?
> —Am I *able*—am *I willing* to send a check today?
> 4–Thank you for reading this appeal.

A little over a month later, the finance committee inserted a notice in the newsletter:

> WE MADE IT!!! Your year-end contributions have enabled us to reach our two goals for 1976. The special drive of $50,000 in May and the budget of $261,500 make a total of $311,500 for the year. We appreciate very much your generous gifts and the fine spirit in which you responded to this challenge. We'll give you all the details later.

Dr. Bowers chose the newsletter of January 19, 1977, for an announcement most of the membership was probably not ready to hear. He revealed that he planned to retire effective with his sixty-fifth birthday month which would be January 1978. His reason for giving a whole year's notice was that he wanted the church to have ample time to "think of the direction in which it wants to go and of the type person needed to lead in that direction." He wanted no gaps in the church's forward progress: "It is my hope we can move into another relationship almost immediately," he wrote. The use of the word *we* was an indication that he meant to make Greenwood his retirement home and First Baptist his church, and that he expected to participate as a church member in whatever choices the church made. The penultimate paragraph is especially revealing:

> I would be very sorry if anyone thought I was trying to be theatrical or dramatic in this or that I was exaggerating the impact of my retirement. As for myself, I would much prefer to delay this announcement. However, I feel, after these years there are some who need to know my plans. I feel the church can move more deliberately, and hence more effectively, in securing a new pastor. I feel this will help us avoid a needless and perhaps costly delay. I believe you understand my motivation. I hope my judgment in this matter has been wise.

As evidence of the pastor's desire to return to "business as usual" as soon as possible after his announcement, the newsletters of the next few weeks reflect a veritable flurry of activity. One particularly intriguing entry concerns an energy shortage so severe that the church actually shared its sanctuary with First Presbyterian and Main Street Methodist for the month of February. Both the other churches heated with gas, while First Baptist used fuel oil, which was not in the pastor's words "so dangerously scarce." The Methodists and Presbyterians would rotate their services between the 9:00 and 10:15 A.M. slots, while First Baptist would move its own worship time forward a half hour to 11:30. Sunday school classes would meet, if they met at all, in private homes, both to conserve fuel and to avoid congestion in the building and parking lots. The system worked very well, far better than anyone had dared hope. Even so, the month must have been rather trying. The rector of the Episcopal church, W. L. Hicks, managed to have a little fun with the situation. He announced one frigid morning to his congregation: "Many are cold, but few are frozen," a wordplay Bowers just had to share in the newsletter. Clearly no one gave a thought to global warming in the winter of 1977.

The church had elected a pulpit committee by the middle of February. John Hollingsworth was named chairman of a group of eleven (eight men and three women) whose job it was to search for a new minister. The committee's first move was to seek input from the general membership. Everything from "thoughts, feelings and desires for our church" to actual names of possible candidates was solicited, and committee members seemed eager for any suggestions as they began their work. As evidence of their sincerity and willingness to listen, names, addresses, and telephone numbers of all the committee members appear in the newsletter of March 2.

Since the question of who would succeed Jim Bowers must have been in the forefront of most people's minds in 1977, perhaps it is not surprising that the year seemed to settle down a bit too much after the initial impact of his announcement had been absorbed. Attendance fell away even more than usual in the summer—one newsletter item begins, "We know you are not indifferent, but . . ."—and Bowers tried a pep talk now and then; still, the big question seemed to hang in the air as the year progressed. The church focused its efforts during this period on physical improvement, purchasing the lot immediately behind the building (North Street and Melrose Terrace to Edgewood Cemetery) and enhancing the grounds with flower beds and landscaping details. Summer camps, beach trips, cookouts, and swimming parties continued to occupy the attention of the younger set, and the record of marriages, births, deaths, and memorial gifts continued to unfold. Ray Beaudrot Young was recognized in late June for thirty-six years of working with the children's group once called Sunbeams (now known as Mission Friends). "Think of the number of lives she has touched through these years," reads an item in the newsletter.

The church also refinished its old silver communion set, the pitcher of which is engraved *November '97*, meaning it was probably placed in service at the time the Bailey Circle building was occupied eighty years before. This set is displayed in a trophy case at the church along with other artifacts from the church's early period.

As First Baptist entered the final quarter of its budget year, the pastor's appeal seemed a little more low-key than usual:

> You have done well with your contributions during the summer. We appreciate this very much. We enter our fall season in a little better shape than usual. However, we do need to realize that in the fall our expenses increase. This will be especially true in this year of transition. If you have gotten behind with your contributions during the summer, we ask you to catch up as soon as possible. Let's face our new year in good financial condition.

The deacons heard a report from the pulpit committee in September. This report, which appeared in the newsletter of September 14, is a gem:

> Last February as we began the search to which you had commissioned us—the search for a new pastor for our church—we asked for your ideas, your recommendations, and your prayers. You responded generously, as always, and we thank you. Our work has been tremendously facilitated by your interest, your many excellent suggestions, your encouragement and support.
>
> As you have participated in our search from the beginning, we want you to be a part of its culmination. We believe we have found the man that you and we together have been seeking. Please come meet him and see for yourself!
>
> Dr. J. William Harris (Bill), his wife Linda, and their daughters Juli (age 12), Heather (age 7), and Jamie (age 18 months) will be in Fellowship Hall from 7:30 to 9:00 o'clock next Saturday night, September 17. The entire church family is invited to drop in and get acquainted, and we sincerely hope that each of you will come.
>
> Dr. Harris, who is at present serving as pastor of the First Baptist Church of Edgefield, South Carolina, will be preaching at the morning worship service next Sunday, September 18. Following the service a business meeting has been called by the deacons for the purpose of hearing and voting on the recommendation of the Pulpit Committee and the Board of Deacons. This recommendation will be to call Dr. Harris as pastor of our church. Further biographical

> and background information will be given at that time, and questions and discussion will be welcomed.
>
> A time of change is always a crucial phase in the life of an individual, a family, a church. The loving, responsible participation you have shown so often in the past can make this a time of growth for us all. Come make it happen!

The additional biographical and background information included the facts that Harris was a native of Laurens and a graduate of Presbyterian College and the New Orleans Seminary where he had earned the degree of Doctor of Theology. Previous pastorates had included an associate appointment at Belton and the post of senior minister of the First Baptist Church of Edgefield.

The thirty-five-year-old Harris was called as the result of a vote following his appearance in the pulpit on September 18. The entire process, from Bowers's announcement in January through Harris's acceptance of the call in September, seems a veritable masterpiece of planning and implementation. If there were snags, and one senses there must have been a few, not a hint shows in the record. It is probably true that Jim Bowers orchestrated much of the process, and it is probably well that he did, particularly since he would be around in retirement and could be expected to take great interest in the church's progress. Harris was slated to come on board as of January 1, 1978.

A new budget was adopted as usual toward the end of 1977. The bottom line was more than $19,000 above that of the previous year, an increase of a little more than 7 percent. The pastor called the new budget "challenging . . . but realistic and necessary" and urged members to share in what he called "an important hour for the church."

The WMU revived the quaint custom of "pounding" as a means of welcoming the Harrises to Greenwood and First Baptist Church. Those who might be bewildered by the term need to know that it means literally gifts of a pound of this and a pound of that item, usually foodstuffs, as a means of helping friends and neighbors in some sort of distress or, as in this case, of welcoming newcomers to an established fellowship. Poundings are right up there with "barn raisings" as expressions of friendship and support. The goal was "a nice box ready by the 11th."

The church's farewell to one pastor and welcome to his successor turned out to be an almost seamless exercise of giving and receiving. The fact that it took place at Christmas and the New Year added even more symbolism to the moments of high drama. Bowers called the holiday *glorious* and *unique*, even as he confessed to a certain sadness at ending a relationship he had found particularly fulfilling over the years. In typical Bowers

The church's farewell gift to Jim Bowers. Left to right: Martha Bishop, Ray Young, unidentified, Leecy Coleman, and Florence Still.

fashion, he blamed himself for any shortcomings in the church's program: "If you have failed to accomplish," he wrote, "it is because I have failed to challenge and to ask. . . ."

A number of gifts, both to Bowers himself and to the church in his honor, marked the occasion of his retirement. The seven-foot "candle standards" used at weddings and other special services were given by Mr. and Mrs. Cliff Fagan; one last stained glass window for the chapel, given in memory of their parents by the daughters of Mr. and Mrs. Herbert Cannon, completed the art glass in Bowers's dream church and gave him great satisfaction; the last service of his official career was communion on Christmas morning; a banquet in his honor was planned for January 6; and the Benson Sunday school class came up with a truly unique piece of textile art as their tribute to the retiring pastor.

Called a labor of love in a newspaper story dated December 20, 1977, the gift was a totally handmade quilt consisting of thirty separate squares, each depicting some symbol associated either with design details of the church itself or with biblical or theological concepts. More than thirty women put in about eighteen hundred hours of embroidery time on the squares alone. Drawing the designs, stitching the squares together, and quilting the whole piece consumed many more. Prominent squares at the bottom and the top commemorate the day Bowers came to the church and the date of his retirement, and the two center panels consist of Ruth Martin's sketch of the church tower, the height of which equals the length of the sanctuary (to demonstrate that the outreach of the church is equal to the upreach of its people).

Bowers himself set the tone for his successor's ministry in late 1977 when he urged his flock to "follow your new leader, the one whom God has sent as your shepherd. He is a good man." And a brief quote from the church bulletin of March 7, 1999, gives an idea of the very special qualities Harris has brought to the pulpit. Minister of music Larry Schultz dedicated that day an original choral response/congregational song entitled "The Windows to God's World" to Harris, "whose fresh theological insight has opened windows of understanding for this congregation for more than twenty years."

CHAPTER SEVEN

Milestones of the Second Century

(1978–)

In a message to the congregation printed in the newsletter of January 3, 1978, Harris called the beginning of his pastorate a "pilgrimage," one he asked members to join on terms of "mutual commitment." Even without a single major thrust, such as the ambitious building program that had characterized Bowers's tenure at First Baptist, the church can point to a number of solid achievements over the first twenty years of Harris's leadership, as well as a few narrow escapes from the slings and arrows of denominational political maneuvers aimed at stripping the church of the convention acceptance and support to which it felt entitled. The story of these and other events will be more fully told when the next writer tackles a church history in fifty years or so. This accounting will be an attempt to capture the essential style of the current pastor and hit a few of the highlights of his tenure in the pulpit.

The church's achievements over the past quarter century seem to fall into a sort of natural outline under topics such as expanded ministries, basic church program development, special events and celebrations, and the broad area of acquisitions and special-purpose endowment funds of various types. Developments in the denominational realm include ongoing difficulties with a state and regional convention, some of whose members seem to have a problem with the church's determination to go its own way. In addition, the record

Dr. J. William Harris, Senior Minister, 1978–.

covers the ebb and flow of new alliances, most of them strictly nonentangling, with similar churches in other places.

The pattern of the worship service itself was among the first changes on the local scene. Not only a trained theologian but also a master teacher, Harris was familiar with the ritual of preparation; he liked to produce his sermons as finished narratives in a series arranged around a unifying theme. The Lenten season during his first year, for example, was fully scheduled as early as February 7 so that members could follow the progression of thought and attain a better understanding of this "deeply meaningful Christian season." In addition, each newsletter contained a column entitled "From the Minister"[1] in which Harris was free to share his views on a variety of topics (one lovely column in the fall of his second year begins, "October refuses to be ignored."). Copies of his sermons were available for the asking.

Russell Comer left the church in the summer of 1978 for a similar position at First Baptist Church of Richmond. His letter of resignation contains a sentence that might sum up the position of the church at the time: "It is not easy to leave this church," he wrote, "where the creative potential is beginning to be expressed in new ways of meeting human need." The church hired David White, a Furman University senior, as interim minister to youth and replaced him with another student when he went on to graduate school fifteen months later.

A gift from L. B. and Angelle Adams enabled the church to complete its carillon with the addition of a "top octave of twelve bells" in 1978. Three of these bells were of the pealing variety, which meant that the carillon could execute a so-called "three bell peal" using large bells, the first in the state with that feature. The newsletter of May 30

Angelle Penn Adams, flanked by sponsor Martha Thurmond Bishop and Dr. Harris, receives the South Carolina Order of the Palmetto, October 22, 1994.

credits the van Bergen Bell Foundry of Greenwood with manufacture and installation. The newsletter also reported that only one city in the country, Washington, D.C., had more carillons than little Greenwood. Everyone was invited to a dedication concert given by Elbert Adams on a Sunday afternoon in early June.

The church began a new schedule of organizational activity when it revitalized its family night on Wednesdays. Dinner (at $.75 per person) was served in the fellowship hall, followed by meetings of graded groups from nursery age up, Bible study for young people, and adult prayer services. The experiment was an instant success; permanent reservations for about two hundred were noted almost from the first. A special feature introduced in 1979 was a family dinner at both Thanksgiving and Christmas for which the church provided the main course and members filled in with side dishes. Family night is still part of the week's opportunities and now includes choir rehearsal. The very nominal charge could not last, of course; family night dinner now costs a maximum of $10 per family, or $3.50 for adults and $2.00 for children, still quite a bargain in anyone's language.

The chairman of the finance committee reported the status of the budget from time to time during 1978. Though surely such was not the case, the appearance was that the pastor would not concern himself, publicly at least, with financial matters. Harris broke his own silence in the newsletter of November when he briefly discussed financial plans for 1979. He called the new budget of $292,446 "a challenge" but pronounced the church "capable of meeting it." He also asked members to think of budgeting in a new way: they were to consider the purpose of the church's expenditures and think in terms of the opportunities these expenditures created for themselves and others. He reminded members that much of the responsibility to make the church program meaningful rested on their shoulders.

Harris called the first *Messiah* of his pastorate "a gift of beauty and inspiration," one presented to the congregation in the spirit of love. There is something quite moving in the idea of a "new" pastor allowing himself to be caught up in an "old" tradition; the church and/or the organ guild had presented Handel's great oratorio more or less regularly for more than twenty years at that point. It must have pleased Harris to realize that he would be part of that tradition in future years.

Charles L. (Chuck) Moates was hired as minister of education in early 1979. A native of Georgia, he brought with him master's degrees from both West Georgia College and the seminary as well as church and convention experience, not to mention a wife and two children, when he moved to Greenwood. Among the innovations Moates introduced during his first year on the job was "A Time for Children" that was added to the worship service once each month; this feature continues to the present day. Moates also endeared himself to the older members of the church when he spearheaded the organization of the NGO (Never Grow Old) group.

The means to solve the church's growing transportation problem materialized when a donor presented a 1980 Dodge van with a seating capacity of fifteen as a gift that year. The church immediately set out to purchase a second vehicle as soon as possible in order to

Dr. Harris and senior members Alma (Mrs. George L.) Johnson and Jessie (Mrs. Carl) Julien pose with members of the younger generation.

satisfy its transportation needs in one fell swoop, a move that many people will view as typical of First Baptist.

Sunday, September 30, was set aside as recognition day for two of the church's stalwarts in the music ministry. Edgar Davis, adult choir director for thirty-six years, and Dr. A. Elbert Adams, organist for thirty-three years, shared honors that day as the membership paused to offer tribute. Pastor Emeritus Bowers was scheduled to preach, and Harris had his say in the newsletter of September 25:

> In honoring Mr. Edgar W. Davis, Jr. and Dr. A. Elbert Adams, not only do we commemorate their long period of service but also we express our love and our appreciation for their dedication and for the high quality music that they have made a tradition in our church.
>
> The fact that Mr. Davis has served as adult choir director for 36 years and Dr. Adams as organist for 33 years is in itself unique. But even more impressive is the faithful way they use and share their talents. They have been of incalculable help to me in planning services of worship. The record of their contributions to other churches and to the community is further evidence of their influence and Christian ministry.
>
> Unfortunately, persons who serve with the greatest competence and reliability often are taken for granted. So Sunday we wish to express to Mr. Davis and Dr. Adams the "Thank you" that many times goes unspoken as we leave the sanctuary. . . .

The responses of the two men appeared in the next week's newsletter. Davis allowed himself to admit to a degree of frustration at times and called his work with the choir a combination of "agony and . . . ecstasy," but a couple of sentences from Adams's response are vintage Adams: "This church is desirous of high calibre accomplishment on the part of its staff," he wrote, "and my effort will continue in this concept toward the enrichment of the worship service through the creative possibilities of music. My kindest thanks are hereby tendered."

The church budget for 1980 topped $300,000. No one seemed to mind, even though the 1979 budget was still short by more than $50,000 as the year came to a close. When all the contributions were finally in, however, the church found itself well in the black. Receipts exceeded the budget by nearly $23,000, and each of the special missions offerings exceeded its goal. Attendance, too, was flourishing. Harris must have seen these statistics as very good omens at the end of his second year as senior minister. The outstanding debt in 1980 was a little over $200,000, an obligation that would be satisfied in less than five years under the pattern of payment in effect at the time.

Only the briefest mention of the 1979 meeting of the state Baptist convention made the newsletter that year; a reminder appeared in the issue of November 6, and nothing further was reported. Perhaps none of the church's quota of twenty-one messengers chose to make the trip, or perhaps no one suspected that a move was in the works to penalize the church for its stand on the baptism and Abbeville Association issues of nine years before. Whether any members were in the audience or not, by the time the 1979 session ended, the first reading of a motion decidedly unfriendly to the Greenwood church was in the record. James A. Howard was the author; the rules called for action on the amendment a year after the first reading.

Thus it was that a serious and pointed denominational challenge to the church loomed in November 1980 just before the annual meeting of the state convention. The amendment proposed in 1979—that an article in the constitution be changed from: "The Convention shall consist of messengers from Baptist churches in the state which are in friendly cooperation with the Convention" to ". . . Baptist churches in the state affiliated with the local Baptist associations which are in friendly cooperation with the Convention"—was reread. This effort to bring recalcitrant churches back in line was not exactly new; similar amendments had been offered before, but the only one to reach second reading and a vote had been defeated in 1972. About thirty churches in the state, including First Baptist, would be excluded from convention fellowship if the amendment passed this time. Harris had calmly assessed the result of a favorable vote before the convention met: "A change of this type in membership requirement would change the convention from a missionary to a doctrinal body, and this would be most unfortunate." As it turned out, Howard withdrew the original amendment and substituted another stating that the convention would consist of "messengers from the Baptist churches composed of baptized believers in the state." This action postponed the issue yet again; a second reading and possible vote would be scheduled for the 1981 meeting in Charleston.

The substitute amendment was duly presented at the 1981 session and its adoption recommended; but instead of a vote, parliamentarian Stewart Simms, perhaps trying to avoid an open clash, offered a resolution strongly urging churches "to uphold by precept and practice our traditional Baptist view that only immersion constitutes true believer's baptism." The resolution was referred to the resolutions committee, and the convention turned its attention back to the amendment. When a standing vote was deemed invalid, the chair called for a secret ballot. The motion failed to carry by the necessary two-thirds majority, and the amendment was defeated. The resolution, however, was approved at the next day's session.

A preliminary report in January 1981 indicated still another very successful year financially. The final report showed that gifts exceeded budget requirements by more than $18,000. As often happens, however, building repairs that year had cost some $14,000 more than the amount projected. Even so, everyone seemed to rejoice in the financial strength of the church.

Carlton E. Allen Jr. was called to the permanent staff in spring 1981. Another Georgian, Allen was also a Furman graduate and had just completed his Master of Divinity degree at the seminary. In an interesting connection with Greenwood, Allen had put in a summer as youth worker at Connie Maxwell Baptist Church a few years earlier. His selection was the result of an eight-month search for a youth minister.

The Reverend Carlton Allen, youth minister 1981–1994.

Librarian June Shaw was invited to participate in the annual conference on church librarianship in theological education in March. Her presentation, entitled "A Church Librarian Speaks to Young Ministers," was a slide program describing the resources of the media center and the way they were used in the church program. This was a noteworthy accomplishment indeed;

Harris expressed pleasure and pride that the media center had been chosen as a model for others seeking guidance in the field.

When the stage in the fellowship hall was completed and the curtains hung, the thespians among the congregation could indulge their love of performing on their very own turf. A dramatization of Annie Armstrong's life and work entitled *Go Forward* was presented in the spring to quite a responsive audience, if the remarks of "A Reviewer" in the newsletter of March 17 are accurate. *Everyman* followed the very next month, this time presented by the Resurrection Players of Greenwood under the direction of Aileen Lau.

Harris's response to the annual meeting of the Southern Baptist Convention held in Los Angeles in the summer of 1981 expressed "the hope that some of the divisive issues . . . [of] recent years have been placed in the background." Clearly, the convention had begun its long slide into controversy and disharmony even in the early 1980s. Both Harris and Moates expressed the hope that members had become a little more tolerant of others' views, but neither was confident that an "era of good feeling" was on the rise.

The church took on a new area of ministry at the beginning of 1981 when it inaugurated a counseling service with the help of Jim Fleming, who was a trained pastoral counselor and a minister as well. Fleming's regular position was clinical chaplain for the Beckman Center for Mental Health Services in Greenwood. A full range of services "for those concerned with problems in living" was anticipated, with fees assessed on a sliding scale. The intention was "quality counseling from a Christian perspective" in an affordable program for individuals and families. The church still lists counseling services among its community ministries.

Once again the church budget was oversubscribed, this time by about $28,000. Actually, this overage was a godsend, since expenses for 1981 had run to nearly that amount beyond the projected budget (the church had determined to convert its heating plant from fuel oil to natural gas that year, and conversion costs had been steep).

Edgar Davis's letter of resignation, effective as of Easter Sunday 1982, appeared as the first item in the newsletter of January 19. Davis's service of thirty-nine years was not unique in terms of longevity in the choir, but he and the church seem to have forged a special bond over a very long period, and his comment that "no church could have been more cooperative or appreciative of my endeavors" probably reflected precisely his emotions at the time. A Baptist minister's son himself, Davis had cultivated a lifelong interest in literature, music, and art, an interest he enjoyed sharing with others of similar inclination. Though he held both the undergraduate and master's degree in English, from Furman and Louisiana State University respectively, Davis's avocation of music landed his first job at Greenwood High School where he taught choral music and directed the band for five years in the 1940s; his parents moved to Greenwood during this time after a heart attack brought the senior Davis's pulpit career to an end. The young man's association with First Baptist Church dates from the same period in the early 1940s.

The combined talents of Edgar Davis and Elbert Adams, both of whom followed other careers at the same time they shared so much of themselves with the church, brought truly *good* music to First Baptist Church. The pastor put it very well indeed in his response to the announcement. He wrote that Davis's ministry had been characterized by "a genuine sensitivity to the place of music and worship in the life of the church." A search committee made up of choir stalwarts Alice Beaudrot, Ora Chaney, Margery Lightsey, and organist Elbert Adams was appointed to recommend a successor to Edgar Davis, and a gala reception in his honor was held on April 18. The church's retirement gift to its longtime choir director[2] was a stereo system. In expressing his appreciation, Davis called the gift "a pleasant and heart-warming surprise."

During the search for Davis's successor, the church changed the job description and title of the position to director of music, a post that would cover the entire spectrum and allow for coordination of effort and continuity of the music program. No doubt a sort of orderly progression through the "ranks" of choirs was anticipated as the ideal. The recommendation of the committee turned out to be Dr. Jane Bolen, an Erskine graduate with advanced degrees from Converse and Florida State. She was at the time choir director at the ARP Church. Bolen agreed to join the church staff as of August 1; Andy Gowan, a member of the music faculty at Lander, directed the adult choir in the interim. Among Bolen's early innovations was the introduction of handbells. The first set of bells and accessories, purchased with memorial gifts, arrived in late September. A mini-workshop to teach elementary techniques of ringing, as well as the care and handling of the bells themselves, was scheduled for the following month. The choir must have made rapid progress; it was heard for the first time as part of the accompaniment for a junior choir performance on October 24. The handbell choir was strengthened in late 1984 with twelve additional units, bringing the range to three octaves (thirty-seven bells). Three separate groups were made possible by this addition: the ensemble ringers, a three-octave choir, and a two-octave choir. All three participated that year in Christmas programs at the church and in the community.

In an innovative move to make the role of deacon more meaningful to the deacons themselves, the church began a so-called deacon family ministry plan in which church families were randomly assigned to deacons in the hope that a mutual relationship would develop. The aim of the entire program was to enhance the spiritual life of every church member and establish a churchwide network of caring.

The pastor expressed the ambivalence of many church members in his remarks after attending the 1982 annual meeting of the Southern Baptist Convention in New Orleans. He confessed to mixed emotions about actions he had observed firsthand, and two sentences in his report to the congregation seem to sum up the divisions he found within the Convention:

> It was good to see attempts to draw the different elements of our convention back together in efforts to witness and to serve without making theological views a basis for fellowship. It was not good to debate so many political and theological issues . . . when resolutions were being considered.

The pastor restated the church "policy" on financial stewardship as he announced the fourth straight oversubscription to the budget. This one amounted to nearly $30,000, and each of the special missions offerings had exceeded its goal as well. Members had every reason to believe that the decision "to develop realistic and challenging financial goals as a congregation and . . . depend upon the commitment of . . . members to meet . . . obligations" had been a good one. They were probably delighted not to be asked for annual pledges, and surely they approved heartily of the "attempt to keep special fund-raising projects at a minimum." No doubt they positively rejoiced that the pastor tried to avoid "talking about money" in meetings and worship services. First Baptist Church had proved itself fully capable of sustaining a program with a price tag of about $400,000 annually.

On senior recognition day in May 1983 the church, as usual, honored the young people among its congregation who were about to graduate from high school. The seniors usually met at the pastor's home for breakfast and a group Sunday school lesson taught by one of the ministers. Then they would sit together, in cap and gown, during the morning worship service at the church. Another graduate was happily recognized that year when minister of education Chuck Moates received the Master of Divinity degree, with honors, from the seminary at Erskine College.

The pastor shared a rather remarkable recital of statistics pertaining to the Southern Baptist denomination as a whole as his message in the newsletter for June 28. These figures might well be hopelessly out of date nearly sixteen years later, but the story they tell is no less compelling for that:

> We have 36,302 churches, 34 Baptist state conventions, and 1,211 associations. Our membership is almost 14 million. The property value of Southern Baptist Convention churches totals more than $14 billion.
>
> In a typical week 3.85 million Southern Baptists attend Sunday School. Each week 5.6 million members hear some 54,000 hours of preaching, sing a quarter of a million hymns, and circulate 150,000 offering plates. They give $60 million per week, of which $10 million goes to missions causes and supports 3,214 missionaries in 96 foreign countries and 3,430 home missionaries. Annual giving in Southern Baptist Convention churches totals $3.1 billion and represents a per capita average gift of $208.56. Each week Southern Baptist Convention churches baptize 8000 persons.

There seemed no end to the variety of activities available to church members in the mid-1980s. A couple of newsletters from May 1984 list, among other opportunities, a churchwide picnic, a musical performance in fellowship hall, a mother-daughter banquet, a golf tournament, several softball games, a handbell festival, a trip to Atlanta, a parent-child dedication service, a baptismal service, and a planning session for Vacation Bible School. Family night on Wednesday continued weekly, as did educational seminars and adult Bible study, not to mention regular worship services and Sunday school. Clearly, the church saw itself as a resource serving a wide variety of interests and needs among its constituency. Many First Baptist families will no doubt remember this period with special fondness; it might have been, in fact, the high-water mark of cooperative participation in total church activity.

The first three paragraphs of the pastor's message in the newsletter of June 19 speak volumes about the continuing slide of the Southern Baptist Convention toward superfundamentalism:

> Last week in Kansas City a messenger to the Southern Baptist Convention was honored for attending fifty consecutive annual sessions. He deserved recognition! I have attended three of the last four conventions, and I feel that I deserve something. It isn't a very pleasant experience any more.
>
> Five years ago leaders of the fundamentalist wing of the convention predicted that they would soon gain control. They have achieved their goal. Charles Stanley, pastor of First Baptist Church, Atlanta, and an active leader in Moral Majority and other New Right groups, was elected president of the convention on the first ballot. Paul Pressler, a judge from Houston, Texas, who has been candid about a fundamentalist takeover for years, was elected to the SBC Executive Committee.
>
> The greatest embarrassment of the week came in the approval (by a vote of 4800 to 3500) of a resolution "On Ordination and the Role of Women in Ministry." The resolution states that "we encourage the service of women in all aspects of church life and work *other than pastoral functions and leadership roles entailing ordination*" [emphasis added]. Such actions make me extremely grateful for local church autonomy and for the non-binding nature of Southern Baptist Convention resolutions!

July 29, 1984, was an extra special day for First Baptist because it was the day the church had chosen to celebrate the final payment on the building indebtedness. Appropriately enough, Dr. Bowers filled the pulpit, and members were urged to be present for this "significant milestone" in the life of the church. The former pastor reviewed the sequence of events that had begun when a committee was appointed to study the question of relocating from the site on North Main Street and ended with the final payment on the mortgage nearly forty years later. Bowers emphasized that the service would not be a traditional "mortgage burning"; rather, he wrote, "We plan to thank God for the beautiful and functional buildings that aid our worship and our Bible study. And we plan to express our gratitude . . . for the faithful and creative contributions of so many in this fellowship who have brought us to this point."

Evidently the commemoration was very special indeed. Harris saw in the day's events a constant theme of "faithfulness," from the comments of members during the weeks before the service to the contributions of the choir who had held a special rehearsal the day before, and especially in Bowers's sermon, which paid tribute to the church's commitment to what it understood to be the leadership of God in the undertaking. Harris wrote afterward, "We have not constructed . . . a 'monument' on which to look with pride. Instead, we have a 'tool' to be used in the service of Jesus Christ."

In spite of this high moment in the life of the church, disturbing signs of decreasing attendance, particularly for Sunday school, began to appear more and more frequently in the newsletter. Almost as numerous were requests for workers in one or another area of church activity. That these two subjects were interrelated could not have been more clear. Modern American life was in another of its endless cycles of change. The concept of an extended family was rapidly evaporating as people moved to new homes and a different sort of life in the suburbs. More and more parents found that both needed to work to make ends meet, and less and less "togetherness" (for want of a better word) as a family was one inevitable result. The trend toward decreased participation in church activities, noted with some alarm in the 1980s, has continued and worsened since that time, and not only at First Baptist Church in Greenwood. When the social history of American life at this period is assessed, perhaps the root causes of what seems to have been the beginning of a turn toward insularity can be identified.

The pastor's message in the newsletter of October 30, 1984, is an excellent thumbnail sketch of the cooperative program to which Baptist churches subscribe through their conventions. Harris had been asked during a meeting of the finance committee, "Where does Cooperative Program money go and what is it used for?" Pleased at the opportunity this question presented and sure that many members would be interested in the answer, he used actual figures for 1984 to explain in the newsletter how the cooperative program worked:

> The Cooperative Program, adopted by the SBC in 1925, is a plan whereby individual churches within the convention cooperate to support all convention ministries. We send our Cooperative Program monies ($45,000 this year) to the state convention where 61.7% is retained for Baptist work in South Carolina. State use of Cooperative Program funds includes Convention and General Board Work, General Board Ministries, and Support Services, 23.92% of each CP dollar; W.M.U., 1.17%; Agencies (*Baptist Courier*, Baptist Foundation), 2.66%; Benevolent Institutions (Connie Maxwell, Hospitals, Ministries for Aging), 16.14%; Educational Institutions (Furman, Baptist College, North Greenville, Anderson), 17.81%.
>
> The remaining 38.3% of the Cooperative Program funds is forwarded to the SBC office in Nashville where it is distributed in this way: Foreign Missions, 18.46%; Home Missions, 7.40%; Seminaries, 8.79%; Commissions (Brotherhood, Christian Life, Education, Historical, Radio & TV), 2.64%; Annuity Board, SB Foundation, SBC Operating, Public Affairs, 1.01%.

A brief item in the newsletter of February 5, 1985, takes on added interest in view of today's headlines. Entitled "Have You Written Your Letter?" the item urges members to write their opposition to a state-sponsored lottery, a bill under consideration at that time by state senators Ryan Shealy and Marshall Williams. Most South Carolinians know that a lottery has been proposed before, but many perhaps do not realize just how long the idea has been around in the State House.

Another venture into unknown territory came the same year when Harriet Dial[3] spoke to a Wednesday evening group about her efforts to provide assistance to "battered family members." In 1985 Dial asked for items such as electric fans and a port-a-crib from First Baptist members who cared about the problem; Greenwood's resources in this area, which now include a full-fledged shelter for women and children, obviously got their start from efforts such as Dial's. The first community social agency to take an interest in this project was the Salvation Army.

Still another fledgling group, Habitat for Humanity, attracted the attention of a number of young people during this period. A group traveled to Americus, Georgia, where the movement got its start, for five days in July to work on a project in that town. The trip was a great success, except that Carlton Allen fell from the roof of the Habitat house on the last day of work. He suffered multiple bruises and a fractured rib, not to mention a few bad jokes after everyone realized he was not seriously hurt. The young people also delivered a check for fifteen hundred dollars to the Habitat group—money that had been collected at their Friday night "socials." Best of all, the youth group found ways to help people in substandard housing back in Greenwood. After the church office received a request for help to buy mosquito netting for the crib of a ten-day-old infant who lived in a house with no screens, the group set out with a roll of screen wire and staples to see what they could do to help these and other rental-house occupants in similar situations. Somebody wrote in the newsletter, "Makes you wonder who owns these houses, doesn't it?"

Church finances lagged all through 1985, though members were reminded again and again that bills arrived with monotonous regularity throughout the year even though contributions did not. The last report of the year, in the newsletter of December 17, pointed out that the Lottie Moon Christmas offering had surpassed its $8,000 goal by about $400, but nearly $78,000 needed to come in over the next two weeks if budgeted commitments of $434,241 were to be met.

Church secretary Janelle Anderson retired in early 1986 after thirty-seven years of service. The pastor, in fact, emphasized that word; "She has *served*," he wrote, "not just worked in the church office, for her contributions . . . have gone far beyond those one would normally expect of a church secretary." A true sounding board for the ministers and blessed with a unique understanding of church dynamics, Anderson's work surely was, as Harris claimed, "of inestimable help" in the day-to-day business of the church. Though Anderson's colleagues had to be a bit sneaky about it, they managed to surprise her with a retirement dinner and the gift of an electronic typewriter (the newsletter reports that her thank-you note was neatly typed). Fortunately, Anderson can still fill in a blank or two on questions of church history when one memory or another falters.

The financial report for 1985, printed in the newsletter of January 14, 1986, contained, as the saying goes, "some bad news and some good news." The church failed to meet its budget by about $20,000, but expenditures fell short of projections by more than $27,000, so that once again the church took in more than it paid out. The newsletter also included a report, by year, of the previous eight years, seven of which had seen an excess of receipts over actual expenditures. The church had been able to build a cash reserve during that time; the reserve fund balance stood at nearly $100,000 as 1986 got under way. Since receipts traditionally lagged behind expenditures, this fund allowed for an orderly cash flow during the year. The church had also greatly increased its missions and building maintenance budgets as its indebtedness was liquidated.

Lay leader Carole Mauldin was selected as Volunteer of the Year in 1986 by the State Department of Social Services. The church shared in this recognition since many of Mauldin's outreach efforts were directed through the missions office. She was honored at an awards ceremony and luncheon in Columbia on April 21. Clearly, First Baptist Church was moving more and more into the mainstream of community missions, in large part through the efforts of caring members such as Carole Mauldin.

The church tried to prepare its members for the Southern Baptist Convention scheduled to meet in Atlanta on June 10. A four-week seminar to study the issues impacting the convention was set for the month of May. Subjects to be discussed were the following:

A historical review of events which led to the current controversy
A look at the SBC lawsuit and the work of the Peace Committee
A review of power struggles related to SBC institutions; i.e., seminaries
A look at the candidates likely to run for president of the SBC

Church secretary Janelle Anderson, who retired in 1986 after thirty-seven years of service.

The church sent its full complement of ten messengers to the meeting that year. In view of the divisions that had become so troubling to churches such as First Baptist, it seemed especially important to be well represented. "Pray for your messengers and pray for your convention at its meeting next week in Atlanta," the pastor urged. Nothing further appears in the newsletter; if a report on the convention was made, by ministers or messengers, it did not find its way to the regular records.

Dr. Jane Bolen resigned as director of music in the fall of 1986. The pastor recognized the "healthy developments" in the music ministry under Bolen's leadership, such as the addition of seasonal music programs and participation in the all-state chorus made up of Baptist youth, as well as the handbell choirs and a general expansion of the music program. Leaders of youth choirs—Linda Harris, Jan Hazel, Joyce Nickles, and Beverly Psomas—were announced in early September, and chancel choir rehearsals continued as usual on Wednesday nights, but nothing about Bolen's replacement appeared until the newsletter of October 7 when the announcement that Steven White had accepted the post of interim director was made. White held a master's degree from the University of South Carolina and was at the time a member of the music faculty at Lander. No dates were mentioned. By the time White accepted the call to a permanent position in early December 1986, the church had acquired yet another octave of handbells, the fourth, this one made possible by gifts in memory of Miriam Smith Wolf, a dedicated choir member and worker for more than forty years.

The disturbing news that the building had asbestos problems, from sprayed-on acoustical ceiling materials in about six thousand square feet of space, hit when the church was considering installing an elevator. The engineering firm of Davis & Floyd conducted studies and recommended removal of all asbestos materials at a cost of $77,000. Since the work seemed necessary, the finance committee proposed to use $25,000 of its reserve funds plus any budget overage for 1986 and borrow the rest. The vote, however, was to delay action pending further study and discussion. Approval came in early November. In the meantime, the elevator project moved forward and was more than half finished by the end of the year. Other projects that year included moving the phone system and installing new air-conditioning in the office area. The elevator, incidentally, was finally ready for use in the spring of 1987.

The two projects were financed very much as the deacons and the finance committee had anticipated, that is, with reserve funds and a short-term loan. The amount of $45,000 for the asbestos project (which came in at only $72,000) was in hand, as was $31,000 of the total cost of the elevator installation, $61,000. The church surely had no difficulty securing a loan for the remaining $57,000. The elevator project would eventually be covered by memorial gifts.

A simple announcement appeared in the newsletter of December 9, 1986:

> The deacons voted . . . unanimously to recommend that the church accept Edgewood Cemetery. The cemetery was recently purchased by Greenwood Mills, and the new owner wishes to make it a gift to the church. The recommendation of the deacons is that the church accept the cemetery and proceed with the establishment of a means whereby Edgewood can become a perpetual-care cemetery. This process would involve interested persons and families throughout the community.
>
> Congregational action will be needed on this recommendation. Therefore, discussion of this issue has been scheduled for this Sunday afternoon, December 14, in the chapel following the Vesper

> service . . . and a motion will be placed before the church on Sunday morning, December 21.

The pastor announced in the newsletter of January 6, 1987, that more than $46,000 had already been given toward a fund to establish Edgewood's perpetual-care status under the control of the church as owner. He called the project one "of immense concern to . . . church and community." The next newsletter contained the wording of the recommendation the deacons planned to make to the church, which included one change and one addition to the church constitution; the vote was set for January 25 at the end of the worship service. Questions and discussion were scheduled for the Wednesday night before the vote.

The news that the church budget for 1986 was once again oversubscribed, as was that of every special mission category, was noted in the interim. Asbestos removal continued apace; adult and youth Sunday school classes located in the affected area were dislodged until after the work was finished. The classes were finally able to move back to their regular rooms in late February. The six-week disruption had caused a real problem with the Sunday school; Moates wrote that attendance had "suffered dramatically" as he asked class leaders to call their members personally in an effort to get back on track.

A different and stronger First Baptist Church began to emerge as a result of the Edgewood acquisition and physical plant improvements. Still another important "first" came when Dr. and Mrs. Jack Parham chose to establish an endowed scholarship fund in memory of their twenty-seven-year-old son Craig who had died in an automobile accident in 1986. Annual awards from endowment income would be made to students enrolled in an accredited seminary. The corpus of the fund amounted to more than $30,000 by the time the program was established. Greg Anders and Joseph Giaritelli, the former a member of the church and the latter a young man with connections to Greenwood, were the first recipients of Craig Holbrook Parham Memorial Scholarships.

A tribute to three staff members during National Secretaries Week in 1987 deserves mention in these pages, at least in part because of its tone of genuine appreciation. The pastor wrote in the newsletter of April 21:

Joyce Williams, Ann Ella Dorn, and Donna Allen perform secretarial duties for our congregation. They answer the telephone, type, file, and see to a myriad of details. And they carry out these responsibilities extremely well.

But these members of our church staff are more than secretaries. They are sensitive counselors. They are able planners. They are problem-solvers. They are caring greeters to everyone who comes into the church office. They are ministers too.

When I left the church last week after the Maundy Thursday service, I saw two cars still in the parking lot. They belonged to Joyce and Ann Ella! I'm grateful for the ability and dedication of these co-workers and fellow ministers. It is a joy to say "Thank you" to each of them on behalf of our church family.

Ann Ella (Mrs. Jackson) Dorn (1923–1997), hard-working church secretary and a great deal more. Harris called her a "minister."

In the same vein, the staff and congregation were pleased to congratulate Chuck Moates on completing the requirements for the Doctor of Ministry degree at Erskine Theological Seminary. Members were invited to attend the graduation exercise; no doubt many did, for Chuck was a great favorite among the membership. His degree meant, among other things, that for the first time in the church's history, two members of its ministerial staff held earned doctorate degrees.

The Southern Baptist Convention meeting in St. Louis turned out to be more of the same and a great disappointment to moderate and progressive churches such as First Baptist. The pastor wrote a full page detailing his impressions (and his frustrations), focusing particularly on the report of the so-called peace committee which had been established in 1985 to study the controversies and divisions within the convention and work toward reconciliation of the warring factions. The committee's "findings" were no more than a statement that theological differences existed among members and that "organized political activity had gone on openly for at least ten years." But the peace committee did not stop there; in effect, it went on to adopt a *creed* and establish a *hierarchy*, two concepts that have traditionally been anathema to Baptists. An amendment to include reaffirmation of long-held beliefs such as soul competency, local church autonomy, and separation of church and state, was defeated by a margin of three to one.

Meanwhile, back in Greenwood, another venture in community missions came about in 1987 when area churches began the operation of an uptown soup kitchen to feed the hungry of the community. Located at the Church of the Resurrection just a block off the square, the kitchen sought volunteers for three hours, one day a week. Money and food supplies were also welcomed. The soup kitchen is still a fixture in Greenwood and still located at the Episcopal church on South Main Street. Someone probably knows exactly how many thousands of hot meals the kitchen has served in its more than ten years of operation.

The newsletter of September 1 contains a most useful listing of Sunday school classes, the enrollment of each, and the number of attendees, presumably at its most recent meeting. Twenty-eight separate classes enrolled nearly 750 members that year, and the most recent attendance had been nearly 61 percent of that number. The largest class, Benson, listed 87 members (!) while the smallest, with only 3, was a brand new class for young adults which had just been organized. Average class enrollment was just under 27, which seems a very reasonable class size.

Dr. Ernest Young, chairman of the Edgewood Cemetery Board, was able to report in September that the endowment fund had grown to more than $100,000 in the ten months of the project's life. A four-grave plot could be purchased at that point for $1,000.

The church arrived at the decision to use a standard Christmas decoration for the church in 1987. Donations to help defray the cost of this "permanent greenery" were sought beginning in October. There is something comforting in the thought that the interior of First Baptist Church looks exactly the same every Christmas. Nothing could be more traditional, nor more reassuring and beautiful, than the large wreaths, complementary greenery, and bright red bows that appear during Advent and stay until the end of the year. Some people hope the Christmas decor will never change.

In view of the disturbing events within the Southern Baptist Convention, Harris's report on the meeting of the state convention in November was positively lyrical. He was pleased at the election of Jimmie Harley as president and believed his emphasis on unity, evangelism, and stewardship was a theme Baptists could embrace without reservation. "The business of the convention was carried out in a good spirit," he wrote, and the messengers seemed concerned with cooperation and support for missions. In short, Harris concluded, he came away with "positive feelings" and saw "signs of hope" at the meeting with Baptist colleagues from across South Carolina.

Perhaps because of the asbestos removal and elevator projects, there had been no performance of *Messiah* in 1986. Steve White and the choir made up for that omission in 1987 with a community chorus and a small orchestral ensemble put together from members of the Greenville Symphony. Harris called the performance that year, believed to be the first with orchestra accompaniment, "a deeply moving experience" and "a wonderful Christmas gift."

The church budget for 1988 reached the all-important milestone of a half million dollars plus. The sky did not fall, and neither did the membership falter, as the vote was taken on November 29. A new note crept into the pastor's financial report at the end of the year. Congress had recently enacted sweeping changes in the tax code, and members were reminded of certain pertinent facts relative to their charitable giving patterns—facts that had to do with improving their standing when tax preparation time rolled around again. Some might say that rendering unto Caesar and rendering unto God had become a little too intertwined for comfort.

The year 1987 was unusually full of activity and solid progress for First Baptist Church. The pastor reviewed his calendar before he put it away that year and recapped 1987 month-by-month as his message to the congregation in the newsletter for December 28. "This list," he concluded, "omits more than it includes. But it reminds me of many things for which to be grateful and many other things to look forward to in the new year."

The church paid tribute to a particularly faithful steward when Paul Burgess retired as treasurer after twenty-six years of service in early 1988. The pastor put together a neat paragraph that describes in a few words the work and dedication of a man who did what he did because he truly loved his church:

> Paul's contributions to First Baptist Church are many. During his term of service he has overseen the receipt and disbursement of more than 10 million dollars. He managed finances during the building of our sanctuary and has helped us come up with ways to pay for maintenance, repairs, and renovations to our facilities. Those of us who work closely with Paul appreciate perhaps most of all his ability to maintain a cash flow even while receipts fall far behind budget needs. . . . [H]e has treated every financial receipt for what it is, a gift dedicated to God.

The church slipped a little in its financial achievements during 1987. A deficit of more than $22,000 marred the record, though three out of four special missions offerings went over the top, and the cemetery fund added more than $20,000 to its fund balance. Perhaps the church was finding its new standard of giving a bit daunting and needed a little time to come to terms with the impact of the financial realities of the late twentieth century.

The WMU, arguably the most vibrant and certainly the most visible of all Southern Baptist subsidiaries, celebrated its one hundredth anniversary in 1988. The pastor (who marked an anniversary of his own that year, his tenth in the pulpit) took special notice of the centennial in his message to the congregation. The Woman's Missionary Union[4] was organized on May 14, 1888, in the basement of the Broad Street Methodist Church in Richmond. Thirty-two delegates from twelve states attended to hear a South Carolinian, Mrs. John Stout, read a paper entitled, "Shall the Baptist Women of the South Organize for Mission Work?" Annie Armstrong moved that organization be considered, and, as Harris put it, "the result is the reason for our celebration this year." He pointed to the clearly defined purposes of the organization which are simply "to promote and support missions, to help a church fulfill its mission, and to lead in missions education." Finally, he reminded members that local church efforts to meet needs in this area before the formation of the WMU were haphazard and ill defined. Usually, a new committee had to be formed to collect contributions every time a special cause came up, with results that were, at best, inconsistent. Missions work through WMU, however, soon took on the virtues of continuity, regularity, and efficiency of operation to the point that it would be difficult to visualize the impact of the convention without it. The denomination simply would not be the same without the immense contribution of Baptist women, much of it channeled through the WMU.

The emergence of the Southern Baptist Alliance and the church's interest in it were announced in the newsletter of May 17, 1988. The group defined itself as "an alliance of individuals and churches dedicated to the preservation of historic Baptist principles, freedoms and traditions and the continuance of our ministry and mission within the Southern Baptist Convention." Believing that the alliance provided an opportunity for "those who share a passion for religious liberty and a zeal for missions," the deacons were ready to recommend that First Baptist sign on as a member of this group.

Harris set forth a number of affirmations the alliance had hammered out, many of them indirectly repudiating Southern Baptist Convention actions, and answered a number of questions he knew would concern the membership. He described the new alliance as a positive voice, one not in competition with the convention, and pointed to growing numbers of Baptists at that point—2,234 individuals and 43 churches with a membership of more than 25,000—who had already voted their support of the group. The church was asked to study the issue very carefully and be ready to act on the deacons' recommendation within 120 days. In the meantime, information would be shared and discussions scheduled as needed.

Deacons made a point of visiting Sunday school classes to answer questions and lead discussions about the proposal that the church join the Southern Baptist Alliance. By the time the vote was taken in

October the church was solidly behind the affiliation with 77 percent of the congregation voting for the measure and 23 percent against. Alliance membership by that time numbered almost 40,000 Southern Baptists. Harris wanted to make sure everyone understood what affiliation meant and, perhaps even more importantly, what it did not mean. He called the act of joining "an expression of concern" and "a statement of dissatisfaction" with the convention, attitudes that might be viewed as negative; still, the pastor saw it as a positive move, one that reaffirmed the true meaning of fellowship with other Baptists who cherished their heritage of religious and denominational freedom.

The sting of the 1988 meeting of the Southern Baptist Convention in San Antonio might have been ameliorated somewhat by the thought that the Southern Baptist Alliance offered a place for moderate Baptists to go when the convention finally achieved the disunity it was clearly bent on pursuing. Harris considered himself and others insulted at the very first session: it seems that the speaker at the pastors' conference began his message with the line that though *liberals* were calling themselves *moderates*, "A skunk by any other name still stinks." (!!) Harris was clearly not the only pastor to take offense at such heavy-handed ridicule. "Before the week was out," he wrote, "quite a few folks were glad to be called 'skunks.'"

Perhaps the most damaging event of the convention was a resolution that effectively denied the concept of the priesthood of believers, a tenet Harris called "a major theme in the Christian faith." The resolution affirmed the authority of the pastor to lead a local church. Harris pronounced himself "amazed that any Baptist could vote for such a resolution."

The church took advantage of the 1988 performance of *Messiah* to recognize Elbert Adams, not only for nearly forty-three years of service as organist but also for the quality of his musicianship and his character. The words used when Adams joined the staff in 1946—*excellent musician* and *consecrated physician*—were echoed in 1988 when the church dedicated the performance to him (he called the dedication "exhilarating") and presented an endowed scholarship to Furman University in his name (this he found "an undreamed-of gift"). Adams called his church work "a prized privilege and a high joy" when he responded in the newsletter of December 6.

The 1988 budget was a squeaker, but once again the membership met the challenge of heavy commitments that included debt service resulting from significant building repairs. Most of that debt was paid in 1988. Harris must have been pleased to note what he called "a most encouraging trend" of more people giving more money to the church than ever before.

The pastor shared a true comedy of errors with the congregation in early 1989; readers might enjoy hearing it again:

> Last Thursday was Jim Bowers' birthday. Earlier in the week all of us on the church staff had decided that we would like to visit Jim together. Our plan was to take a dessert with us and to surprise him with a little party. We told Louise, of course, and asked her to have a pot of coffee ready. We thought it would be impressive for a group from the church to arrive in a van for [a] late morning birthday celebration.
>
> Jim was surprised! So was Pogo, the Bowers' pet Boxer. Pogo got very excited as seven strangers trooped into the den. Pogo got rather protective as the noise level gradually increased. Jim decided that Pogo really did not belong at the party. When requests that he leave did not work, Jim took Pogo by the collar to escort him out. That was a mistake! The result was either a bite or a scratch on the arm. Louise had no trouble; she simply opened the door and Pogo left.
>
> After that episode the party resumed. As coffee and dessert were being served, someone noticed that Jim's arm was bleeding. In the effort to attend to the wound, we spilled his coffee all over him and the chair. We staff members did our part. We worked on the arm; we helped clean the chair and the floor; we called the doctor to see whether Jim would need a tetanus shot. I think the high point of our celebration was our promise not to come for a surprise party next year. . . .

Surely no one will be surprised to learn that one of the church's most significant ministries began with a simple appeal from Carole Mauldin and the missions office to the board of deacons on a Sunday morning in February 1989. The case she made that day centered around the need for a shelter for abused children in the Greenwood community and was backed up by some stark statistics: eight children in one day had to be taken into protective custody by law enforcement officials, and a total of thirty-six children had been subjected to the same process in the first six weeks of 1989. Foster care was the accepted remedy in these cases, but there was a shortage of foster homes; one Department of Social Services (DSS) official stated that they could not be licensed fast enough to meet the need. The account in the church newsletter of February 14 continues:

> Wouldn't it be wonderful for a church, *our church*, to provide a place where children who have to be removed from their homes could come and find love and care until their situations are resolved? That's an idea, a concept, that was described to our deacons Sunday morning—the idea that our church could sponsor such a shelter; that literally everyone in our congregation who is willing could donate something to supplying shelter, food, clothing, and love to children under extreme duress; that we could make a major impact on a major problem of our times.
>
> This idea is just that—an idea! Implementation would require a tremendous commitment of time and resources. This idea came to our deacons from missions coordinator Carole Mauldin. The deacons recommended last Sunday that the missions committee study this concept in detail. During the coming weeks the missions committee will visit facilities of this type in other communities, study licensing procedures, and continue to examine the need and how it best can be addressed.
>
> Please take this idea and give it your careful thought and sincere prayer. Share thoughts about it with the deacons, members of the missions committee, or church staff.

The missions committee set to work at once and in all directions on a feasibility study. A follow-up report from Carole Mauldin was ready for the newsletter of March 28. Three members of the committee visited an experimental program in Spartanburg, the only children's shelter in the state run by the DSS. The first director of that facility, who happened to be the daughter of church members Buddy and Mary Hamrick, visited First Baptist to offer suggestions and answer questions. The meeting, according to Mauldin, was well attended and very informative. "We learned what *not* to do as well as what to do," she wrote.

The next step was checking into licensing requirements at the state level. The help of two church member/lawyers was recruited for this step, as was the expertise of another professional, this time a CPA, who offered accounting advice. Two church members, Elizabeth Moss and Jean Ricketson, agreed to attend a workshop on grants writing as an aid in seeking any special funding that might be available for the project. Advice was solicited from Connie Maxwell Children's Home which operated an emergency shelter for teenagers at the time, one, however, that was open to all counties in the state so that little space was available for strictly local needs. Still other volunteers looked at the availability of suitable houses in the community. Finally, Mauldin reported a gratifying level of support from community agencies: United Way and Parents Anonymous had expressed interest, as had several churches, individuals connected with Lander College, Girl Scout troops, and the court system.

The urgency of the need and the thorough investigation of the missions committee emboldened the church to move quickly, and a plan came together in an amazingly short time. The deacons voted on April 9 to recommend that the church undertake sponsorship of a shelter for abused children, and the issue was scheduled for a vote by the congregation on April 23. The support for this new ministry was overwhelming, as reflected by an 87 percent favorable vote. The pastor viewed the impact of this decision as great and far reaching. Someone pointed out that this ministry would direct the resources of the church toward the needs of others instead of itself. The actual recommendation was to approve the establishment of a nonprofit, tax-exempt organization to operate a shelter for abused children, to be controlled by First Baptist Church. The vote also elected as a partial board of directors A. C. Fennell, Richard Jackson, Carole

Mauldin, Kenny Poston, and Chuck Watson. Ten additional directors were elected a month later.

In still another act of serendipity, Paul and Helen Baker donated a house on Elm Court that was almost ideal in size and location. The missions committee was also ready with a name: The Bowers-Rodgers House would honor both the pastor emeritus and Mrs. Baker's parents, Thomas E. and Pearl R. Rodgers, both of whom had been faithful members of First Baptist Church. Events had moved very quickly indeed; a little more than two months had elapsed between Carole Mauldin's initial appearance and the vote by the church. The pastor's response, however, contained an element of caution: "The work is just beginning," he wrote, "How we shall meet all the needs that lie before us I personally cannot say. However, I believe that God is guiding us to take on this effort, and I believe that He will provide a means to carry it out."

In the meantime, Chuck Moates resigned his dual position as minister of education and church administrator in favor of the top job of executive minister at Smoke Rise Baptist Church of Stone Mountain, Georgia. His ten years at First Baptist had been fruitful years indeed; he took with him a wealth of experience (as well as a solid doctoral degree) to a new post in his home state, one that would afford him the opportunity to manage and administer a total church program. While Moates would definitely be missed, First Baptist members wished him well in his career and threw a churchwide reception honoring him and his family on March 19. Moates's new duties were scheduled to begin the following week.

The long-range planning committee viewed Moates's departure as an opportunity to try to determine some direction for the church; accordingly, a membership survey was conducted in an effort to tap into the needs and desires of the church family as it stood at the time. Church leaders felt that such a survey could help them settle on a replacement for Moates, as well as reveal other possibilities for growth and service.

When the Harrises's daughter Juli was married to Reel Robertson in 1989, the pastor considered it his privilege as father of the bride to invite simply everyone to the ceremony, which he did in the newsletter of May 9. Other than that, however, the wedding was treated in the usual First Baptist way: the flowers for the ceremony were left as a gift to the church for services on Sunday, May 14, and the young couple was wished "much happiness" as usual in the newsletter of May 16.

Carlton Allen's doctorate, awarded in late May 1989, meant (but only in part) that the church narrowly missed being able to boast of *three* staff ministers at one time with earned doctoral degrees! Allen's Doctor of Ministries was awarded by the seminary in Louisville on May 26, 1989.

The pastor's assessment of the Southern Baptist Convention after its meeting in Las Vegas (a "most unlikely place" indeed) came in the first sentence of his June 20 message which pronounced it "suicidal," albeit by the "slow death" method of extreme polarization. Harris deplored the growing distrust and gradual loss of spirit among messengers, a trend that had been discernible for at least ten years. An Associated Press report printed in *The State* of April 22, 1999, confirms the view that convention controversy has damaged the denomination. Membership in the Southern Baptist Convention dropped in 1998 for the first time in seventy-two years, though church attendance and Sunday school enrollment registered an increase, as did offerings and other gifts. A convention spokesman cited any number of possible reasons for the decline, but Nancy Ammerman, professor of sociology and religion at Hartford Seminary in Connecticut and author of *Baptist Battles*, probably got it right when she attributed the decrease to "concern among local churches over the convention's shift toward a more conservative leadership."

The church called Roger Dale McAbee in October as associate minister with responsibilities in music and education. A graduate of Furman, McAbee held a master's in pastoral care and counseling. He had gained valuable experience in youth work and music at several churches during his undergraduate and seminary years. McAbee was also a Craig Holbrook Parham Scholar. The job description specifically excluded the chancel choir. The church had gone back and forth over the years trying to get the music ministry just right; this time, it appears that the adult choir would be considered in a class by itself. Unfortunately, McAbee's tenure was to last only six months. It seems he suffered a certain "separation anxiety" from leaving Louisville and when an opportunity came to return, he grabbed it. As a young and single man, McAbee was evidently unable to carry out his initial desire "to put down roots" in Greenwood, even though he tried hard. The church was most gracious in accepting his resignation to be effective at the end of March. As usual, volunteers moved in to take up the slack with youth choirs as Holy Week approached.

In the meantime, First Baptist pitched in along with the rest of South Carolina to help clean up after Hurricane Hugo hit in September 1989. One church member cleaned out a store's entire supply of charcoal and sent it to Charleston on the first relief truck along with food supplies from another church. Others went to towns and communities along the coast to offer direct assistance, such as clearing debris from yards and driveways. Groups of volunteers left the church at 5:00 A.M. for several straight Saturdays armed with their lunch, chain saws, rakes, and shovels. They surely returned to Greenwood physically exhausted, but with the satisfaction of *knowing* they had made a difference.

Work on the Bowers-Rodgers Home continued throughout 1989. Much of the actual labor involved had been supplied by volunteers, but serious renovations to the house were left to professional contractors. A director, Janet Bishop, was named in November, and the opening date was tentatively scheduled for February 1, 1990 (later revised to early March). The church budget was expected to cover only $50,000 of the projected annual operating costs, while the rest would come, or so everyone hoped, from other sources. A number of grant proposals were in the works, and the Abney Foundation's gift of $25,000 was part of the report to the deacons on November 5. The Bowers Sunday School Class had determined as early as the previous August that one of the rooms in the shelter would be dedicated in honor of Carole Mauldin.

The arrival of Advent was the signal for another performance of *Messiah*, the annual Lottie Moon Christmas offering, family participation in lighting candles on the Advent wreath each Sunday, special family night programs, and something just a little bit different in 1989: a traditional Moravian lovefeast of buns and coffee. The Moravian Church had begun this practice in 1727 in an attempt to revive the spirit of the early Christians who would break bread together to signify union, fellowship, and love. Two church members who had belonged to a Moravian church in Pennsylvania helped Dale McAbee plan the service of hymns, readings, and prayers. The church also presented that year "a First Baptist version of the traditional service of lessons and carols," a program of scripture readings and music first performed as a Christmas Eve service at England's Truro Cathedral in 1880. Finally, there was for the first time a "mitten tree" to be decorated with dozens of handmade or purchased mittens in children's sizes, part of the effort to "fill the drawers in preparation for the opening of the Bowers-Rodgers Home." Taken all in all, 1989 was quite a year for First Baptist Church. And there was more to come.

The church was able to open more space in the sanctuary when pews were placed in the gallery. A longtime project, but one with a rather low priority, the installation was finally completed with financing from several memorial gifts. Most people agreed that the result was a more "finished" look to the sanctuary, and members were encouraged to find ways to fill up the additional space.

Plans for the opening of the Bowers-Rodgers Home were announced in the newsletter of February 13, 1990. The pastor reviewed the yearlong activity that had begun with a discussion of the need for temporary foster care in Greenwood. As Harris pointed out, this ministry was clearly an idea whose time had come; he wrote that it was rare for a project to receive the sort of widespread support this one had attracted, not only from within the church but from the wider community as well. Open house was set for March 1–3 with a formal dedication ceremony to follow on March 4; service to children would commence on March 5. The pastor pointed out that the ministry represented a sizable investment—renovations alone had cost $100,000, and operations were projected to cost at least $10,000 above that figure annually. Though the ongoing needs and costs meant a formidable challenge, clearly most people felt that the opportunities outweighed the difficulties ahead. Dedication day, "a glorious day for . . . church family and . . . community" went off without a hitch, and a performance by the Furman Singers the same night seemed to cap a period which, in the words of the pastor, radiated "wonderful spirit and enthusiastic involvement."

The Bowers-Rogers Home on Elm Court, dedicated in 1990.

Bowers-Rodgers had served a total of forty-five children by early August of its first year, and twelve youngsters, four of them teenagers, were in residence at the time this report was heard by the directors. As evidence that the facility was meeting a real need, the home's license was amended in September to increase its maximum allowable occupancy from twelve to fifteen.

The church began initial explorations of the feasibility of forming its own association of churches when the deacons met with their counterparts from the First Baptist Church in Clemson. A national convocation for those moderate-to-conservative Baptists who were dissatisfied with their convention, particularly the funding of its cooperative program, was called for August 1990 in Atlanta. The pastor reported that nearly three thousand people attended. The group chose a title—Baptist Cooperative Missions Program—and named a sixty-member committee to develop a mission statement and work on recommendations for missions support. Back in Greenwood, church leaders planned a series of forums so that First Baptist members could discuss these events and share their thoughts and feelings as the movement evolved. Local Baptists rejoiced when Furman's board of trustees distanced the school from the excesses of the state convention by voting to give itself the sole right to elect trustees.

Barbara Tucker of Fort Worth, Texas, joined the church's staff in 1990 as minister of education. Trained at the master's level as an early childhood teacher, Tucker also held a master's in religious education from the seminary. She was fully experienced in both church and school work. Tucker's hiring brought the church full circle in the sense that its very first education director hired in 1949 was a woman. The time span between the employment of Elizabeth (Gravlee) Moss and Barbara Tucker was just over forty years.

Carole Mauldin's very special and intensely personalized work in community missions was recognized again in November 1990 when she received the E. A. McDowell Award for Distinguished Christian Service from the South Carolina Baptist Convention. Mauldin's association with the Bowers-Rodgers ministry might have been the most obvious reason for this honor, but church members were well aware that she had built the missions office of First Baptist Church into a vital resource for meeting community needs in any number of areas.

When the Harris family vacationed in Europe in the summer of 1990, they were able to attend a performance of the famous Passion Play presented every tenth year in Oberammergau in southern Germany. But it was another event on the same trip that resonated most directly in the life of First Baptist Church Greenwood. Harris's tour group attended a Sunday morning church service conducted in English at a Lutheran church near their hotel in Lucerne, Switzerland. The group was recognized and introductions made prior to the service, everyone was caught up in the feeling of warmth and goodwill, and the worship leader invited Harris to read one of the lessons and offer the common cup during communion. Writing about the experience in the newsletter of July 17, the pastor recalled the emotions of the moment. "The feeling of celebration and sharing," he wrote, "was profoundly moving." The memory of that event inspired him to add communion—but communion with a difference—that year to the church's longstanding tradition of a late Christmas Eve service. The difference was that worshipers would receive communion one-by-one at the altar during the half hour of music that opened the service. Members responded positively to the addition, and communion is still a component of Christmas Eve at First Baptist.

The church faced the crisis of the Gulf War in January 1991 with a call to prayer and an open chapel where a listing of names and prayer requests could be found. The pastor's line, "War does not have to be the only way of solving problems," probably reflected most people's thinking at the time, especially in the fiftieth anniversary year of the Japanese attack on Pearl Harbor.

As the music committee worked to find the right person to lead the music program of the church, choir members assigned themselves the task of directing, one month at a time, in late 1990 and early 1991. Margery Lightsey, Reel Robertson, Ora Chaney, and Elizabeth Moss provided leadership and continuity. The pastor's tribute was genuine: "The ability and dedication of our choir members have never been more evident," he wrote. "Each week the choir area is filled, the choir is prepared, and the music is superb."

By the time Jim Bowers died on February 15, 1991, he had invited members of his beloved church family to come and say goodbye. "For several days," the pastor wrote, "a stream of friends . . . [spent] a few moments, one or two at a time, with him." The worship service that was his funeral was led by people of his choosing; he also chose the musical selections nearly a year before his death. Harris called the service a "celebration of a life and an expression of gratitude to God." Bowers had made Greenwood his home, and First Baptist his church, for forty-eight years. He was deeply gratified that the Bowers-Rodgers Home, which he pronounced "the very kind of thing the church should be doing" would be a lasting memorial in his name.

A special music search committee wrote a job description for a full-time minister of music to direct and coordinate all aspects of the church music program. The only problem was the impact on the budget of funding this position (projected at the $30,000–$37,000 range) at the same time the church was coming to terms with the reality of the ongoing expense of the Bowers-Rodgers Home. Deacon Kenny Poston laid out the problem in the newsletter of April 2, 1991: "We've become spoiled at First Baptist," he wrote, "because until last year, we've never had serious budget problems. The funds always seemed to come in. We took it for granted." Poston predicted that the membership would accept the dual challenge of a new staff position and the Bowers-Rodgers commitment in true First Baptist style after a little serious consideration of the implications of retrenchment. The church was scheduled to vote on this issue, as well as on a statement setting forth a position on denominational affairs, at a conference set for April 21. Both recommendations received overwhelming approval.

The vote to adopt the congregational statement of faith in Jesus Christ and its expression through historic Baptist principles meant that the church could move forward on its feasibility study of a new Baptist association. The church at Clemson had broken with its association in 1976, and First Baptist had been without affiliation at that point for twenty years. Groups from the two churches had voted to form an association for purposes of fellowship and mutual effort in ministry, education, and missions. When the membership agreed with this position, the way was cleared to write a covenant and invite other churches to be part of the new venture. The first meeting of the Covenant Baptist Association was held at Clemson in October. Harris saw the gathering as "a genuine celebration" of unity and fellowship, of Baptist heritage, and of new opportunities. A committee headed by Kenny Poston had written a constitution which became the founding document of the organization when approved by those in attendance and signed by each church's deacon chairman. The first officers were as follows: Carlton Allen, moderator; Butch Trent, vice-moderator; Joyce Williams, secretary; and Jacque Herndon, treasurer. Appropriately, two officers were from Greenwood and two from Clemson. When the new association was refused recognition by the general board of the state convention, which happened the following spring, Harris's response was that the board had missed yet another chance to affirm Baptist heritage and tradition and was therefore the real loser from the vote. "We will go on being Baptist," he wrote. "We didn't lose a thing."

Deirdre Francis, a native of Anderson, a Furman graduate, and an alumna of the famous Westminster Choir College in Princeton, New Jersey, became the first full-fledged minister of music on August 1. The music project had required a full six months from the earliest phase of dreams and discussions to hammering out a final job description, collecting resumes, conducting interviews, and settling on the candidate with ideal credentials. The job of the search committee from beginning to end was, in effect, no less than preparing the way for the church to expand its ministries through a comprehensive music program.

The pastor reported on the progress of the Southern Baptist Alliance in the newsletter of September 24. Organized in 1986, the alliance consisted of 134 congregations and more than 72,000 members when it held its fall meeting in Washington, a meeting that Harris attended. The group had not been idle: a new seminary in Richmond had just opened its doors with thirty-one students in the first class, and the alliance had also produced entirely new Sunday school literature entitled "Formations."[5] Discussions of future possibilities with any number of Baptist groups were also under way. A convocation was scheduled for March 1992 at which participants would be asked to approve a name change to "Alliance of Baptists" in order to reflect the inclusive nature of the alliance as well as its growth in scope and mission.

The church budget for 1992 topped $600,000 and was subdivided into seven ministries: Missions, Pastoral, Christian Education, Youth, Music, Support, and Building and Grounds. A full quarter of budgeted expenditures was earmarked for denominational and local missions; topping the list was the church's own Bowers-Rodgers Home.

The holiday season in 1991 capped a turbulent year for the Baptist denomination, on both the regional and state levels. The state convention meeting in Columbia that year was marred by unrest over "the Furman question." Messengers voted, in fact, to pursue a court ruling regarding the legality of the trustees' decision to become a self-perpetuating body, a move that seemed not only futile but self-defeating as well. "Furman will prosper with or without the South Carolina Baptist Convention," the pastor wrote. Meanwhile, the church moved smoothly into its own well-loved routine of family night at Thanksgiving, followed by Advent, Deedy Francis's first *Messiah* and other music performances, trips, parties, and the myriad activities of a large church family. An expanded *Messiah*, featuring choruses and arias not included before, was presented that year; four guest soloists, mostly from Greenville, performed with the local chorus and a regional orchestra.

The pastor used his first column of the new year to report that the budget for 1991 was met, even oversubscribed by the munificent sum of $198![6] He believed this milestone in giving was a clear indication of growth, understanding, and commitment on the part of the membership. He also announced that a series entitled "Know Your Church" would inform members and others about the variety of ministries and the scope of activities and opportunities available, as well as the meaning of certain symbols and rituals adopted over the years. The first was an explanation of the antependia colors of white, purple, red, and green and their significance to the church year.

A provocative article appeared over the signature of youth minister Carlton Allen in the newsletter of April 28. "First Baptist Church Greenwood is a special place," he wrote, and added, "We are indeed a unique Baptist congregation." While the defining characteristics of the denomination itself mean that these statements could be made about any Baptist church, Allen clearly had something else entirely in mind when he wrote the article. His point was the possibility that the church could lose sight of its rich Baptist heritage by concentrating too strongly on the increasingly diverse religious backgrounds that could be found among the congregation. Though he recognized that new ideas and new views, many of them characteristic of other denominations and other creeds, could enrich fellowship and enhance Christian growth, he also wished to remind members that the name First *Baptist* Church meant something quite specific, something that new members might wish to explore in more depth than was possible in a Sunday morning sermon. For that reason, an orientation study over four Sunday evenings would cover very basic questions focusing strictly on Baptist beliefs.

The first, *Who Are We?*, would discuss early Baptist movements and the development of the Southern Baptist Convention. *What Do We Believe?* would examine Baptist doctrine, while *What Have We Become?* would explore the radical changes in the convention since 1979, the reasons for the changes, and their implications for the future. Finally, *What Makes Us Unique?* would concentrate on First Baptist Church itself, its mission, and its evolution over more than a century. At the same time, the deacons were working on a statement regarding the state convention and the burning question of what it would do about Furman's defection. Clearly, denominational matters occupied center stage in the early 1990s. Allen might have been more prescient than he knew when he wrote, "And, perhaps, there are some [members] who have been here for years and [still] struggle to define who we are and what we believe."

When the convention voted "to sever legal and financial ties" with Furman in May, the pastor called the action "the best option available" to the nearly five thousand messengers who voted on the question, but not the solution many had wished. The school had worked out a specific "covenant relationship" with the convention's relations committee, but when that option was removed from consideration it seemed that setting Furman free was the best way to go. Harris reminded the membership, however, that the situation did not apply to individual churches who remained free to continue their own ties with Furman in their own way. The last paragraph of the pastor's message made an important point: "In time, 'legal and financial ties' will likely prove to be unimportant. Ties of faith and practice are much more significant. They come from common goals and from mutual feelings. Ties of that nature are very much intact."

Several staff members retired in the summer of 1992, among them secretaries Joyce Williams and Lois Grice. C. J. Hendrix, who had been the church's first maintenance supervisor, also retired after seventeen years on the job; he was replaced by current supervisor Alan Bishop. Grace Burton came on board to join Nell Morton as a full-time employee, while Williams continued to work in a part-time capacity.

The year 1992 marked the end of annual performances of Handel's *Messiah*, which had become almost a signature of the church's presence in the community as well as a clear sign that the holiday season had begun. There was no explanation of the reasons for moving to a biennial schedule, though it is true that attendance had been dropping for several years. One could speculate also that the amount of time and work involved had simply become too much. Most people agree that "American family life" has become something of a misnomer in the 1990s. Every family member seems gradually to have developed his or her individual schedule—each timetable vitally important to someone—and a great deal of coming and going and rushing around to meet that schedule is now the norm. Something as basic as pulling off a full family dinner a night or two a week had become difficult by 1992; it should not be surprising that fitting rehearsal times for a major production into people's lives was nearly impossible.

The church moved into new territory once again with a proposed budget of $614,500 for 1993. The pastor noted that the figure represented "a modest increase" over the 1992 total of $605,000. That budget, however, had not been fully subscribed as of the end of the year; the first newsletter of 1993 reported a shortage of $31,000. The deficit had shrunk to $26,558 by the middle of January, and the deacons voted to call on cash reserves to meet budgeted commitments; oddly enough, reserves and shortage roughly equaled each other. Members responded by oversubscribing budget needs in early 1993. Receipts had outstripped budgeted needs by more than $4,000 at the end of the first six weeks.

An intriguing ministry called "helpinghands" was inaugurated in March 1993. Patterned after a similar program at a church in Spartanburg, the purpose was to offer members a chance for hands-on involvement in the work of the church for four days each year. The day's work for an individual might be anything from phoning shut-ins to driving someone to a doctor's appointment or the supermarket, but it was work that was meant to make members feel part of something larger than themselves. Carole Mauldin called it a "tithe of time and talents" and emphasized that the program was for everyone in the church—a chance for many people to "do a little bit" to help with the missions effort and make the church program their own. About ninety people had signed on by the time the effort got under way on June 1. Volunteers during the first week provided forty-two hours of service, the equivalent of a week's work of a full-time home missionary. The duties were completely fluid from week to week and even from day to day. The program was expected to grow and change as needs were identified and as the ministry skills of the volunteers became apparent.

The pastor reported on the status of the church's scholarship ministry in the newsletter of July 20. The Craig Holbrook Parham Scholarship Fund provided scholarship assistance to twenty-two seminary students for 1993–1994, bringing its total disbursements to nearly $37,000 and the number of recipients to sixty-five in its seven-year history.[7] The Furman Scholarship Program, a budgeted item at $4,400, was the result of direct giving after the state convention severed ties with the school. In addition, an award in memory of Tony Stokes was established in 1990 and given annually to an outstanding high school senior. The pastor reminded members that these ministries were congregational in scope and provided a significant service to individuals who were preparing themselves to render services of their own.

The combined choirs of First Baptist and First Presbyterian Churches presented John Rutter's *Requiem* in November 1993 with Charles Gaines, music director at Presbyterian, conducting. A small orchestra provided accompaniment, and Deedy Francis was soprano soloist. The performance took place on All Saints Sunday "in honor and in memory of those who have gone before."

The budget for 1993 was oversubscribed by about $20,000, an accomplishment the pastor termed "highly significant" in view of the previous year's experience in which the church's cash reserves were entirely depleted to meet budgeted commitments. Harris praised members' responsiveness to early "catch-up" calls and noted that 1993 was a year of growth in both missions consciousness and financial stewardship.

An item in the agenda for the deacons' meeting of January 9—that the missions committee was considering a "united ministries" type of program—was surely the real beginning of the community-wide Greater Greenwood United Ministries we know today, a program described as "a partnership of denominations, community groups, and congregations" whose purpose is to assist individuals and families in need. Though the helpinghands program also played a role in the church's desire to find more effective ways of meeting needs and helping families in crisis, a full-fledged move to join with other community agencies was clearly the final goal. Missions chairman Carole Mauldin was authorized to work toward a recommendation as to funding and services. The next step, one that would formalize the church's continuing involvement, was to place Mauldin on salary for six months during which time the church missions office would function as a center for community missions. At the same time, the Bowers-Rodgers Home was moving forward on a number of fronts, one of them a thrift store which opened in 1994 and which continues to provide significant revenue to the facility.

The format of the newsletter became a little more sophisticated with the issue of April 5, 1994, thanks to the computer skills of George Cone and Ken Anders. Primarily a means of communication but also an important record of church and community events, the newsletter, in the words of the pastor, "binds us together as a congregation." The change, the pastor noted, was the first since 1953; no one could call it extreme or premature. Another change—a small one this time—came when new hymnals were placed in service in August, and the "Amen" was omitted at the end of most congregational hymns.

When Elbert Adams retired after forty-nine years as organist, the church needed a little time to adjust. "It is difficult for us to imagine coming to worship and not having Dr. Adams at the organ," the pastor wrote. "We are conditioned to expect his service and to appreciate the excellence he brings to the music program of our church." Though his official retirement came in July, the church chose a Sunday in September to designate Adams organist emeritus after a service during which the choir presented four anthems of his selection as well as several of his favorite congregational hymns.

Greenwood native Elbert Adams and First Baptist Church shared a mutual regard that apparently never wavered. Adams accepted with appreciation the church's "total cooperation" in everything he did and called the experience "one of the great joys of my life." He considered himself especially fortunate to have designed three separate organ installations during his tenure on the (organ) bench.

Adams had studied organ and piano at Lander College even before he entered Furman University where he earned both the BA and BS degrees and graduated with honors. Though he majored in the sciences as a premed student, Adams's college career included five years as piano accompanist and soloist for the Furman Glee Club; he also won the Fallaw-Wesner music medal and played the organ at Pendleton Street Baptist Church. Even as a medical student at Emory, Adams was able to indulge his artistic side as organist for the university's Little Symphony Orchestra.

Adams's medical career in Greenwood, beginning in 1941, was interrupted almost immediately by four years of military service in World War II. After seven months in England and North Africa, he returned to the United States for study at the Air Force School of Aviation Medicine and a later appointment as lecturer in field medicine and field surgery at the School of Applied Tactics. Adams left the Medical Corps with the rank of major and returned to Greenwood where he resumed his professional practice and began an association with First Baptist Church that would last until his death in December 1995.

Adams was a founding member of the Greenwood chapter of the American Guild of Organists and served terms as both southeastern regional and state chairman of the organization. The Greenwood Community Theatre and the Lander-Greenwood Performing Arts Association named him to their boards and elected him president. He served his church also as deacon and chairman of the building committee during the first phase of the building campaign from 1953 to 1956. And always Adams was a regular on the recital stage, performing as both soloist and in two-piano programs.

Elbert Adams was a man of taste and refinement, a bit of an aesthete but possessing a practical side as well. Many people credit Adams with masterminding a great deal of the "high church" image of First Baptist Church Greenwood; one member believes he must have come from an Anglican (or at least an Episcopalian) background. Actually, that explanation is rather doubtful since Adams's roots in Greenwood County lie in the Phoenix section where his grandfather practiced medicine. Phoenix is a "good news–bad news" sort of place; Louis Booker Wright, perhaps Greenwood's most distinguished native son, grew up there. On the other hand, the Phoenix Riot of 1898 links the place with a particularly violent post-Reconstruction lynching episode.

Carlton Allen resigned in the fall of 1994 to accept a call to the First Baptist Church of Claxton, Georgia. His thirteen-year tenure as minister to youth was marked, in the words of the pastor, by dedication, competence, and faithfulness. Though he gave first priority to his work with young people, Allen's influence had actually been felt throughout the church; he was called a gifted preacher, a talented storyteller, and a compassionate counselor. Always there are mixed feelings when a popular staff member moves on; the wrench of saying goodbye is balanced by the realization of greater opportunities and a bright future in another place. So it was when the Allen family left Greenwood and First Baptist Church. The youth minister filled the pulpit on his last Sunday; the sermon topic that day was "I Thank My God for You. . . ."

Along with sixteen other charter churches, First Baptist was ready in October to announce the formation of the Greater Greenwood United Ministries. Financial support was recommended at 1 percent of the budget (about $6,500 annually). Formed as a crisis ministry to provide emergency assistance—such as food, clothing, and shelter—to people in need, the program was also designed as an opportunity for members to become involved in the larger community. Prayers, volunteers, financial support, resources, and talents were actively sought as preparations for the ministry moved from the planning stage to full implementation.

E. W. Milford (1892–1982), member of the church for seventy-five years, whose bequest of $1.25 million funded a permanent endowment in 1995. The majority of the Milford estate of more than $11 million was left to Baptist institutions in South Carolina.

Nearly a quarter of the proposed budget for 1995 was designated for missions ministries, both denominational and local. Clearly the church viewed itself at this juncture as willing and able to manage its own commitment in this vital area. A shift of more than $10,000 between denominational and local missions occurred from 1994 to 1995, but the bottom line increased only nominally, from $638,087 to $641,119, less than ½ of 1 percent.

In early 1995 First Baptist Church announced that it had received the amount of $1.25 million from the estate of Eugene and Louise Milford, part of a $10 million bequest the Milfords left to five religious and educational institutions. This gift meant that the church was able to set up a permanent endowment fund, the income from which would be used to fund some of its ministries. At the same time, the 1994 budget came up short by nearly $11,000 as the new year got under way. The record contribution of more than $113,000 in December was still not enough for the church to meet its budgeted obligations.[8] It was inevitable, of course, that someone would assume, aloud, that the Milford bequest must have ended any worries about the church's finances. When that actually happened, the pastor used the opportunity to remind members that no part of the gift, nor any income it might generate, could be used for operating expenses. His reminder was terse and to the point: "Our church budget is still our guide, and our personal gifts support the church budget." Even so, it is difficult to avoid wondering whether the receipts for January 1995, called the weakest showing ever, might have reflected some lingering confusion among the membership.

The church was presented with a statement of concern as part of its long-range planning committee report delivered in early 1995. Not surprisingly, a major concern was what seemed to be a record of declining attendance at both Sunday school and worship services. Financial stewardship was another troubling issue, since the pattern of giving continued to be uneven. A third problem was a perceived lack of involvement among the laity in leadership and service roles. A formal plan was laid out—from objectives to strategies—and responsibilities fixed, with timetables, to address these concerns. Long-range planning was a new approach for church leaders but one that fit rather neatly into the scheme of American life in the 1990s. The pastor was obviously pleased with the committee's work; he seconded the note of urgency and significance the deacons had brought to tackling the focus area of spiritual growth, commitment, and attendance. He also believed that an emphasis on faith and service would serve members well as they worked together on congregational goals.

The newsletter of January 31 also announced a celebration of the 125th anniversary of the church's founding planned for September. Several former staff members would share in the program, an anniversary directory was in the works, and a formal church history would be undertaken. The job of the congregation would be to inform friends and former members, anticipate the celebration in ways meaningful to their own households, and invite family members to "come home" for the event. A number of displays were also planned to depict "the way it was" in a number of areas when the church (if not its members) was a good deal younger.

The personnel committee hoped to be able to announce a replacement for Carlton Allen by June 1, 1995. A new title, minister of students, had been worked out, as well as an expanded job description; the new minister would be expected to work with middle school students as well as with those of high school and college age. The committee's choice turned out to be Richmond native Graham Cheek. The church approved the recommendation, and Cheek reported for work in early September. He held an undergraduate degree in history and religious studies from Virginia Commonwealth University and a master's from the seminary at Richmond. He also had extensive church experience and had developed a thriving youth program at the Carlisle Avenue Baptist Church in Richmond. The church was pleased to recognize interim youth director Robert Cone who, along with Christy Coleman, had performed yeoman service with the student ministry for the past year.

Carole Mauldin undertook an explanation of the relationship between the helpinghands program and the United Ministry in the newsletter of February 21, 1995. She pointed out that the two programs were actually quite different—one was a crisis ministry committed to help with permanent solutions to chronic family problems, while the other had been set up to deal with minor chores such as providing transportation around town, handling deliveries of one kind or another, and rendering small services to individuals in less than dire circumstances. Mauldin believed the answer to whether both types of effort could be sustained lay with the members themselves and asked them to join in pondering questions about the church's role in the community. She was willing to state her own belief that the church was fully capable of handling both ministries.

A small group from First Baptist attended the fifth annual general assembly of the Cooperative Baptist Fellowship which met in

Fort Worth, Texas, in the summer of 1995. The pastor chose to expand on the three-word name of the organization as a means of briefing the membership on the meeting. The word *cooperative*, he wrote, describes the fact that members freely join their fellow Baptists in missions work in a "world without borders." He added that the word *Baptist* is absolutely vital, standing as it does "for the freedom of individuals and churches, the priesthood of all persons (including women), and the effort to understand and practice what the Bible says (not just to praise the Bible)." Finally, he declared that "*Fellowship* is simply what we are, . . . a group of people who love and serve Christ together [with] . . . no concern for power." Harris concluded the article with the hope that the fellowship would remain just that and not become a "denomination."

Deirdre Francis resigned in August after a successful tenure of four years as minister of music, and Jean Wood agreed to step in as interim director of the chancel choir. In other news on the music ministry front, organist Brenda Fairbanks announced the gift of a new set of chimes and a nine-bell cymbelstern[9] to the organ installation. She also announced a series of classes designed to acquaint members with the finer points of the church's instrument, including the loft area.

The church found itself struggling once again with needs in the music area, specifically the question of whether the position of music minister should be part- or full-time. The work of a committee appointed to study this question went on for months and resulted in the recommendation that the church employ Larry Schultz, a native of Oklahoma and a seminary graduate, as the full-time minister of music. Schultz joined the staff in early 1996. Even as the personnel committee was working on the music vacancy, Barbara Tucker resigned her position as minister of education to return to the classroom in Texas where she planned to teach English as a second language (ESL in academic terminology). Tucker characterized her tenure of five years ("one of the great adventures of my life") as a time of great change in denominational relationships and literature resources. Tucker's replacement turned out to be Kenneth Standley, another Texan and seminary graduate, who moved to Greenwood from Nashville, Tennessee.

At the time of the 125th anniversary celebration—September 1995—the church staff was in something of a transition phase. Committees worked to revamp job descriptions in an effort to rethink both the needs of the church and the constantly evolving emphases in the world of work. The fact that the church was actually somewhat shorthanded makes the scope and quality of the anniversary celebration even more impressive.

The three-day event planned for Friday through Sunday, September 22–24, was conceived as a sort of combined Homecoming/Thanksgiving/Rededication for the church. Former staffers and members who had gone on to careers in ministries of one kind or another were invited to participate in worship services, musical performances, reunions, and even a very special book-signing event in the fellowship hall. Bill Treadwell came from Texas, Carlton Allen and Chuck Moates from Georgia, and Jerry Keeney from Missouri. Russ Comer, a victim of severe kidney disease, was too ill to travel from his home in Virginia, but he sent his regrets "with pain and tears" in a letter to the pastor. The Reverend Johnson Dorn, who grew up in the church, Angela Wyndham Powers, Gloria Lightsey, and Chuck Beaudrot, all of whom shared long memories of activity in the youth program of the church, also participated in very special ways, as did the church's favorite professional singers Nat Chandler and Keith Richard.

The schedule for the weekend was nothing if not comprehensive. The media ministry sponsored a book signing by Greenwood native Robert Seymour on Friday afternoon. Reunions for participants in the youth program were held at different times on Saturday afternoon at the lake homes of the Bill Allreds and the Bill Eatons; youth leaders Bill Treadwell, Jerry Keeney, and Carlton Allen were guests of honor at these gatherings. Members of the NGO group met in reunion with their special friend Chuck Moates, who had served as staff advisor during the early development phase of the seniors' organization. Chancel choir alumni met for early breakfast and a special rehearsal on Sunday morning. Historical displays calling attention not only to the past but also to a record of growth and service in Christian education, library and media, missions, and music, were set up around the fellowship hall. The Sunday school emphasized a high attendance day for Bible study and worked to have all current members, as well as former members and prospects, present on Sunday morning.

Finally, three formal worship services—during which Allen, Dorn, Moates, Keeney, and Treadwell spoke—were scheduled for Friday and Saturday evenings and Sunday morning (Julie Jay Carter also participated on Sunday morning). Chuck Beaudrot composed a special anthem, "This Is the Day," for the occasion; other special music offerings were presented by Powers, Lightsey, and a brass quintet; and a full concert by Chandler and Richard set the stage for the Saturday night worship service. Capping everything off was an old-fashioned picnic ("dinner on the ground") at noon on Sunday.

Notes of appreciation came in from former and current members alike. Chuck Beaudrot, writing from his law offices in Atlanta, called the celebration "extraordinarily rich" and "one of the best things I have ever seen done at First Baptist." Noonie Fennell, who had moved her membership to another Greenwood church, attended in part to represent the Ray family (her father, Robert Ray, had been a member at that point for more than fifty years); she wrote that the music and worship services, particularly on Saturday, had left her speechless. Elizabeth Byrd found the program "glorious" and "a great thrill," while Rena Bailey wrote that it was all she could do "not to get up and go" with the choir during its processional down the center aisle. Bailey added that the happiest days of her life had been spent in the choir loft of First Baptist Church. Judy Cheek Ethridge wrote that she had "spent most of the weekend . . . with a lump in my throat."

The anniversary celebration was, of course, the result of a great deal of work and dedication by a great many people. Guidance had come from professionals in a number of areas (brochures from the Historical Commission of the Southern Baptist Convention had played a part), and everyone seemed to have caught the spirit of the occasion. Even the pastor's "debriefing" in the newsletter of September 26 used terms such as *impressed*, *inspired*, and *strengthened* to describe the lingering effects of the weekend, particularly the "loving contributions" of all who had made it so special. The theme of emotion—a state of strong feeling—was everywhere apparent, from the "touching" quality of the formal messages to the "relaxed fellowship" of the communal meal that followed the last service. "We are a people dedicated to Christ and to each other," the pastor wrote, "That's worth celebrating at all times, not just on anniversaries."

But anniversaries—and other high holy days—cannot in and of themselves define a church. The cumulative effects of its day-to-day impact on real people and real communities must be analyzed for that purpose, and the myriad responses and contributions of literally thousands of members over months, years, decades, and centuries must be added to the mix. Perhaps the most significant aspect of First Baptist Church Greenwood is that it lives and its story is ongoing. Graham Cheek, a new staff member at the time of the celebration, moved back to Virginia in the spring of 1998, and Jamie Harris (eighteen months old when her father assumed the pulpit) joined the staff in early June upon graduation from Furman University. Established ministries grew and changed as well; some, such as the Bowers-Rodgers Home and United Ministries, became full-fledged community entities not officially connected to the church, while others, such as Habitat for Humanity, AIDS Awareness, the Food Bank, Greenwood Soup Kitchen (named in memory of Margaret Ray, a dedicated volunteer from its beginning in 1987 until her death in April 1995), and Meals-on-Wheels, continue to attract volunteers from within the church family. Helpinghands remained in the church program as a ministry for all church and community members. The budget continued to grow to its current level of just under $662,000. Major repairs to the organ installation were made in 1997, and the sanctuary was repainted for the first time the same year. The deacons could not seem to agree on plans for a covered walkway on the building's lower level; the notion went back and forth for at least a year and the project has not been implemented as of this writing, but the downstairs carpet installation received the green light at a meeting in 1997.

The pastor continued to deliver his masterfully crafted sermons as a series around a central theme—the Psalms was one unifying topic; God as Father, Son, and Holy Spirit another. A series on the parables and miracles as depicted in the church's own stained glass windows is currently under way. Under the aegis of its worship committee the church moved into the study and practice of the concept of corporate worship, defined as the worship of God through the actions of a gathered body, in the summer of 1997, a move that led to a change in the order of service. The aim of the change was to bring about greater understanding and appreciation of the concept of worship and an attempt to view every element of the service as a call to God. Part of this emphasis took the form of a most informative twenty-page booklet entitled *The Worship of God at First Baptist Church* that defines every aspect of the church program, both the tangible and the intangible, in terms of the underlying philosophy of corporate worship. Of particular value is a glossary of worship-related terms to assist those who wish to understand the historical context of a number of elements in the church's physical design, as well as its form of service.

Running like a golden thread throughout the life of First Baptist Church as it moves inexorably deeper into the second century of its existence are the words of the vision statement printed in a shaded box in most issues of the church newsletter:

> As the body of Christ living in today's world, we celebrate Christ's love by coming together for worship, study and fellowship and by going out to serve and to minister to those in need.

The Eddie Lieberman story has come virtually full circle since the bare bones account in the church's minute books of more than fifty years ago. Many members remembered his name, and when word of the author's search for more information reached the ears of Robert R. "Buddy" Jay, whose family had known Lieberman well, his own curiosity was aroused. He vaguely remembered hearing at some point that Lieberman lived in retirement in Greenville and decided to do a little detective work of his own.

In addition to his willingness to help research the church history, Jay had another reason to look for Lieberman. By an odd chance, he and his wife Liza had attended the 11:00 A.M. service one Sunday in the summer of 1998 when Johnson Dorn filled the pulpit as guest minister. Jay was amazed to find that a story about his mother, Lucile Parks Jay, was part of Dorn's sermon that day. Naturally he was pleased, and even more touched when Dorn followed up with a personal note and an essay entitled "Mrs. Jay" that he had used as background material for the sermon. The essay is dated 12-7-95. Both are presented here just as he wrote them:

July 24, 1998

Buddy:

It was truly good to see you again, after so many years, this past Sunday. The Lord really is interesting in His ways. I had not planned on telling that story about your mother. I did not use it at the 9:00 am service. For some reason it just seemed to fit at the 11:00 service.

Your mother was indeed a remarkable woman. I hate I did not avail myself of her while she was alive. Yet, the Lord is full of grace because, even beyond the grave, she speaks now. One of these days I may write a book about the people the Lord placed in my life but at the time seemed relegated to the periphery, but who now loom so much more in the center of my life. Your mother was one of those people.

I hope the enclosed story ministers His grace and encouragement to you as she did to me.

Bless you,
Johnson Dorn

Mrs. Jay
12-7-95
jgd

I deemed Mrs. Jay eccentric at best. She was the little old lady who stood at the end of her church pew every Sunday when the people of God filed out of church. It was her calling to greet the saints, admonishing them, encouraging them, and in the midst of it all, as old saintly women are apt to do, she always praised the Lord.

As a teenager, I did my best to avoid Mrs. Jay. She scared me. I didn't understand her ways nor her words. Her joyful demeanor was a mystery I could not come close to penetrating. Her wise and wonderful words bounced off a heart hardened with self-assured immaturity. So I did what most of us do in the presence of unrecognized holiness. I walked away.

Most Sundays I was able to slide out of church elusively, slinking down the aisle opposite Mrs. Jay, seizing the moments she was engaging some unsuspecting member of the congregation. Occasionally though, my Father, bless his soul, would grab me by the arm, flinging me at the Lord's mighty little servant. And there I stood on those occasional Sundays, when I was within Dad's arm's reach, in the presence of Mrs. Jay, begrudgingly listening to a word from the Lord. Words I wasn't prepared to hear for many years.

My teenage years gave way to years at college. Yet even in the distant security of a school many miles from home, I could not elude the awakened and persistent heart of Mrs. Jay. She wrote me letters. Letters filled with clippings from devotional writings. Letters filled with the wisdom that comes from many years of walking faithfully with the Lord. Letters filled with sincere and appropriate warnings about the dangers of my studies and how they might lead a young and unripened heart astray. Letters that spoke of her prayers, prayers for me.

In the blindness and pride that often comes with youth, I took Mrs. Jay's letters and prayers and I laughed. Not mockingly, but condescendingly. The laugh accompanied by the shaking head. You know the kind. And, I gathered her correspondence and quietly buried it all in some hidden manila folder and went on about my business of getting smart.

> In the gospel of Luke (2:36–38), there is a story about a woman named Anna. It was said of Anna that she was very old. A widow. And, that she never left the temple but worshipped night and day, fasting and praying. Interesting thing about this Anna, she recognized Jesus when he was a baby, when all the world didn't recognize a thing. The scripture says she gave thanks to God for Jesus and spoke about him to all who were looking forward to his redemption.
>
> Mrs. Jay. A modern day Anna. A woman of worship. A woman of prayer. A woman found faithfully in the temple of the Lord. A woman giving thanks. A woman speaking prophetically to anyone who listened.
>
> I wasn't listening years ago when Mrs. Jay uttered her prophecies from the rear of First Baptist Church, Greenwood, South Carolina. I did not see that my life with the Lord, a life that I treasure so deeply now, would be preserved by the likes of Mrs. Jay. During years of desert wanderings that took me far from the Lord's holy temple, there was old Mrs. Jay praying and living a life of praise before the Lord. And I, for one, am now deeply thankful.
>
> Look closely now and see the eccentric ones. The ones who are strangely in this world but not of this world. The ones who glow with the light of mystery and fear. The ones who love the Lord and the Lord only. The ones whose lives are so unlike ours. The ones whom we would prefer to dismiss. The ones who live on the periphery, who take their place at the rear of the church and hold forth girded up by a cane. Oh, see them now, and if you are able become as they, for even though now they sit in the rear of the church, then they shall be first.

With this background, it is easy to understand why Buddy Jay was eager to see if he could find any trace of the Eddie Lieberman he remembered so well in connection with his mother. He called his friend Bill Martin and asked him to read off the list of Liebermans in the Greenville telephone book. Sure enough, an Eddie S. Lieberman was there. Buddy called that day and spoke to the very gentleman he remembered from his mother's Sunday dinner table many, many years earlier. Neither wasted much time; Jay received a brief note in November 1998 and a longer communication meant for the church history only a couple of weeks later. Both deserve reprinting in their entirety:

17 November 1998

Dear Buddy:

Memory—what a wonderful thing it is, especially when it brings back joyous experiences. That's what your phone call did and is still doing to me.

I'm truly sorry that this note is so delayed, but with my physical condition, plus my mental & emotional state due to my wife's sad condition, I was unable to get on time the information you requested on behalf of church history.

Johnson Dorn's reflection on your dear sainted mother was touching. *I owe her much more!!*

Please keep in touch.

Love in Him,
Eddie

* * * * *

3 December 1998

Dear Buddy:

Here at last is something you asked for about [your] Mother and a short biographical sketch of myself. Actually both are interlocked. Here goes.

Lucile Jay was to me "the gospel in shoes." She was more than a hearer and believer—she was a doer of the gospel. My first encounter with Mrs. Jay, oddly enough, was when I was behind bars as a federal prisoner in Greenwood. That was before they moved the federal jail to Atlanta.

In May 1932, four p.m., three women came to the jail to hold services for the inmates: Mrs. A. F. Hagan, Carrie Hagan and Mrs. Jay, all members of the First Baptist Church. Mrs. Hagan was the spokesperson, Carrie sang and Mrs. Jay who "amened" Mrs. Hagan.

I was a nineteen year old Orthodox Jew who attended the service out of curiosity. It made no impression on me. To my amazement, the three women returned the following Sunday. Since I had never heard the gospel before and the name of Jesus was forbidden in my home, I started to argue with them. But their patience and loving attitude toward me, a Jew, made a deep impression.

The next Sunday, in anger, I told them that this Jesus could not be the Jewish Messiah. It was Mrs. Jay who suggested that she would bring a Bible to let me read for myself and see that Jesus was the Jewish Messiah, fulfilling the prophesies in the Old Testament. I agreed to read it, knowing that it could not be possible.

In her spiritual insight she brought me a complete Bible (I had never seen a New Testament) and had written on paper some nine prophesies in the Old Testament and how Jesus fulfilled all nine. Wisely, she wrote the page numbers, chapters and verses for me to read. My whole conception of Jesus (he was a false god) radically changed. After two and a half months of reading the New Testament, I believed that Jesus was the Jewish Messiah, had been raised from the dead and offered me eternal life. I accepted him as such and promised to follow him to the best of my ability.

After my trial and the results (which made headlines in the "Greenwood Index,") Mrs. Hagan took me into her home. My family in New York City cast me out, declaring me dead. This was in response to my letter to them that I had become a Christian and had been baptized.

The pastor, Dr. Sims, and the congregation took me into their hearts and homes. Mrs. Jay had me over almost every Sunday. The one dish that she prepared for me every Sunday—how could I forget it?—was her famous macaroni pie. At the depth of the Depression I was living in joyous expression. As Jesus taught, I had more than life. I was experiencing abundant life!!

Mrs. Hagan, Lucile Jay and many of the members prayed that I would become a minister which was the farthest thing from my mind. I was set on getting an education. My journey along that road brought me to our Baptist seminary in New Orleans for further study of the Christian teachings. Then quickly followed Mars Hill College, Baylor University and the University of Tennessee for a doctorate in psychology. My special field would be clinical psychology.

Sometime later, I was invited back to the seminary to set up the first classes ever taught in personal counseling, family problems and social case work. They made me an associate professor in the Religious Education Department, not certain in what department my subjects belonged. Two of the subjects I introduced at the seminary are still being taught. Over fifty years!

Through my student days in New Orleans and Mars Hill College, Major R. B. Curry had his Sunday School class loan me a total sum of three hundred dollars. This was a large amount of money in those days. Years later, I paid it back to the class.

The prayers of Lucile Jay and others finally were answered. I accepted God's call to the ministry, resigned my professorship and pastored my first church in Alabama.

Before Mrs. Jay went to be with the Lord, I came to see her and asked for the Bible she had let me use while I was in prison. It is in my library right next to the Bible that the First Baptist Church gave me on the day I was ordained to the ministry. Numbers of times I have perused through both Bibles to recall the early days of my Christian beginnings.

Now, in my eighty-sixth year my memories of the members of the church from the early nineteen thirties through the seventies remain crystal clear, with special thoughts of God's three angels who introduced me to Jesus Christ, the son of God. To him and our Heavenly Father be honor, glory and thanksgiving.

Yours and Always His,
Eddie S. Lieberman

By this time, readers are surely aware that they have a perfectly splendid introduction to Mrs. Jay through the words of two people who knew her in different ways and at different times of her life. They might, in fact, believe they know all there is to know about this remarkable Greenwood character. But they would be wrong to think so, since she was as multifaceted on one level as she was singleminded on another. The singlemindedness was, of course, her simple and straightforward faith. A Christian in the sense that she walked daily with her Lord and Savior, Mrs. Jay was truly, as Lieberman put it, "a doer of the gospel."

But she was even more. Born in 1889, Lucile Parks lost her mother to typhoid fever when she was only two years old. From a churchgoing family, she was baptized early (in Cuffeytown Creek) by her home church, Bethany, at Liberty Hill in what is now McCormick County. Having spent a great deal of time with her Sheppard,[1] Yeldell, and Parks relatives as a young girl, she must have been pleased when her father remarried and moved with his new wife to Orangeburg and a job on the newspaper in that town. But there would be no lasting new family for young Lucile, who was by this time completing high school in Columbia. Her father was shot down on the town square one day by a man who had taken offense to a story under his byline in the newspaper. Unfortunately, this type of behavior has not been nearly so uncommon in our state as we might wish. We do not know what happened to her father's murderer nor to his second wife; we are told only that Lucile was "nearly crushed" by the tragedy.

But life moved on. Fortunate enough to be able to go away to college, the young woman studied music and shorthand for a year at Limestone. Though her teachers urged the family to see that she received conservatory training, it seemed more practical to everyone that she leave school in favor of a job to earn her living. That venture led her to Greenwood where she worked as a secretary for the Southern Cotton Oil Company at its site on the edge of town where the old Greenwood High School building now stands. Troy native Eddie Jay came into her life soon thereafter; her eventual decision to build a future with him apparently surprised no one, least of all Lucile herself. They were married in Greenwood in 1912.

The new Mrs. Jay had transferred her church membership to First Baptist when she moved to Greenwood, and it was primarily through the church that she lived a life infused with faith and good works until her death at the age of ninety-six. Along the way she reared five children and helped her traveling salesman husband with the paperwork his job required. Mrs. Jay also made time for music, both in her home and her church. The instrument she favored most was the piano, but she was also adept at the classical guitar, a choice that might seem rather unusual for the time and place she lived. She was able not only to read music but also to play by ear. Buddy remembers his early exposure to classical music, particularly opera, as well as the family Victrola in the living room, and he attributes his own interest in music to his mother's talent and example.

The family lived very near the church on Bailey Circle. Buddy remembers a childhood that allowed him great freedom to roam East and West Cambridge Avenues, downtown, and the residential side streets where many of his school friends lived. To avoid the indignity of shouting, Mrs. Jay hit on a unique way of calling her wide-ranging brood to the supper table at the end of the day. In a perfectly normal fashion, at least to her, she developed a different whistle for each child, and each child was quick to respond to his or her individual call. Buddy says she had other whistles for the family cat and dog, to which each responded as readily as the children.

Mrs. Jay's whistling ability was not restricted to rounding up children and pets, however. As musical as she was artistic and bright, and blessed with perfect pitch as well, the young woman once actually whistled her way through a solo hymn tune as part of the church service. Buddy admits to a sort of horrified embarrassment at his mother's performance that morning; he says he crawled under the pew and refused to show his face until the service was over. Nothing daunted, his mother followed that feat with another virtuoso whistling performance at a PTA meeting when she hummed her own accompaniment in a two-part duet with herself!

Mrs. Jay's days were filled with "church work" of both the organized variety, such as Sunday school teaching and WMU work, and that of her own devising which took the form of personal witness, as well as writing poetry and letters to old and new friends, young people, family, and others to whom she wished to bring the good news of the gospel. It was actually a mixture of the two that led her to the young Eddie Lieberman in 1932.

Mrs. Jay always liked to follow the news of the day, particularly as reflected in political cartoons. She had her favorite cartoonists and collected their work in the form of newspaper clippings, not only for herself but also to share with others. As she grew older she began fashioning unique scrapbooks for her grandchildren. Though she was an ardent tither, Mrs. Jay saw no reason to limit her financial contributions to the church program alone. Buddy remembers a special muffin tin in his mother's kitchen which was used in a careful distribution of small change meant for her favorite charities. She also continued to put her typewriter to good use, pulling together a collection of original poems in a small volume entitled *Miscellaneous Musings* that was privately printed in 1940 and revised with an introduction by granddaughter Julie Jay in 1982. No false note comes through in about a hundred verses that speak to her involvement with family, friends, nature, and her Lord. One is entitled "In Memory of My Beloved Friend, Mrs. A. F. Hagan," and another, "The Valley of Baca," based on Psalm 84, was read by Dr. William Harris at her funeral on December 4, 1985.

APPENDIX B

When the clerestory windows in the new sanctuary were announced as "giving opportunities," many individuals and groups responded. The announcement of one of these gifts, from the Benson Sunday School Class in honor of Mrs. R. E. Gaines, struck a chord. The Gaines name was familiar from the early history of Greenwood County when J. M. Gaines, who represented Edgefield in the state senate at the time the county was formed, not only supported Greenwood's bid but also was elected the new county's second senator in 1900.[1] Perhaps there was a connection between this early good citizen and the Robert Edwin who was Mrs. Gaines's husband. In addition, the words of the dedication, delivered by Mrs. Byron (Dora C.) Burns, were so appealing they needed to be quoted in the church history just as they were in the newsletter of September 1, 1971:

> When women get our age we are sometimes hard to please! Things don't go to suit us at home, and when and if we get to church on Sunday morning, the room is either too hot or too cold, the chair in class hurts our back, and even God himself may seem far away! But on the fifth Sunday morning everything is all right—for that's the day for Mrs. Gaines to teach! Seriously, though, we do feel out of touch with God, too often, I'm afraid. But Mrs. Gaines is able to help lift us up to God who is ever reaching down to us—and make us feel—really feel—His Presence and His Power.
>
> Because of her keen intellect and inquiring mind, because of her knowledge and understanding of the Bible, we gain insight and understanding. Because of her faith and inward strength in the face of numerous adversities, we too are strong and brave. Because of her determination to keep serving in spite of loss of health, sight and hearing, we too are inspired never to give up. Because of her humility, her gentleness and her poise, we too would gain serenity. Because of her deep concern and love for people, we too have more compassion and love for others.
>
> At a moment like this, I truly wish I were gifted with a silvery tongue and could properly express the deep feelings that are in your heart and my heart this morning. But then, we are not trying to impress each other—we are simply trying to tell Mrs. Gaines how we feel about her! We want her to know that we hold her in the highest possible esteem.

> Her leadership and the influence that she has exerted in our lives for 20-odd years cannot be measured. She has been deeply interested in the Building Program of our church and so this morning we would like to dedicate a clerestory window in the sanctuary in her honor. And as we dedicate this window, may each of us seek anew to dedicate our lives in the service of our Lord. We love you, Mrs. Gaines, and because of you, we love our Lord even more.

Surely anyone would want to know more about the person who could inspire such a tribute. Mrs. Gaines's daughter, Mrs. Harold (Mary) McCord, supplied the essential facts of her mother's long life, among them the information that her father Edwin, who was called Ed, was a son of J. M. Gaines, one of eight children in that family. Born in 1877, he was a young man of twenty when Greenwood became a county.

Mrs. Gaines, a native of Hampton County, was born in 1891, the fourth of eight children of Mr. and Mrs. Edwin Hansford Fitts. She was named Winifred which, naturally, was soon shortened to Winnie. At first thought it seems she must have been something of a prodigy since she entered Winthrop at the age of fifteen, but her early schooling was probably about the usual for the time; that is, the young woman received the equivalent of a ninth-grade education. It should be remembered that the last three years of high school came very slowly in South Carolina; the twelfth grade, for example, was added as late as the 1940s. Miss Fitts entered college on a four-year state scholarship, and she was among several who led their class as marshals at graduation in 1910. A teaching position brought her to Greenwood where she met Mr. Gaines and married him in 1912. The Gaineses reared a family of three daughters.

Mrs. Gaines left teaching for a time to be with her children, but she maintained a long and active membership in Delta Kappa Gamma, the Lotus Garden Club, and the Cateechee Study Club, all well-established Greenwood women's groups. She was also more than just a member of First Baptist Church; according to her daughter, she "loved her church devotedly throughout her life." Having been born into a family of strong Christian faith, perhaps it is not surprising that she became a student of the Bible early in life, particularly since it is abundantly clear that young Winnie was of an intellectual turn of mind. Like many young women of her day, she developed a great love of literature that lasted throughout her life; she was considered quite well read among her family and her peers, so much so that McCord remembers her friends gathering to listen as Mrs. Gaines read or told them stories from classical literature. She also taught a Sunday school class for many years. Her daughter added that when she returned to teaching in 1941 she found time to sponsor a Bible Club at Ninety Six High School.

With a background suited to learning and a natural instinct in that direction, Mrs. Gaines herself probably saw nothing at all unusual in her interest in the Bible as literature and history.[2] Biblical scholarship must have satisfied her on any number of levels, not least the spiritual, and one can imagine her proficiency increasing as she grew in understanding and maturity. Still, women from later generations might see the picture somewhat differently and might attribute her special knowledge to the fact that women's roles in that era were much more circumscribed than they are today. With fewer outlets outside the home and with the Bible readily accessible inside it, surely it is perfectly natural that inquiring minds, whether they belonged to men or women, would turn in that direction for mental stimulation as well as spiritual consolation. When we speak of biblical scholars among the laity today, we generally mean people such as Mrs. Gaines and in many cases our own grandfathers and grandmothers. Hardly ever are we talking about ourselves or our neighbors.

One of Mrs. Gaines's daughters believes strongly that her mother would not have felt her opportunities were limited. She points to the fact that Mrs. Gaines did volunteer work with the Red Cross in World War I, played an active role in a large family, and achieved full accreditation as a flower show judge, among other activities of a fruitful life. McCord adds that her mother also "was a person people trusted, one from whom many sought advice and counsel." It would be difficult to think of a better assessment of integrity and usefulness.

Mrs. Gaines, along with her daughters, had already given a church window in memory of her husband, who died in 1962. She must have been thrilled indeed when the Benson class returned the favor with a window in her own honor a few years later. As it happened, she was to live on for many years beyond that day in spite of a variety of infirmities associated with age. She was fortunate enough to manage in her own home until 1979. The last eight years of Mrs. Gaines's life were spent at the Methodist Home; still, in the words of her daughter, "Her mind was clear and her interest in public affairs was keen until her death just before her ninety-eighth birthday."

Though a number of Greenwood's oldest families can point to strong ties to First Baptist Church, the Beaudrot family seems to occupy a special niche in both county and church history. Many people agree that the wife of the original Charles Louis Beaudrot, née Mary Amelia Bond, deserves her own place in the pantheon of community and church notables. The fact that she was also a member of the Crews and Waller families, both well-known in early Greenwood history, only adds to that distinction.

A native of Greenwood, Mary was born in 1853 to Sarah Frances Crews and Sobeski Louis Bond,[1] who had come to the village from North Carolina. Her birthplace was the old Crews home which still stands at 711 East Cambridge Avenue. The family moved to the Columbia area when Mary was a girl; she remembered ever after the sounds of Sherman's army as it plundered and pillaged (and, some say, burned) the capital for three days in February 1865. Mary joined the First Baptist Church of Columbia as a teenager.

Mary Bond and a blacksmith from Charleston named Charles Louis Beaudrot met in Columbia and married in 1873. The couple moved to the upstate soon afterward, lived in Ninety Six for a time, and finally settled in Greenwood where Beaudrot opened his own blacksmith shop in 1879. The business prospered and eventually evolved into a modern mechanical repair and welding shop known as C. L. Beaudrot & Son (the son was Joseph L.). Their seven children—four sons and three daughters—formed the nucleus of a close family group, many of whose descendants still call Greenwood home.

Mrs. Beaudrot joined First Baptist Church in 1876 when the little congregation had been in existence only six years. Granddaughter Ray Young calls the C. L. Beaudrots "pioneers in the Baptist movement in Greenwood" and believes they worked all their lives to build and strengthen First Baptist Church. Mrs. Beaudrot, for example, began her career as a Sunday school teacher there in 1892. A notice in the church bulletin of February 3, 1935, states that she had taught continuously at that point for forty-three years. With such a record it was almost inevitable that her class, originally known simply as the adult women's Bible class, was renamed the Mary Beaudrot Class. Another signal honor was accorded when the Sunday school presented to the church a silver urn bearing the inscription, "To be used / for / Memorial Flowers / This vase is presented / by / The First Baptist Sunday School / in honor of / Mrs. Mary Beaudrot / A Devoted Servant of God." The dedication called the vase "a fitting symbol of her own beautiful life of consecration and usefulness." The Mary Beaudrot silver urn is part of what might legitimately be called the church's "treasury" contained in a trophy cabinet located in the main corridor near the offices.

Ray Young believes the words *consecration* and *usefulness* are apt descriptions of her grandmother's life. Somehow she had picked up a good working knowledge of medicine (not really an unusual skill and a virtual necessity for housewives and mothers in the days when medical science was not far advanced), but Mrs. Beaudrot's expertise in this area extended beyond the family circle; she was regularly called upon to assist friends and neighbors when illness struck. She also served as midwife when the occasion demanded. Her home, too, was a haven unlike any other. Originally there were six Beaudrot houses on both sides of the railroad track along a stretch of present-day Calhoun Avenue; the section was actually known as "Beaudrot Row" or "Beaudrotville." It is not difficult to imagine family members in and out of each other's houses all day long; perhaps this proximity helps to account for the solidarity and stability of this remarkable family. A number of these houses still stand, but only one has been occupied continuously by a family member—John C. and Russie Beaudrot Young live at 420. The land had originally been part of the Crews property; streets named Charles, Stanley, and Crews are reminders of these families.

Ray Young remembers vividly the beauty and fragrance of flowers and shrubs from her grandmother's house and garden. Even today, a whiff of banana shrub or tea olive instantly recalls her childhood and her grandmother's imaginative plantings. Perhaps this love of flowers explains the fact that members of the next two generations of Beaudrots were themselves identified with an interesting piece of Greenwood's business and social history called Beaudrot's Flowers.

The heart of a large and close family—there were fourteen grandchildren—Mrs. Beaudrot presided over a well-ordered household, always occupied but never too busy to help a friend in need, dry a grandchild's tears, or hurry to the side of any neighbor, family or not, who called. A good wife, devoted churchwoman, and concerned citizen, she could be a bit of a disciplinarian as well. When members of the younger generations were learning how to be still and pay attention during church services, sitting by

Granny Beaudrot was the best way to make sure, in her words, that "order was had." One can almost see the twinkle in her eye when that line was delivered; a keen sense of humor is another well-remembered trait.

Teaching Sunday school to the conscientious Mary Beaudrot meant a great deal of time spent in preparation. Her grandchildren remember that ritual; Saturday afternoons found Granny studying her Bible to be ready for the Sunday morning class. Many Sunday school teachers grew ever more knowledgeable from such close and regular scrutiny of the Bible, and Mary Beaudrot was no exception; in view of the scope of this knowledge it is not far-fetched to call her a biblical scholar. Ray Young acknowledges her grandmother's skill as a teacher of the Bible, but honors her equally as a "teacher of life."

Mr. and Mrs. Beaudrot's time together ended with his death from pneumonia in May 1916. A family history records that among Charles Louis's last words were: "Tell Brother Burnside he will have to get someone to assist him in the communion service, I will not be able to do it." Mrs. Beaudrot lived on another twenty-four years, but she did develop health problems as she grew older. She was stricken, for example, at the age of seventy-eight with a serious kidney infection. No one remembers who the doctor was—the date would have been the early 1930s—but an operation was clearly necessary to save her life. Granddaughters Ray and Russie (both of whom married men named Young: Ernest and John C. respectively) remember their fears that she might not survive general anesthesia and major surgery at her advanced age. The operation was performed and Mrs. Beaudrot recovered fully, though perhaps "fully" is not precisely accurate. Another strong impression that remains with both Mrs. Youngs is their grandmother's beautiful posture as a younger woman. She held herself erect and always walked with her head held high, but both remember a stoop that seemed to date from soon after the operation and that became more pronounced every year. The stoop might have been the result of the loss of a kidney, osteoporosis, or simply old age—it is impossible to say conclusively—but both granddaughters seem to carry a similar mental picture of their Granny Beaudrot's stooped posture and slow gait toward the end of her life as she moved about her tasks.

Mary Bond Beaudrot died, after a singularly useful life, in April 1940. She rests beside her husband in Magnolia Cemetery.

Russie Beaudrot Young passed along two original pieces of church memorabilia when I asked her for materials to be included in this book. One was a handwritten, very personalized history she had prepared as a program for her garden club a few months ago. The other, entitled "Historically Speaking," is a history of the Woman's Missionary Union of the First Baptist Church during the period 1941–1958, written by Mrs. H. R. (Ora) Higgins who served as treasurer of the organization during that period. Actually, her length of service was much longer than the sixteen years covered by this memoir; Higgins's name continues to appear in the yearbooks at least through 1967, meaning she served as treasurer for more than twenty-five years. Both of these manuscripts are genuine artifacts written by people who were deeply involved in the work of the church. They are presented here for that reason.

FIRST BAPTIST CHURCH
Greenwood, SC

"Boll Weevils and Baptists taking Over the Country."

[The church] was organized on September 25, 1870. First church was in what used to be called "Old Greenwood" which was on East Cambridge St., about where the railroad crossing crosses the street. My daddy joined the church in 1893 (at 14 years of age) when it was located there.

The next church building was built on Bailey Circle in 1896. This is the building where I went as a child. [The first pastor] I remember [was] Dr. William Vines. . . . He baptized me about 1929. Before Dr. Vines became pastor Dr. DeMent served in that capacity. Often I heard my dad say how much he enjoyed having his pastor drop by his blacksmith (later welding) shop which was close to the church, on what is now Beaudrot Ave. to ask how he was. He seemed to be a "down to earth" pastor. Following Dr. Vines came Dr. Charles F. Sims who was there many years. Dr. James Bowers was next and he retired in Greenwood and he was followed by Dr. J. William Harris, who is our present minister.

Thinking back about our old building I remember in many ways it was very inadequate. It all centered around a semi-circle sanctuary & Sunday School assembly room (which had wooden doors between that could be pulled down to separate the two sections). The Beginners Room on Bailey Circle was usually where we went in. There were only about 5 large Sun. School rooms in the building. Downstairs was the Baraca—men's class—Room which served as our general meeting room & where meals were served (very few) as compared to now. To get downstairs you had to go down some stairs which was like going into a cave. I was impressed with the way the men only class . . . [registered their attendance at] Sun. School. There was this wooden board in the front of the class that had electric light bulbs on it & each member would turn their light on to show their presence.

Our first "minister of youth" was Mr. Gerald Smart. He never married & he loved children and more or less adopted us. Many times he carried us on outings & on mountain trips. He would some way get someone to loan him an open truck, we would stand up in [the back] and invariably it would break down & we would have to wait for it to be fixed. For years he played the organ.

The church had no air condition[ing]. Blyth [Funeral Home] fans could be seen being used to stir up a little cool air. There were several electric fans up high but [they] didn't help the situation.

One of my favorite classes in Sunday School was the Primary Dept. My aunt Sarah Mauldin was Director. She was a wonderful storyteller.

Our choir loft was small and I remember the ladies wore big hats.

My favorite teacher was Mrs. E. F. (Lucile) Jay. She taught a class of girls when we were in High School. [Her motto came from an entry, "Light From Many Lamps," by L. E. Watson, quoted in the *Mission Action Handbook*]: "It is the greatest of all mistakes to do nothing because you can only do a little. Do what you can."

When members first started talking about building a new facility, some of the older men in the congregation began to balk, saying we didn't need one. They were wrong, I believe. The tower steps were already sealed off because they were unsafe. [Three] of the men who raised so much fuss were former Mayors Mack Marshall and DeVore Andrews and my uncle Clarence Beaudrot. There were many heated committee meetings beforehand.

We purchased property on Grace St. which we had several years before building. Our church annual picnics were held on the grounds. We used a temporary sanctuary (now Fellowship Hall) for about 15 years, moving into our present one on April 4, 1971.

HISTORICALLY SPEAKING
Woman's Missionary Union of the First Baptist Church
Greenwood, S.C.
1941–1958

In 1941, when time came to appoint a nominating committee for the WMU of the First Baptist Church, the following were appointed: Mrs. Lucy Sigwald, Mrs. Sarah Imboden and Mrs. Joel P. Burnett.

Mrs. Charles F. Sims, wife of our pastor, was elected president and Mrs. H. R. Higgins was elected treasurer.

The facts that I am about to present to you concern the presidents that I have served with beginning January 1, 1942.

* * * * *

Mrs. Sims knew the work of the WMU well and made a good president. When Mrs. Sims and I began our term of office, the former treasurer gave me the balance on hand, which amounted to 86 cents and a list of unpaid bills!

At that time money was not plentiful and the circles were having a hard time giving to the WMU Treasurer 50 cents per month to carry on the work. We had ten circles and fostered a Sunbeam Band, GA and YWA organizations.

The amount received for all causes for the year was $1,044.00. Of this we gave to the Lottie Moon Offering 224.76; Home Missions 106.80 and to State Missions $51.10. We were giving through The Hundred Thousand Dollar Club to help pay the large debt of the Southern Baptist Convention caused by a dishonest treasurer.[1] This was continued for two and a half years, or until the shortage had been taken care of.

It was during this year that Camp Rawls was being built. We were apportioned a certain amount but Mrs. Sims had very little cooperation. She told us that whether we helped or not Camp Rawls would be built. She was so right! Many young people have been won to Christ and dedicated their lives to full-time Christian service since the camp has been in operation.

Dr. Sims resigned in 1943 so Mrs. Sims had to resign also. Mrs. A. J. Snead served for a few months and because of her health resigned, and Mrs. Sarah Imboden served the remainder of the year. We entertained the State BSU Convention and the Abbeville Association WMU during that year and both Mrs. Snead and Mrs. Imboden served well during their short terms. Mrs. Imboden passed away May 10, 1944.

During 1944–45 Mrs. G. E. Hawkins served as president. One word would describe her: *Humility*. She said at the very beginning that she knew nothing about the WMU work and she imagined there were others who knew no more than she did, so we could all learn together. She asked all who would, to secure a Year Book and we would have a class and discuss the book and learn something about WMU work. We had this class, in the Beginner's Department, sitting around a big open fire on a cold afternoon. No longer could it be said that we knew nothing. Mrs. Hawkins was a most competent officer and a fine person. She died as the result of an automobile accident, May 26, 1953.

In 1946 Mrs. R. E. Seymour began serving as president. More different things happened during the three years she served than in any previous time. It was in this year that our WMU year was changed to October 1 through September 30, so 1946 was a nine months' year. Money was getting more plentiful and our circle dues were increased to $2.00 each per month.

Mr. G. H. Smart gave to our WMU $1,000.00 in memory of his Mother and in honor of his three sisters, all being so very active in WMU work. This money was to be invested and the interest given to our special seasons of prayer offerings each year. It is invested in the Mutual Building and Loan Association and we receive a dividend check for $15.00 each January and July. This is given equally to our three seasons of prayer offerings as requested by Mr. Smart.

At the end of the first quarter of 1946, and time for reports to be made, Mrs. Seymour came to my home for me to help her make up this report. I had done this many times before, and she had not, and of course, had to learn. She said she would never learn and told me if I would do this for her she would love me forever. She has kept that promise.

At this time the Ladies Parlor Fund was started so that we could have a place for our meetings. Later these plans were changed but we continued to give and now the Ladies Parlor is furnished.

During Mrs. Seymour's term, our last Charter Member passed away; Mrs. E. F. Waldrop, who was 99 years, 5 months and 1 day old. We had named a circle in her honor and we now have a circle named in her memory.

During the last year of Mrs. Seymour's term her health began to fail and for about six weeks of her last year she had to take a complete rest. Mrs. Seymour was a faithful and efficient president. Mrs.

Raymond Smith, first vice president, served as president for the remainder of the term, which ended September 30, 1948.

1948–49, Mrs. G. H. Byrd was our president and served for two years. During this time we entertained the Western Division (now Region). Mrs. D. C. Bomar was superintendent and later was elected president of our State Woman's Missionary Union and served ten years. We were honored by having our president serve on the State WMU nominating committee.

During the year Camp Rawls had grown and was in great need for more accommodations. We were apportioned a small amount but it was not until the very last of the year that we decided to contribute. However, we did give the amount apportioned. Mrs. Byrd's term ended September 30, 1950.

1950–51 Mrs. W. G. Bishop was elected as president and served for two years, ending September 30, 1952. She was interested in missions and missionaries. We had more missionaries with us and did more for them than ever before. We had Miss Inabelle Coleman with us for a Sunday morning service and it so happened that we were broadcasting that month, so many people had the privilege of hearing and enjoying her by radio. Also we helped Miss Coleman entertain the Chinese Students in colleges in the States one Christmas. Dr. M. T. Rankin provided the place in Richmond, Va. and other organizations like ours helped provide food for them. We also had Miss Martha Franks for an afternoon meeting. We sent money as a Christmas gift to Miss Clifford Barratt.

We were hostess to the Abbeville Association WMU and it was during this time that our gifts to missions were greatly increased. Money was getting more plentiful and we were made conscious of the great need for missions. Mrs. Bishop made a splendid president.

1952–54 Mrs. G. L. Johnson was elected president. She was a fine executive. The most outstanding thing done during her term was having our WMU adopt the budget plan. It took her six months to get us started but we would not do without it now for anything. Of course, Mrs. Johnson was interested in more than the money. Perhaps she did more than anyone because she gave her daughter to be the wife of a Foreign Missionary. Jean and Jack Glaze are stationed in Argentina, South America.

1954 through 1957, Mrs. E. W. Carpenter was our president. She served for three years which was the longest term of any. While Mrs. Seymour served three years, one of the years was a nine months' year due to changes in WMU plan of work. Mrs. Carpenter's term was three calendar years. She was a fine officer, always pleasant and never wanting to say or do anything that would hurt anyone. During her term we were hostess to the Abbeville Association WMU and had as guest speakers Miss Hattie Gardner, missionary to Africa, and Mrs. James F. Burriss, at that time our State WMU president. Also, we had Miss Martha Franks, missionary to Formosa and Miss Hannah Plowden, missionary to Hawaii.

Again we were asked to make a contribution to Camp Rawls. Three circles gave $5.00 each. Our gifts had greatly increased and we received for all causes during the year around Five Thousand Dollars.

We now have sixteen circles, each circle giving to the WMU Treasurer $4.50 per month for carrying on the work of our WMS and full graded youth organizations which we foster.

When Mrs. Imboden asked me to serve as treasurer, I told her that the committee would never have cause to regret having asked me to serve, that I would do my very best and be faithful. I have kept that promise. These have been sixteen happy years, rich in experience and increased knowledge of the work of the Woman's Missionary Union.

Now we are in the beginning of a new year, 1957–58, with Mrs. William F. Mauldin our new president. Having worked very closely with her when she was Director of Youth Organizations, and later when she was second vice president, I'm sure that we will have that beautiful cooperation that is so important to make a success of the work.

May we pledge to Mrs. Mauldin our support and help make this a great year in His service.

Respectfully submitted,
(Mrs. H. R.) Ora H. Higgins

This brief history covering the tenure of only one WMU officer is a clear indication that the work accomplished by the women's missionary effort of the church over the years has been, to steal a phrase, "unstinted and multiform."[2] Another tireless worker, Christine Penn Henderson, turned over a whole box of church-related memorabilia, among which were yearbooks, financial records, correspondence, minutes, lists, recipes, menus, and the like, all compelling evidence of both the scope and the quality of the work performed by these remarkable women. The church owes an enormous debt to the people who chose to take the missions aspect of church work as their primary focus. The bulk of Henderson's collection covers the period 1956–1973 and her own work as a committee chairman and active circle member. Miss Olive Baxley served terms as both WMU president and missions chairman during this period. Her frequent letters to the various circles (which numbered between fourteen and seventeen at the time and which were renamed *groups* toward the end) are marvels of information, inspiration, and instruction. Corporate CEOs could take lessons from the organizational skills and coordination of effort these women achieved.

Many of us are guilty of using the phrases *Woman's Missionary Union* and *Woman's Missionary Society* interchangeably. This is incorrect. Actually, the Woman's Missionary Union (WMU), officially classified as "an auxiliary to the Southern Baptist Convention," consists of one overarching organization whose focus includes a number of smaller age-level groups formed within local churches, from Sunbeam Bands for infants and young children, through GAs and YWAs, to the adult group which is called the Woman's Missionary Society (WMS). Local churches were intended to have one society, with circles, or more than one society. Either way, the plan of work comes from the WMU through the state organization to the local groups which adapt it to their particular program emphasis. The names of the various groups underwent a significant change in 1970. Sunbeams, for example, became *Mission Friends*, GAs were to be called *Girls in Action*, and the YWA organization was renamed *Acteens*. The emphasis on missions remains the same.

* * * * *

Still another piece of WMU material showed up in someone's cache of First Baptist Church memorabilia. Internal analysis reveals it to be a report (probably given to the writer's own group back home) on the annual convention of the state organization held in Greenwood in 1909. This report, handwritten by an unnamed delegate from an unnamed church and obviously copied many times, is important for several reasons, not least of which is the fact that it is a firsthand account of the proceedings as well as a look at the town of Greenwood, the church, and the local WMU at a moment in its early history (the piece required some editing for clarity):

> As I was the only representative from our Society at the opening exercises of the Woman's Missionary Union Convention, although I was not the delegate appointed, I will try to give you some idea of what was done during the session. When the crowded train reached the

Depot, the place was alive with the good people of Greenwood to receive their delegates & a committee of ladies was there to pin a badge on each one as they left the train. In that way the delegates could be distinguished everywhere, and there was a goodly number of them, amounting to over 500. The Baptist women of the State had a great meeting at Greenwood, which was the 7th annual Convention of the Woman's Missionary Union—auxiliary to the South Carolina Baptist Convention.

Tuesday at 2:45 p.m. the first session began. The President, Mrs. I. W. Wingo, called the Convention to order and introduced Rev. G. N. Cowan, the pastor of the Greenwood Baptist Church. He gave the Convention a hearty welcome to the church & made an appropriate address and in an earnest prayer asked God's blessing on all that was to be done in the meeting. After Rev. Cowan's devotional service, the Mayor of the City, Mr. Kenneth Baker, was introduced and on behalf of the City of Greenwood gave a most cordial welcome to the women of the state—to the city and to their homes in Greenwood. Then the men *all* retired & the President, Mrs. I. W. Wingo, took charge of the Convention. The beautiful & impressive way in which she talked of the missionary work & the ways of doing things for Christ was so clear that everyone could understand. I never saw a crowd more in earnest and eager to hear what was to be said, and to know what was to be done. Mrs. Wingo did not mind one bit addressing that body of 800 or 900 ladies & her voice could be heard distinctly all over the house.

Mrs. A. L. Crutchfield, the Corresponding Secretary, gave a report of her work showing advancement all along the lines of missions; she too was a good talker and had such a sweet and pleasant manner [that] she commanded undivided attention. She told of the different amounts given to every object—foreign, home & state missions, the Orphanage, Training School, Margaret Home, and to China—in such a way that showed she was familiar with her duties, and she has served the Convention for 3 years without one cent of pay and without one day of vacation, so the Convention this year voted to give her an assistant to be paid $100, and Mrs. Crutchfield [is] to have one month's vacation each year as long as she holds the office of Corresponding Secretary.

Miss Lula Whilden, the guest of honor of the Convention and our missionary to China, told of her work in China, the pleasure she had had in teaching the heathen, and the privations she had endured in order to help those poor unenlightened souls. She told how eager they were to be taught when they once got them interested, and how they would work and give & suffer to help others after they were converted themselves. I could not help but wish you *all* were there to hear her. She told a right touching little story—she did not have a written report, just told things as they occurred to her & things that came under her own observation. She said there was a Hospital built in a city where she worked, and the missionaries could do a great deal of work among the heathen patients. They called the Hospital Jesus's house. One poor lame & almost blind fellow who had never heard of God but had heard of this Jesus house thought he would go there, so he started & by traveling a few miles a day and begging what he could to eat as he went along he managed to reach the Hospital, this Jesus house as they called it. Of course he was taken in, but he had to wait his time to be served & while he was waiting he heard the preaching & praying for the other patients & when his time came he was given a good bath & clean clothes & put on a nice clean cot, the first time in his life he had ever been in a clean bed. The poor fellow looked up at the nurse and asked her if he was in heaven now. Just think of it—a grown man who had never heard of Jesus & heaven. She says we need no longer pray for the heathen to receive the missionaries, but [need] to pray for more missionaries to be sent to them, that they are ready & willing to receive the glad tidings.

At the close of her talk a collection was taken up for the missionaries in China, or for the girls school in China. A contribution of $78.87 was given, and in the collection basket was found a card signed by Miss Sallie McGee of Honea Path. On the card was written, "I give my life for my master's cause wherever it may be, at home or abroad, wherever he calls I am willing to go." When it was found that this girl had given *herself* to her master's work she was asked to come on the rostrum & tell why she had decided to give her life for Christ's work. Without any hesitation she came forward & her bright young face was just beaming with joy. She told how she had entered the high school & somehow she could not get in with the girls, but she did not get discouraged. She undertook to start a band of workers, with just a few to start with, but in a short while others began to take an interest & it was not long before quite a number joined. Before she left school there were three of those girls that volunteered to go & help carry the gospel to the heathens, so she thought as she had been the means of bringing these three girls to work for Christ perhaps that was her mission, so she freely gave herself. After her talk the President said perhaps there were others in the Convention that would be willing to follow Miss McGee's example, if there were to rise, and about 15 young ladies rose to their feet. Of course that did not mean that they were going, but that they would be willing to go if called upon. This shows how mission work is growing.

The mornings & afternoons were devoted to the Convention's work & no men were allowed, but at night everybody was admitted & some men would either preach or make an address. Dr. Derieux, Dr. Poteat, Dr. A. J. S. Thomas of the Baptist Courier—and I will state that it was insisted upon in the Convention that the Baptist Courier should be in every Baptist house in the state, especially where there were children—Dr. S. J. Porter of Pennsylvania, Field Secretary of the Foreign Mission board, preached a fine sermon. The house was filled to its utmost capacity. He preached on missions & why we are commanded to send the Gospel to foreign lands. A collection was called for after his sermon, which amounted to $64.05.

Wednesday A.M. Mr. Jamison of the Orphanage addressed the body and invited the Convention to visit the Orphanage that afternoon after we had had our lunch. There was a large hall near the church & the whole crowd of delegates, over 500, and all of the visitors were invited there to lunch. There were plenty of seats and a committee of Greenwood young ladies waited on everybody. [We] were [each] given a plate with a ham sandwich, crackers & pickles, and a cup of hot coffee; it was a plenty, and so much easier to feed the crowd than the way we do it. When the lunch was served a little bow of red ribbon was pinned on each one, & in that way none were overlooked. It was at the lunch hall that some of us enjoyed ourselves most. There we met old acquaintances and made new ones and had a good time generally. When lunch was over & we went back to the church we found just lots of conveyances that the gentlemen had provided to take all who wished to go over to the Orphanage. Mr. Jamison received [us] very kindly and at each house the matron & little children met us on the porch and some child would show [the visitors] all over the house. Everywhere was as clean & neat as could be. The floors were spotless, the stoves or ranges—for every house had a nice range—looked like they had never been used. The cooking utensils, dishes & everything [were] in their proper places & the children were required to do all of this work. The children looked happy & contented and were neat & clean but plainly dressed. I noticed in several of the houses a *high chair*, and I always asked to see the baby. Somehow an orphan baby always touches the tenderest spot in my heart. In one of the houses in the reception room, life size oil paintings of Dr. & Mrs. Maxwell, the founders of the Orphanage, were hanging, also one of a sweet faced little girl for whom the orphanage was named, Connie Maxwell. This reception room was where the children were taught music on the piano. Everyone that visited the orphanage was asked to register & page after page was filled with names & where they were from. Greenwood has just cause to be proud of her orphanage and the Superintendent seems to be the right man in the right place.

Thursday A.M. The opening exercises of the Convention was in charge of Mr. Jamison & he had all of the orphans at church with him. He stated to the Convention that they had not made any preparations whatever for that occasion but that he would just call on them to sing or recite what they had been taught before. They sang several songs & did it well, and they repeated in concert several psalms & chapters in the Bible & it was surprising to hear those little children. Mr. Jamison called one of the smallest boys & the little fellow was too small to be seen by the ones in the back of the church, so he stood him on the desk & told him to recite a piece he had been taught for Thanksgiving service. The little fellow did not hesitate to recite several verses.

After the orphans were through with their exercises a collection was called for. Perhaps you all know that the different Societies all over the State were asked to give silver knives, forks & spoons for the Orphanage, & I wish you could have seen how liberally so many of them gave, just page after page was sent up until there was more knives, forks & spoons than they needed amounting to $250 in silverware, besides $170 in cash to buy silver, making in all $420. Remember this grand offering was given by the *women* of the different societies of South Carolina. After they had such success in getting the silverware someone said a Chapel was needed at the Orphanage (they use the School Building now for devotional service) and it went through the crowd like an electrical shock & in less than a half hour $1000 was raised in that body of women to begin to build a $10,000 Chapel at the Connie Maxwell Orphanage in the next 4 years. Some gave cash from 5 to 25 dollars, some gave *personal* pledges from 5 to $100, and some pledged their societies for different amounts. They seemed just in the humor to build a Church for those children right away. Mrs. C. E. Watson, about the oldest and I think one of the wisest officers of the Convention, advised that they would not go into that Chapel building too hurriedly, that she thought the delegates ought to take the matter back to their Societies and agitate the question and study over it and pray over it and at the next Convention in 1910 they would be better prepared to say what they would do. So Mrs. Watson's advice was taken.

Miss Lucy Cureton of Union spoke of our lady missionaries and their work in their different fields & when she had finished the nine missionaries that were present were requested to come to the platform. The whole assembly rose to their feet & gave them a Chautauqua salute. Each one gave a short talk & all seemed to have their hearts in their work and although some of them had endured hardships they seemed willing to labor on and really enjoyed it. One of them spoke of having to part with her wedding ring because she had no other means of living when her money failed to come from the board. Miss Eliza Hyde who has been our state worker for 25 years was present and is always an inspiration, even in her writings. Mrs. E. A. McDowell made a resolution which was heartily accepted that we as a body set our disapproval on wearing big hats to church. She said if you couldn't buy a small one, why just make one *like she did*. It was decided that the 2nd week in November be the time hereafter for the Convention to meet, and the next meeting will be held in Greenville in 1910.[3]

List of Pastors

Thomas H. Pope	1872–1875
J. S. Jordan	1876–1878
J. K. Fant	1878–1879
H. C. Smart	1879–1886
G. H. Carter	1887–1891
E. J. Forrester	1891–1902
H. A. Bagby	1902–1908
George N. Cowan	1909–1914
Byron H. DeMent	1914–1917
John R. Jester	1918–1922
William N. Vines	1923–1927
Charles F. Sims	1928–1943
James A. Bowers	1943–1977
J. William Harris	1978–

A small brochure was compiled in 1947 to celebrate the fiftieth anniversary of the church in its building on North Main and Bailey Circle. The author, Gerald H. Smart, called the work a "fragmentary historical sketch." Because we have so few actual church records from the period 1917–1938, Smart's little booklet takes on added significance with its precious few paragraphs on the pastorates of Dr. John R. Jester, Dr. W. M. Vines, and Dr. Charles F. Sims. These paragraphs are presented as Smart recorded them, sometimes as quotations from someone else:

Dr. John R. Jester succeeded Dr. DeMent and remained with the church four years. Under his guidance great advances were made in every phase of church work and Kingdom causes. His greatest achievement, perhaps, was the fine way in which he put over the $75,000,000 campaign, securing pledges amounting to $132,000, while our apportionment was only $75,000.

Dr. W. M. Vines: "After the departure of Dr. Jester," writes Mr. Sproles, "we had a pastorless period of several months. However we had able supplies and were not idle ourselves, but busy casting about for his successor. To be sure we were not fishing for minnows nor yet a whale,

> but the indications are that we have accidentally or providentially bagged one of the latter off the coast of Virginia when that preeminent preacher and pastor Dr. W. M. Vines of Norfolk accepted our call and entered upon his work on Feb. 1, 1923. Dr. and Mrs. Vines endeared themselves to the hearts of all our people most wonderfully. Mrs. Vines entered into the work of the church and Sunday school at once, and as a trained leader and teacher her work has been productive of much fruit. During Dr. Vines' pastorate the increase in attendance was phenomenal, both at church services and at Sunday School. To care for the congregations, chairs were placed permanently in each of the aisles and the partition separating the Sunday School rooms was entirely disposed of. The Sunday school, part of the time under the leadership of J. C. Burns, later of Julian Bolton reached an average attendance of 650, with a peak on one Sunday of over 1000.
>
> "Fostered by a live woman's missionary society, organized simultaneously with the church, the missionary spirit of the church has been dominant among the members, their contributions at all times being commensurate with what they conceived to be their duty and ability; their conception of both however was materially changed as time went by and their vision enlarged, with a notable increase in their contributions. The most noticeable one came with the adoption of the duplex envelope system. Today this church ranks among the foremost in its per capita giving to all the interests supported by our denomination. Only three churches in the state exceed in gifts to missions and benevolence, the average for the past three years being $16,000 per year for our church." (Written in year 1923).
>
> **Dr. Chas. F. Sims:** Dr. Vines remained with the church until March 3, 1927, leaving to become an evangelist under the Home Board of Southern Baptists. Dr. Chas. F. Sims followed Dr. Vines, and began his pastorate on Jan. 1, 1928, remaining as pastor for 15 years. He left the church Feb. 1943 to accept work with the State Board in Columbia, S. C.

Dr. Jester resigned in 1922. His farewell to the congregation appears in the church bulletin for June 25:

> "Probe a little deeper and you will find the Emperor," said one of Napoleon's wounded soldiers to the surgeon who was searching for a bullet which had pierced his body near the heart. In the heart of the pastor, and also of each member of his family, this church is enshrined now and forever. Four and one half years ago we began our work

together. The pastoral relationship is now closing, but the ties of friendship and affection which have been formed shall be as deathless as love, which is by nature eternal.

The pastor is profoundly moved by two feelings: on the one hand that of gratitude to God for His blessings upon our work together; and on the other hand heartfelt grief that these relations must close. Impelled by obedience to what seems to be the call of God we turn from the church which has been the Philippi of our ministry, thus far in life, to a great and difficult task in another city. We shall continue to pray that our Father's blessings may abide upon this church, and crave a continued interest in your prayers for the work to be accomplished at Winston-Salem.

Another tribute to Dr. Vines was found in the church bulletin for August 29, 1943:

About twenty years ago Dr. W. M. Vines came to Greenwood to serve this church as its pastor. He did not stay with us a great many years but while he was with us a lasting bond of friendship grew up, which abides to this day. It has been said that "True friendship is the manifestation of the finest quality of love." Dr. Vines loves people and because of that precious gift people love him and are drawn to him in the bonds of loyal and lasting friendship. Since Dr. Vines resigned the pastorate of our church, to enter a greater field of usefulness, it has been our custom to invite him to spend one Sunday with us each year. That has grown to be a red letter day for us in the calendar and as the season for his coming approaches the question is often asked, "When is Dr. Vines coming?"

Some one defined a friend as one who knows our faults but loves us still. Dr. Vines lived with us long enough to learn of our faults yet notwithstanding our shortcomings he has borne with us and loves us still. May we be more worthy of his great friendship and love.

First Baptist Church Staff—June 1999

J. William Harris, Senior Minister
B.A., Presbyterian College
B.D., New Orleans Baptist Theological Seminary
Th.D., New Orleans Baptist Theological Seminary

Jamie Harris, Minister to Students
B.A., Furman University
B.S., Furman University

Lawrence E. Schultz, Minister of Music
B. Mus., Oklahoma Baptist University
Master of Church Music, Southern Baptist Theological Seminary

Kenneth R. Standley, Minister of Education
B.S., Tennessee Technological University
M.Div., Southern Baptist Theological Seminary

Kathy Claphan, Church Secretary and Clerk
Nell Morton, Education and Financial Secretary

Brenda B. Fairbanks, Organist
B.S., Winthrop College
M.M., Furman University
B.M. Organ Performance, Furman University
M.S.M., Emory University

Horace Culbertson, Treasurer
Gwen Laucis, Hostess
Alan Bishop, Building Superintendent
Jesse Bolden, Maintenance

Chapter One: In the Beginning

One hopes no one would undertake to write a history of a Baptist church anywhere in South Carolina without consulting Joe King's excellent work, *A History of South Carolina Baptists*. Bill Harris was kind enough to lend me his personal copy of the book; of course it was the very volume I needed to get me started, but I never got over feeling a bit intimidated by King's credentials and scholarly touch. Because he and I have very little in common, this is a different sort of work entirely. I was intrigued to learn from a couple of his friends that King has tended to move his church affiliation from place to place since the Baptist work was published; I have suffered no such trauma, at least not yet, though I fully understand his quest.

Harris also provided copies of other important church histories, among them *Adventure in Faith: The First 300 Years of First Baptist Church, Charleston, South Carolina* (1982), by Robert A. Baker and Paul J. Craven Jr.; *Saints of Clay: The Shaping of South Carolina Baptists* (1971), by Loulie Latimer Owens; and *A Centennial History of the First Presbyterian Church, Greenwood, South Carolina* (1983). I happened, quite by accident, upon *First Baptist Church, Laurens, South Carolina* (1984), and my friend Fred Holder sent me a copy of *Pickens: The Town and The First Baptist Church*, by Jane Boroughs Morris (1991). Holder cares so much about the South Carolina upcountry that he continually nudges (prods?) those of us who labor over local history projects to keep plugging away. I didn't know, and neither did he, that the Pickens book would supply a quote for my chapter notes, but one of his paragraphs from the foreword might easily have been written about First Baptist Greenwood:

> The tone of Baptist thought in the Pickens Baptist Church has always been governed to greater and lesser degrees by its pastors. Although the relationships of the congregation with the pastors were not harmonious in every instance, the church records reveal little internal strife; and the oral history of the town concerning the First Baptist church is generally characterized by a tradition of placidity.

The Presbyterian church history, *The History of Main Street United Methodist Church, Greenwood, South Carolina* (1992) by Harry Mays, and

Bryan, Rush, and Shannon's *History of Callie Self Memorial Baptist Church, Greenwood, South Carolina* (1977) were strong reminders that my own church was something of a latecomer to the business of producing a written history. A phone call to the Mays household, in fact, helped us to settle on a publisher for this volume.

---

1. Joe M. King, *A History of South Carolina Baptists* (Columbia, S.C.: R. L. Bryan Company, 1964), 10.

2. Harry Tolliver Cook, "A Compendium of Colonial Baptist History in South Carolina 1683–1776," *Baptist Courier,* 8 Dec. 1921; no p. Cook was also the author of a valuable little local history/genealogy book, *The Hard Labor Section,* published in 1923.

Chapter Two: A Church Is Born

Chapter 2 sent me back to *Greenwood County Sketches* (1970) by Margaret Watson and my own work with Don Herd in the late 1970s. These references, along with more of King and a little of Louis Booker Wright's bicentennial history of South Carolina, got me through the first part of the chapter, which consisted mostly of setting the stage for the small group of Baptists from Mount Moriah who wanted to establish a church in town. Greenwood's two Baptist schools—one for boys and one for girls—had come and gone before First Baptist Church was founded, but it seemed important to profile the early ministers for whom they were named, Nicholas Ware Hodges and Richard Fuller. And when I learned that one of the earliest supply pastors was the great preacher John A. Broadus, whose book on preaching is considered a standard in the field, I was sure I wanted to include a biographical sketch of this gentleman as well. The story about Broadus and the other faculty members trying to decide whether to reopen the seminary after the Civil War was one of my favorites.

The fledgling church had a building committee, but no lot and no building, by the end of its second year of existence. Those deficiencies would be remedied during 1873.

---

1. E. Don Herd Jr., *Mount Ariel-Cokesbury, South Carolina,* vol. 1 (Greenwood, S.C.: privately printed,1979), 3.

2. John Asplund, *Annual Register of the Baptist Denomination in North America.*

3. King, 143.

4. King, 148.

5. James H. Wade Jr., *Greenwood County and Its Railroads: 1852–1992* (Columbia, S.C.: privately printed, 1993), 45.

6. Louis B. Wright, *South Carolina, A Bicentennial History*. (New York: Norton, 1976),186–87.

7. Jane Elizabeth (Betsy) Creswell Waller, daughter of Elihu Creswell and mother of the first senator from Greenwood County, C. A. C. Waller. These names link Greenwood's First Baptist Church with prominent early families. Waller Hall was the second story of a wooden store building which stood at approximately the site of the Chipley Building, the former Masonic Hall, at the head of Waller avenue (now The Exchange).

8. A listing of charter members in the church bulletin of September 9, 1923, does not coincide exactly with the names found in the original minute book. Mr. and Mrs. W. H. Whitlock and Misses Nancy and Edna Hughey are named on that list; Isaacs, Norrel, Silks, Arnold, and Farrow are not.

9. Dr Williams was the second superintendent; the first was W. P. McKellar.

Chapter Three: Years of Growth and Service

Nobody was quite sure, or so I thought, exactly where on East Cambridge Avenue the first church building was located. Perhaps it is only natural that I assumed it must have been in the general neighborhood of the original Green Wood; that is, at some point near where Cokesbury Road intersects East Cambridge just below the railroad tracks. Evidently Russie Young assumed the same thing, judging from her little memoir reprinted in the appendix. Fortunately for me, I found in my files a communication from John Blythe who had researched the matter in his characteristically thorough fashion a number of years ago and found that numbers 215, 223, and 229 East Cambridge Avenue mark the location of the first church building erected in 1873. Jack Parham visited one of these residencies, number 223, to check out its windows which are said to be from the original church. Blythe's research indicates that this is the Mattison house erected in 1899. The Sproles house next door at number 229 is supposed to contain lumber from the church building. Opinion seems to be divided as to whether number 215 or 223 is the actual site of the church. Perhaps we could settle the matter by assuming the building occupied part of both lots and that wagons and buggies were parked under the trees at number 229.

Chapter 3 also contains information on Connie Maxwell's Children's Home, though the story is in no sense comprehensive. The history of this unique Greenwood institution has been well documented in at least two books. My chief interest was the interlocking story of Dr. John Maxwell/Greenwood Baptist Church/Connie Maxwell Orphanage from the earliest days of all three (Maxwell moved to Greenwood from Newberry soon after the Civil War). Following is an account of a most intriguing episode from the church's early period; this is the "mystery" mentioned in note number 5.

The story goes that one Saturday evening sometime in the winter months of an unknown year that must have been rather early in the life of the church, Dr. John C. Maxwell's horse and buggy were spotted in the little village of Greenwood slowly making their way to Maxwell's home on what is now East Cambridge Avenue. The doctor could be seen on the buggy seat, in his rumpled black suit and creased shirt, slumped over with his chin on his chest, very much out of it. The immediate reaction was that the doctor was drunk, and the word got out and spread until the deacons and other leaders of the Baptist church determined they had to call him to account for the incident. He was, as the saying goes, "called before the church" and given the opportunity to defend himself against the charge of public intoxication.

It is easy to imagine Dr. Maxwell, one of Greenwood's most prominent and respected citizens, taking his own sweet time and looking squarely at each of his inquisitors in turn, as he told his story. It seems he had been called on a Thursday to Ninety Six where he treated a man who had caught his arm in some part of the machinery at the cotton gin. It was touch-and-go for awhile, but the patient rallied and the doctor was nearly ready to leave his bedside when a horseman arrived from Kirksey with the news that a problem pregnancy was about to end in a problem delivery, and the doctor was needed at once. Feeling his services required in spite of fatigue, Maxwell left Ninety Six and headed to another patient's side where he worked for many more hours to save the life of a mother and her new baby. When he felt it was safe to leave, the doctor moved on to the White Hall section to treat a man who had split his leg with an axe. After still another errand of mercy in Troy, Maxwell was finally free to go. By this time it was Saturday and he had slept hardly at all for two nights. To make matters worse, the weather was miserable; a freezing rain began to fall as the doctor made his slow way from Troy to Greenwood. Maxwell freely admitted that, in an attempt to get warm, he had taken a number of swigs from a jug of whisky he kept in the buggy as part of his medical supplies. He conceded that he might well have taken a swig or two too many; his only excuse was that he had not slept or changed his clothes at that point for more than forty-eight hours and was in a state of exhaustion. His horse, fortunately for him, knew the way and got him home safely. Pronouncing himself perfectly ready to accept whatever penalty the church wished to impose, Maxwell rose and left the meeting.

The church interrogators, though somewhat chagrined and decidedly uncomfortable after the doctor's explanation, still believed they had a duty to withdraw fellowship from an admittedly erring brother and proceeded to do their duty. Some weeks later, a story about Maxwell's handsome gift to the orphanage committee was reported in *The State*. When the news reached the church leaders in Greenwood, they lost no time in contacting Maxwell to offer reinstatement of his membership. To his eternal credit, he is supposed to have agreed to come back.

Boykin Curry told me this story even before he and I discussed the possibility of my taking on the church history. He said he had read the account himself in the church minute book and thought people could learn a valuable lesson from it; he wanted the story to be included in the history. He also remembered that each line of the entry, which was originally recorded in ink, had a single line drawn through it, a gesture indicating to him that the church would prefer this embarrassing incident not be picked up and used in any way.

My interest piqued, I could hardly wait to see that part of the official record for myself when I set to work on the church minute books. I was very curious to see how the recorder had handled the story, and I looked forward to deciding how I would handle it myself more than a hundred years after the fact. To my intense disappointment, there was no accounting anywhere in the official record book of bringing Dr. Maxwell before the church on an accusation of public drunkenness; indeed, there was nothing to indicate anything at all except the cryptic notation that Maxwell had tried to resign his membership and the unexplained blank spaces in the minute book, both of which I recorded in chapter 3.

When I told Curry the story was not there, he thought I must have overlooked it, while I thought it might have been in another place. I asked if perhaps the deacons had kept separate minutes of this sort of episode. Everyone agreed that no separate minute books existed. Curry recalled further that the church secretary, Janelle Anderson, had actually handed the minute book to him the day he read the famous story; he suggested I call to check her memory of the episode. Anderson's recollection was that she had heard the story many times but had never actually seen it in writing. The tale had been particularly troubling to Dr. Bowers, she says, who used it as an example of the excesses of early churchmen who viewed themselves as arbiters of other people's behavior. He was horrified also at the damage such stories could do to innocent people.

Curry also remembers that as time went on he liked to tease both Bowers and Dr. Sam Smith of Connie Maxwell about the time the church shot itself in the foot while trying to shame a member. Bowers and Smith did not enjoy the teasing, according to Curry. They believed the story would just "go away" if people would stop bringing it up.

Is the story true? If so, what happened to the official record of the incident? Nobody knows, really, but the best guess would have to be that someone with access to the minute book decided to expunge the evidence to protect the reputations of both the church and Dr. Maxwell. Ironically, that action might have ensured the very thing the perpetrator was trying to prevent. It remains to be seen whether the next church historian will honor the noble intent of the censors. In the meantime, the story that someone seems to have tried hard to kill lives on in the record of the church's first 129 years.

The story of the Giles family came from a University of Pittsburgh dissertation written by Lucile Snyder Deutsch in 1978. I had touched on this family in the county history, and when I realized that one of its members, E. S. F. Giles, had First Baptist connections, I seized the opportunity to explore his story, and that of his mother and sisters, more thoroughly. I still find it quite remarkable that the first three female graduates of Duke University once lived in the house next door to Angelle Adams and are buried in Magnolia Cemetery.

I always enjoy trying to describe an important building, particularly if that building has historic connections and most particularly if it is no longer standing. In the case of the Baptist church, the dedication of its second home was one of those special Greenwood events—as well as the lead story in the first issue of the *Greenwood Index.* I always liked the church building on its leafy lot on North Main Street—with its arched entryways, tall steeple, and memorial windows—almost as much as I liked the Presbyterian church, designed by my favorite architect, Reuben Harrison Hunt, just down the street. When I accidentally discovered Ralph Ray's 1951 watercolor of this 1897 building, nicely framed and leaning against the wall in Ruth Martin's gallery (a Sunday school class was selling prints as a fundraiser, and Martin had supervised the project using Martha Bishop's original), I knew I had found the perfect image for the dust jacket.

This wonderful building, alas, grew too small too soon; perhaps the church was a victim of its own success in gaining converts, or perhaps its membership split over matters other than the form of communion, but only twelve years after the dedication of the building on North Main, some members began to grumble about the lack of space for both the congregation and the Sunday school. Soon afterward, a group of seventy-eight members joined in a resolution to form a new congregation at another place, all the while expressing "brotherly feeling" toward the church but adding that they wished to leave "for the good of the cause" in the community. There simply had to be more to the story than appeared in the record, but just how much more would not be revealed until the next building wave hit in the 1950s.

---

1. A periodical for South Carolina Baptists established in 1869. Its title defined the character of the paper, according to researcher Robert Ivey, and its aim was "to stir up the pure minds of Christians and provoke them to love and good works." The periodical was the direct forerunner of the *Baptist Courier.*

2. Old-line Baptists know that Cat Fish is in Dillon County, near the town of Latta. King names a Catfish Church established as early as 1752 in the same general area.

3. It is impossible to escape the note of condescension that creeps into Maxwell's report. Class consciousness was alive and well in the Greenwood of 1896. On the other hand, it is also true that a college education was not the normal expectation in the late nineteenth century that we enjoy today.

4. The minutes show that Mr. and Mrs. Sproles presented themselves "at the conclusion of the regular prayer meeting" on November 22, 1911, requesting restoration of membership. Happily, they were unanimously received into fellowship after an absence of fourteen years.

5. It is quite possible that Maxwell's desire to leave the church was linked to the references to "blank spaces" and "application of ink eradicator" in the next paragraph. For a full account of this "mystery," see above.

6. Lucille Snyder Deutsch, "The Giles Sisters' Contributions toward the Higher Education of Women in the South 1874–1904" (diss., University of Pittsburgh, 1978).

Chapter Four: The Middle Years

The events of the period covered in chapter 4 might be said to have moved the United States from its pre-World War I stance of complacent isolationism to a leading role in world affairs, thanks to World War II, presidents such as Woodrow Wilson and Franklin D. Roosevelt, generals the likes of George Marshall, Dwight Eisenhower, and Douglas MacArthur, and the development of the atomic bomb. Greenwood's First Baptist Church, too, changed a great deal from 1912 when its membership was reported at 638, to 1950 when the congregation numbered more than 1,200. Its financial strength grew accordingly, so much so that the 1951 budget, when integrated with the building fund, topped that of the previous year by more than 179 percent.

Another artifact, one that I did not know existed, came to my attention after the manuscript was finished. Brian Benjamin brought me a copy of *These Ninety-three Years,* a little memoir by George N. Cowan, privately printed in 1961 and given to Brian's family by Cowan himself. In addition to describing how the eight-year-old Napoleon Cowan became George N. when a couple of female relatives decided he needed two names, Cowan gave his own assessment of his years in Greenwood.

It seems that after four years in Bristol, Tennessee, Cowan found Greenwood a most congenial place to live and work. He called the people "interesting and wonderful" and was especially pleased with Connie Maxwell Children's Home which sent all its workers and children to First Baptist with the result that the church "just overflowed with men, women and children on Sundays." Best of all in Cowan's mind was "the expansion of our . . . work in Greenwood" when the number of Baptist churches grew from two to six during his time in the pulpit. Three—South Main, Connie Maxwell, and West Side—were daughter churches of First Baptist.

Cowan also singled out the Jones Benjamin family, who lived four miles in the country along the railroad, as special friends during his time in Greenwood, which he called a "splendid little city." Cowan frequently walked on pastoral visits to the Benjamin home, "only an eight mile walk for that afternoon. God gave me two good large feet. . . ." And he would stay with the Benjamins, who had moved into town by that time, when he returned to supply the pulpit at First Baptist.

Cowan's career in the pulpit lasted more that fifty years. He continued to serve in interim and supply capacities long after retirement.

The bad news about the period covered in this chapter is the lack of official church records from May 1918 to September 1937 and the resulting dearth of information on pastors Jester, Vines, and Sims. Still, it is clear from such records that remain that each of these three men played a significant role at First Baptist Church, if only to pave the way for the pastorate of Jim Bowers, who came to the pulpit at the age of thirty in 1943 and promptly began laying the groundwork for a large building program.

The Eddie Lieberman story is covered so thoroughly in both text and appendix that nothing additional is needed here. Corresponding with this gentleman directly was an added treat to learning about his connection with the town and the church in the 1930s and 1940s. It was also great fun to renew an old friendship with Buddy and Liza Jay. I came away from a morning's interview regretting that I never knew Buddy's mother, who figured prominently in the Lieberman story as well as in the lives of a remarkable number of First Baptist Church members.

---

1. Cowan returned to supply the pulpit in Dr. James Bowers's absence in April 1958, some forty-four years after he left Greenwood. He was described as "advanced in years" but still active in a supply capacity. A circle of the WMU, named in his honor, sponsored a reception on the Sunday he preached. Cowan died in 1966 at the age of ninety-eight. At that time he was the last of the former pastors of First Baptist Church.

2. For a brief description of the pastorates of Jester, Vines, and Sims, see appendix E.

3. Dr. R. O. Lawton was a Methodist preacher and professor of English at Lander College.

4. Dr. Wil Lou Gray's famous school moved to a permanent home in Columbia a few years later.

5. Dr. Barnwell Rhett Turnipseed, Methodist minister and third president of Lander College.

6. Ramsay was president of Greenville Female College, now part of Furman University. He had filled the pulpit at Greenwood a number of times before; the earliest recorded date is 1893.

7. Lieberman himself explained this discrepancy in a letter to the author dated February 27, 1999: "When first apprehended, I gave the name Lee to the sheriff. In the South at that time (1932) blacks and Jews were far from welcomed. Lee was not a Jewish name. The same name was given to the church, not knowing their reaction to someone with a Jewish background. . . ."

8. Lieberman never forgot Mrs. Hagan. A notice in the church newsletter of October 17, 1957, credits him with sending flowers in memory of "Mother Hagan," who died in 1938. The pastor noted that Lieberman "was converted under her ministry and . . . encouraged in his spiritual pursuits by her interest." Nor was 1957 the last occasion for memorial flowers from Dr. Lieberman. He continued the practice throughout the 1960s and 1970s and even into the 1980s.

9. Clifford Irene Barratt, *My Life on the Mission Field,* (Greenwood, S.C.: privately printed, 1999) 103–05.

10. Valley Forge, Pa.: Judson Press, 1991.

Chapter Five: Maturity

Chapter 5 covers the era of Elbert Adams, who was to the music and building program what Jim Bowers was to the pulpit of First Baptist Church for more than thirty years. Bowers and Adams made a formidable team, one that not many members seemed to care to challenge;

even so, it is plain from church records that considerable trauma accompanied the decision to give up the building on North Main and Bailey Circle in favor of a totally new physical plant more than a mile away in the 700 block of Grace Street.

As it turned out, the decision to go "totally new" meant not only the destruction of the old building but also the abandonment of its memorial stained glass windows, most of which had been given in honor or in memory of early members and pastors. This episode seems to have been the only time Bowers displayed anything like a cavalier attitude toward his flock. A rather cold and terse announcement in the church newsletter appeared to offer the windows to anyone who might want them: "The windows will be removed from the building and placed outside. Those who wish to get them will please notify the church office of their desire. . . ." While the records are not completely reliable in the matter—no further mention of windows appears—other sources indicated that the windows were finally crated and trucked to Connie Maxwell Children's Home where John Murdoch thought perhaps they could be used in a church then in the planning stage. When that idea went nowhere, the windows went to . . . wherever they went. Jack Parham is currently tracking them down; he has managed to secure one—the Enoch Simmons window—which will eventually be displayed in the archives room at the church. Another is currently for sale in an Asheville antique shop; Parham has every expectation of bringing that one home as well. Evidently the building materials of the old church were equally fair game; Buddy Jay reports that most of the bricks in his house in Sheffield came from the structure. A photograph in the newspaper shows the half-demolished church as it appeared in April 1957, some months after the new building was occupied. The steeple still stands incongruously intact over a building that appears to have been skinned. The caption reads, "Old First Baptist Church Structure Comes Down."

It seems odd that the ever tactful Bowers would have dropped the ball so completely in this matter. On the other hand, perhaps he understood the situation very well indeed and threaded his way as carefully as possible under the circumstances. From the first, Bowers had seemed every bit as much diplomat as minister; he appeared to know instinctively how to move the congregation slowly but surely toward the objectives he had in mind. Everybody in Greenwood knew Jim Bowers. I knew Jim Bowers, though I was not a member of the church during his pastorate. As it turned out, that was a very good thing. When I took on the church history project I was able to deal with the Bowers question from a totally objective viewpoint. I do not think such objectivity would have been possible had he been my own pastor. Similarly, because I am definitely not neutral about Bill Harris, I actually tried (quite unsuccessfully as it turned out) to end the church history in January 1978 when he assumed the pulpit. Of course that would have been a great mistake, and I am grateful to those who insisted that I must deal with the last twenty years if the history were to have any validity.

Chapter 5 is, fortunately or unfortunately depending upon one's point of view, primarily the story of Phase One of the building complex that now houses the program of First Baptist Church, Greenwood. Because they are virtually interchangeable, it is also the story of Jim Bowers and one of his colleagues, minister of education Bill Treadwell. Largely because of Treadwell's interests and energies, the church made huge strides in both its youth program and its emphasis on education during this period. The chapter ends with the beginning of Phase Two of the building program, the new sanctuary.

---

1. David Alvarez, "Vatican," in *Encyclopedia of U.S. Foreign Relations,* ed. Bruce Jentleson and Thomas Paterson (New York: Oxford University Press, 1997), no p.

2. It is equally interesting to note that compensation and related costs amount to almost exactly half the budget for 1999.

3. *Collier's Encyclopedia,* 1959 ed., s.v. "Stained Glass."

4. The shorted item that year was the church's contribution to the Bethea Home.

5. Local car dealer Paul Davis recalls that air-conditioning was listed as an option on new cars until sometime in the 1980s, but as a practical matter his company ordered factory-installed air on virtually everything they sold from sometime in the early 1970s.

6. Russie Young added the names of a few others, among them Ben Nickles, Josh Arrington, Clyde Simmons, and Arthur Culbertson, as sometime singers with the quartet. Women guest singers included Elizabeth Moss, Margery Lightsey, and Jean Wood.

7. This was Jack Glaze, a career missionary and Mississippi native whose wife was (and is) the former Jean Johnson of Greenwood. Glaze was named president of the Baptist seminary in Buenos Aires in 1967. Now retired from the active missionary field, both Glazes are veterans of both classroom and pulpit, as well as a great deal of First Baptist Church life. No names appear more frequently in church records.

Chapter Six: New Directions

The title of chapter 6 carries a double meaning: it refers to the changes in American society during the 1960s and 1970s, changes that profoundly affected people's attitudes toward churches—along with every other institution previously taken for granted—and to the innovations churches adopted to try to neutralize the damage. In the case of First Baptist, the title also refers to the first period in more than twenty-five years without a single-minded emphasis on stone-and-mortar issues and the debts engendered by a building program.

Stained glass windows loomed large again for a time, as did kindergarten and the music ministry, but the absolute biggest challenge in the church's hundred-year history came when its members chose to look within themselves to determine where they *really* stood on questions of fellowship with each other and with potential new members. A committee worked for six months to hammer out recommendations to the church that centered on questions of criteria for membership—specifically, whether the southern tradition of "whites only" would continue to apply and whether immersion would continue to be the sole form of acceptable baptism for potential members from other denominations. A "new direction" indeed, and one whose implications reached much further than most church members had anticipated, this question placed the church squarely in the middle of controversy that spread from church to association to convention and that still rears its head from time to time.

This issue alone, it seems to me, would have been quite enough to convince anyone that First Baptist's was a story worth telling. I could hardly wait to find what treasures the official records of this period contained or, perhaps, omitted. Would they downplay the drama? Would they be less than candid on the race issue? Were there undercurrents within the membership that threatened to erupt at inopportune moments? Of course what I found was simply the record of what had actually transpired—verbatim committee reports, pastoral interpretation of association actions, even official minutes of convention sessions—all spelled out in sober and thought-provoking terms to a mature and decent and thoughtful congregation. I loved it all, and as the story almost wrote itself I felt more and more proud to be a part of First Baptist Church. I make no apologies for presenting in rather substantial detail an episode that might easily be viewed as the church's finest hour.

But there were other "fine hours" as well. The church also began a new emphasis on local missions during this period, one that would lead directly to several very significant and active ministries in place today. By the time Bowers retired just before his sixty-fifth birthday at the end of 1977, he could point to thirty-four years of solid achievement for First Baptist Church; and it was he who paved the way, in still another "new direction" for the church, for the era of Dr. J. William Harris.

---

1. About $15,000 of this figure represented interest and dividends on investments.

2. Originally Glenhaven Apartments, now New Haven, on New Market Street.

3. Treadwell left for a smaller church, but Washington, it seems, wanted a larger field.

4. South Main was larger by thirty-one members (1969 statistics).

5. It is impossible to escape noticing that 16,000 must have represented every "consenting person" in Greenwood County in someone's mind.

6. It was announced that this space would henceforth be called the Great Hall.

7. The pastor noted that Davis's gift meant the church owned a complete set in all four colors of the church calendar.

8. For an account of the window given in honor of Mrs. R. E. Gaines, see appendix B.

9. What a disappointment to learn from the newsletter of April 5 that a "sudden illness" prevented Harris's scheduled appearance.

10. For a fuller sketch of Benson, see *Greenwood County: A History* (1992).

11. J. B. Phillips, trans., *The New Testament in Modern English* (New York: Macmillan, 1958), 459.

Chapter Seven: Milestones of the Second Century

Notes for chapter 7 would likely be considered extraneous since Greenwood people like to make up their own minds about institutions as uniquely their own as First Baptist Church. Thus, my "poor power to add or detract" is in no way required and might actually amount to a distraction as readers consider this review of the events of the last twenty years, many of which they shared as full participants.

Similarly, only a philosopher—or at least an astute observer of human behavior—would feel the urge to make observations containing the word *millennium* at this point in a work of this nature. Certainly I shall not do so; still, after months of close attention to the first 130 years in the life of this particular "organization of religious believers," a period that just happens to span the years from 1870 to 2000, surely I am qualified to come up with a few descriptive phrases of my own.

On second thought, Bill Harris has done it for me, many times in fact, with lines such as *inclusive . . . the love of God . . . the table is large . . . we are one in Jesus Christ . . . the joy of fellowship . . . mutual commitment . . . faithfulness . . . celebration and sharing . . . dedicated to Christ and each other.* The events of Sunday, June 20, 1999, will surely remain in the collective memory of the congregation as proof that these are not mere empty phrases. A group of young people who had just returned from a missions trip to New Mexico had charge of the worship service that morning. The presentation was low-key—no robes, no anthem, no sermon—but extremely powerful, coming as it did from the young people themselves. Those who spoke managed to convey the message that while the purpose of the trip was to minister to others it was the young "missionaries" who had benefited most from the experience. This spirit might well sum up what Greenwood's First Baptist Church is all about.

---

1. The column was renamed "From One of the Ministers" as the staff expanded.

2. Davis called himself *choirmaster,* a term with subtly different connotations.

3. Both Carole Mauldin and Joyce Williams remember Dial as a community activist and not a professional social worker.

4. Grammatically, of course, the word should be *Women's*, but the official name is definitely Woman's Missionary Union.

5. Six adult classes at First Baptist adopted the series that fall, while other classes chose their teaching materials from a variety of new resources.

6. Final figures reflected an overage of more than $12,000.

7. The most recent report, in the newsletter of August 5, 1998, reveals that more than 250 students have received Parham Scholarships totaling more than $120,000 since the program began.

8. The final report submitted somewhat later showed receipts within $5,000 of budget needs.

9. "a box with untuned, high-pitched bells that give a 'tinkling' sound when revolving."

Appendix A

1. Among her Sheppard relatives was John C., who served as governor of South Carolina from July 10 to November 30, 1886. Elected lieutenant governor, Sheppard succeeded to the office when Governor Hugh S. Thompson resigned upon appointment as assistant secretary of the treasury under President Grover Cleveland.

Appendix B

1. Gaines is believed to be the only person ever to serve as senator from two South Carolina counties.
2. An excellent example of this interest was the gift of maps to the Benson class in November 1974.

Appendix C

1. The Beaudrot family is noted for reusing family names generation after generation, but Ray Beaudrot Young noted with a laugh that she had run across no Sobeskis other than her great-grandfather Bond.

Appendix D

1. No official church record mentions this incident.
2. In a never to be forgotten tribute to Samuel Lander, his daughter, Kathleen Willson, applied these words to his work over many years with the South Carolina Methodist Conference.
3. Another copy of this document was found, this one annotated, "Report of State WMU Convention given by Mrs. C. C. (Lily Adams) Fuller to Bethany Church Society, McCormick-Liberty Hill, S. C."

INDEX

The First Baptist Church

GREENWOOD, SOUTH CAROLINA